"I know first hand [...] with it. I was an u[...] habitual violence t[...] ironically, was a m[...] sions to which batt[...] help. He was a cler[...]

"I grew up in fear of the wifebeater's power. . . . It was made clear that I must keep silent. . . . I lived through its incapacitating grip on daily life and its long-reaching after-effects."
—Author Terry Davidson

What kind of man beats his wife? He feels powerless and possesses little self-esteem. Unable to express his dissatisfaction with himself, he directs it toward his wife. And often, once his hands have stopped hitting his wife, he cannot even recognize or admit his violent behavior.

What kind of woman is the battered wife? She is often a "good" wife—loyal, mothering, and sympathetic to her husband, accepting physical punishment for the sake of the marriage. The marital bond is a violent one, yet, to her, separation seems even worse.

"The seriousness of America's most under reported crime of violence is at last confronted in this moving, carefully researched, and important book." *The New York Times*

"Mrs. Davidson provides us with an important primer on a subject about which we can no longer feign ignorance." *The Kansas City Times*

"CONJUGAL CRIME is a valuable resource for battered women who need to know where to turn . . . For anyone who wants to understand the psychology of the wifebeater as well as the problems the battered woman faces, CONJUGAL CRIME should be required reading." *The Trentonian*

"CONJUGAL CRIME is an orderly, clear, and extensive exploration of the subject, painfully disturbing in its exposés, encouraging in its reportage of progress." *Vogue*

Conjugal CRIME

Understanding and Changing the Wifebeating Pattern

TERRY DAVIDSON

BALLANTINE BOOKS • NEW YORK

Copyright © 1978 by Terry Davidson

All rights reserved under International and Pan-American
Copyright Conventions, including the right to reproduce this
book or portions thereof in any form, except for the inclusion
of brief quotations in a review. All inquiries should be ad-
dressed to Hawthorn Books, Inc., 260 Madison Avenue, New
York, New York 10016. Published in the United States by
Ballantine Books, a division of Random House, Inc., New
York, and simultaneously in Canada by Random House of
Canada, Limited, Toronto, Canada.

Library of Congress Catalog Card Number: 76-56524

ISBN 0-345-28611-1

This edition published by arrangement with
Hawthorn Books, Inc.

Manufactured in the United States of America

First Ballantine Books Edition: April 1980

Especially for
Doe Lang and Irving Markowitz . . .

And for all the dear, loving friends
and caring Significant Others
who gave me a sense of trustworthy family
and lifted my spirit, I give thanks. *Amen.*

To the devoted women of the first shelters and services—and especially the
Women's Advocates of St. Paul, who
pioneered the American concept of shelter and continue to struggle to keep their
House open to battered women despite
ever uncertain income—I dedicate this
book in the hope that the acute need
will be acknowledged and answered
with dependable funding.

Contents

1

Conjugal Crime:
It Happens in the Best of Families

America is a violent country. It is also a country that places high value on God and family. By law, the national motto In God We Trust is inscribed on all the currency. By custom, marriage and home are elevated to sacred, inviolate institutions, not to be interfered with by laws.

The large middle class and its values form the backbone of America. Values, however, are sometimes more proclaimed than practiced.

This book uncovers a shocking dichotomy between proclaimed values and practiced way of life. It may be the first ever to portray middle-class battered wives and wifebeating husbands and the psychology and life-styles of both. Conjugal crime is estimated by law enforcement officials to be a phenomenon few people are willing to discuss, touching perhaps 50 percent of American marriages at one time or another and seriously threatening the safety of a significant percentage of women and their children on a nightmarishly recurring basis.

The problem of wifebeating has always been with us, from the days when women were considered chattel: but in our "civilized" times, the problem has been hidden.

Wifebeating is not to be confused with sadomasochistic behavior on the part of two consenting adults. Wifebeating exists when the wife is in fear of the husband's superior strength and combative ability and has no means of matching or beating him or effectively defending herself or stopping him. She has not agreed to the behavior. Further, the woman has no option for reversal, postponement, discussion, or escape. The wifebeater has seized the occasion, set the rules, and

1

intends to cause injury and pain. His assumption is that no retaliation will be possible.

If a male intruder were to inflict the same injuries on this man when unable to use his strength—when ill or outmatched, for instance—the injured man would then have full access to the law and to the sympathy and concern of his world. No one would suggest he accept the violent behavior or learn to live with it or cover it up or try to appease the molester so it wouldn't happen again. He could expect that his assailant would be charged with a crime. Moreover, he would be *believed* as he recounted his experience.

The battered wife does not yet have the same advantages in our society.

Here is an example of wifebeating, followed by no significant deterrent, from the "Assaults, Felonious" files of a midwestern county sheriff's department:

> Victim stated the first argument started over a pack of cigarettes. Victim states accused (her husband) held her against the bathroom wall by the hair and continued to beat victim with his right hand. Victim is six months pregnant at that time. Victim stated accused kept telling victim, "You are going to lose that baby," and then accused would beat victim in the stomach again. After the assault in the bathroom, accused told victim to cook dinner.
>
> Victim states the accused picked up a butcher knife and put it to the victim's throat and told victim, "I am going to kill you and you know I can do it, too, don't you?" Victim answered, "Yes," and accused laid the butcher knife down on the table and turned around and hit the victim in the face with his fist and knocked victim on the floor. . . .[1]

On hearing such a story, many people would react with: "But nice people don't do that!" Until very recently, that has summed up the prevailing attitude —much as with rape, child abuse, and drugs. There was no concern for those three social evils until public consciousness realized that they were not confined to the slums alone.

2

Little by little, people who *know* have spread the word that the problem does exist for the middle-class wife and that help must be created for every battered woman. Although very few statistics or surveys have been available, wifebeating is considered by law enforcement officials to be the single "most unreported" crime in the country.[2]

In the last few years, the existence of wifebeating in all strata of society has been increasingly recognized, and solutions are beginning to be developed. In December 1975, CBS-TV found the problem significant enough to run a series on the Morning News, nationwide. Channel 13, the New York area educational television station, did a program on what little help was available. NBC-TV followed with a Clare Crawford–produced *Weekend* segment in the spring of 1976. In 1977, *Glamour* magazine—whose readership is largely young, sophisticated career women—ran a piece on the subject, and *Family Circle,* the world's largest-selling magazine sold exclusively in supermarkets, published the first popular article on the psychodynamics of the middle-class wifebeater. I wrote it. September 28, 1977, marked New Jersey's first Conference on the Battered Woman, held at Trenton, the state capitol. Paula Webster, of the United States Commission on Civil Rights, spoke out against society's tolerance of conjugal crime, stating that wifebeating statistically is three times as frequent as rape. In 1979, *Vogue* magazine's review of the hardcover *CONJUGAL CRIME* emphasized the special problem the middle- and upper-middle-class battered wife has. The General Federation of Women's Clubs, with more than 600,000 members in 12,000 local clubs, selected domestic violence as a priority for help, 1978–1980.

One of the nation's most affluent communities, Montgomery County, Maryland, reported having seven hundred incidents of assaults against wives by husbands each year. The community realized that even more incidents of the "too humiliating" crime go unreported and formed a Wife Abuse Task Force to look into it. Findings showed that incomes of reported wifebeaters ranged up to $40,000 a year, educational levels up to the doctoral degree. The county council began considering the need to establish a shelter for abuse victims.[3]

In middle-class, conservative Suffolk County, New York, an agency dealing with victims of spouse abuse and sexual assault logged more than 4,500 hotline calls, and had 468 clients in the Counseling Center during the first year after opening June 1976; 96 percent were victims of spouse abuse. In upper-middle class/upper-class Westchester County in November 1977, the Chiefs of Police Association endorsed the establishment of a shelter for battered women.

"Violence hardly seems absent from middle-class families." That was the conclusion of Dr. Murray A. Strauss, professor of family sociology at the University of New Hampshire and a past president of the National Council of Family Relations.[4] A recent survey found that 23 percent of middle-class wives charged physical abuse as a reason for seeking divorce. Generally, however, members of this socioeconomic group are loath to report conjugal crime to the police, courts, or social workers. And if they tell a therapist, or discuss it with their pastor, they want their "chagrin" kept secret.

"When the wealthy or the middle class . . . beats up their wives," said an administrator at New York City's Family Court, "it never gets to court. The wife is ashamed to let people know. If it happens, they go for private counseling or get a quiet divorce. We know that it goes on all over."[5] This book will show that many of these wives are too terrorized to get a divorce or even seek counseling.

In Chicago, a police commander spoke from his experience: "Wifebeating has been categorized as a lower-class crime, but that's wrong."[6]

In Cleveland, a cross section of six hundred couples applying for divorce showed that 37 percent of the women gave physical abuse as the grounds.[7] They were the lucky ones, not immobilized by fear of what would happen if they tried to end the marriage.

Pollster Louis Harris, in a survey for the National Commission on the Cause and Prevention of Violence, found 5 percent *more* college-educated people approved of slapping their spouses "on appropriate occasions" than the national average did. "Physical violence is

4

reported equally common among all income groups," Harris found, but "if anything, the middle class is more prone toward physical assault than the poor."[8] The prestigious National Institute of Mental Health considered the problem of domestic violence serious enough to commission a study of it and announced its findings in 1977. The estimate was that an episode occurred "at least once" in "50 to 60 percent of all couples." And in Canada, a newspaper reporter found that "police and social workers will tell you that some of the most inveterate wifebeaters are lawyers, doctors, and business executives."[9]

Detroit-area police records and local chapters of the National Organization for Women (NOW) indicate that there is a significant number of assaults and that the justice system is of very little help to the victims. There is no police category for "wife assault" or "spouse assault," for instance (although women's groups are now working to correct that). But FBI figures indicated that in Washtenaw County in 1974, at least 751 complaints of physical violence were filed by women against the men they lived with.[10]

The university community of Ann Arbor, Michigan, is representative of the need for a change in the mental stance of our entire culture. A local social worker, Vera Conrad, feels that re-education is needed toward the point of view that "it's not all right to beat your wife." She relates the following incident:

"A young woman being beaten by her husband ran out into the street, screaming for help. What was interesting was the response of the neighbors. Not only were they *not concerned* with offering any help to the woman, but they were annoyed with her behavior and felt she had no right to disturb the neighborhood peace.

"The result is that the police bear the brunt of all the unpleasantness without the benefit of any backup services or community support."[11]

The way this community and its university responded was heartening, and representative of the fact that some of our society is taking action at last. Local members of NOW did not delay in volunteering to open their homes to battered wives with no place to turn. The movement in Ann Arbor became one of the foremost in the country, offering a wide range of services. Innovative ideas coordinated with established community functions. Community support is necessary for true effectiveness, to provide a program for developing viable alternatives for these women who must start all over again.

For many of these wives, the husband who had once declared his love in courtship had become, with marriage, the woman's closest relative and her best friend, the focus of her world. When this same loved one became a Dr. Jekyll—Mr. Hyde, turning from a beloved husband into a wifebeater, the battered wife was thrown into a split situation where she no longer had her friend to confide in. With no outside world to count on, she had no one to save her from her undreamed-of new enemy. If she were to survive, she had to reorganize her once-familiar, comfortable life—but with no emotional support at all and with very few inner resources left intact.

This book will provide an understanding of the wifebeating pattern and the larger family and the larger community affected by it, and point to many ways of changing it. A recurring theme is the culture that sustains the crime. Man's assumption of violence as a way to deal with woman has its roots in history and in some of the institutions we most revere. The fact that he still gets away with it so readily in this enlightened age is the responsibility of our legal system and of our conflicting moral attitudes about man-woman relationships and the criminal's versus the victim's rights.

America's tacit acceptance of violence contrasts sharply with the dictates of its religious values, which minimize or actually deny its existence. The battered wife is pressured not to leave the marriage, and not to "bother" society about her predicament.

This acceptance/denial mix pervades the attitudes of the public as well as the policies of social institutions, which in turn reflect the attitudes of the good middle-class people involved in them. It serves to keep the plight of the battered wife and her frightened children invisible.

A recent Gallup poll showed that for over half the Americans surveyed, their religious beliefs were "very important." And "nearly all people" questioned said they belonged to some church.[12]

The latest FBI statistics available show that aggravated assault (one of the categories, along with felonious assault, under which the specific crime of wifebeating is swallowed up) occurs on a crime-clock average of one every sixty-five seconds.

As for the violent/religious society existing under the gun of this aspect of American life, the 1975 FBI report notes that "criminal homicide is largely a societal problem beyond the control of the police. . . . Murder within the family made up approximately onefourth of all murder offenses.

"Law enforcement agencies have difficulty in obtaining convictions based on the original charge in the aggravated assault category," the report continued.[13] Only 68 percent of every one hundred adults arrested for aggravated assault in 1975 were even prosecuted, while 12 percent of those were plea-bargained to a lesser charge.

Wifebeaters, if jailed at all, get only a few days. A battered woman's story is often met by dubious outsiders with an accusatory, "But why does she put up with it? . . . Why doesn't she leave? . . . Why doesn't she have him jailed and throw away the key?" A detective in Yorktown Heights, New York, recounts the story of a woman who tried to escape and obtain justice.

In 1973 Thomas beat Loretta, leaving a wound of her left ear so severe that it required twenty-three stitches to save it. Loretta filed charges. Police arrested Thomas. The criminal court judge, however, released Thomas, bidding him stay away from Loretta.

She moved to her own apartment, completely breaking the relationship. In April 1974 he waylaid her on her way to work, beating her savagely. She filed charges. Police arrested him. The judge released him, bidding him stay away. He promised to comply. In June 1974 Thomas broke into Loretta's apartment.

7

This time she had to file her charges from a hospital bed. The judge paroled Thomas without bail, exacting the usual promise. Loretta complained to the police that no one was helping her.

In November 1974 he broke into her apartment again for the same purpose. This beating was so vicious her eye had to be removed surgically. The unidentified judge, however, paroled him on his own recognizance. No bail was required. Loretta complained to the police and the district attorney, who responded that "only the courts had any jurisdiction to put him away permanently." And that is the unfortunate truth.

In February 1975 the wifebeating pattern resumed, even worse than before. It was at this point that a concerned detective decided to make the case known by writing it up on *The New York Times* Op-Ed page. Although the night court judge was apprised by the police officer and the assistant district attorney of the previous assaults, a travesty of a fair-minded public servant was sitting on the bench. He was unmoved by the hopeless sobbing of the battered, maimed plaintiff, doomed to an endless round of unhampered victimization, unmoved by the long record of the violent defendant—and he paroled Thomas. Was the judge a woman-hater? A wifebeater-lover? One of those Americans to whom religious beliefs were "very important"?

All we know of this unnamed upholder of the laws is that he required no bail of the wifebeater. And he listened to another promise.

"The purpose of a judicial system," the detective quoted at the beginning and at the frustrating conclusion of his incredible account, "is to ensure equal and just treatment to the citizens of the state and to protect the rights of the individual . . ."[14]

What would change the odds in favor of the victim instead of the criminal? "All that is needed for evil to triumph," Edmund Burke observed two centuries ago, "is for enough good men to be silent." Historically, the battered wife has been relegated to invisibility because of the silence of good men.

If strong public outrage does not replace the silence with a mandate to legislators and courts to acknowledge the reality and to act to correct the imbalance, the system will continue to favor and foster the sociopath.

In the wifebeating subculture there are multiple victims. The battered wife is victimized not only by her assailant but also by the tolerating/denying society, which cavalierly permits her suffering and intimidates her into staying with him and effectively blocks her from making a break.

All over the country battered wives tell how indifferent the police have been to their plight, refusing to inform them of their rights, take them to the hospital, guard them while they pack to leave for safety, or arrest the perpetrator. Of course, there are exceptions, and it is not entirely the law enforcers' fault. Legally, the police are prevented from accomplishing much "rescue." As we have seen, neither laws nor courts have favored the victim. Studies show that some police, as well as some judges, tend to put more emphasis on the injured wife's possible "fault" and on urging her to be the one responsible for "patching up" the "quarrel."

Commander James Bannon of the Detroit Police Department acknowledges that "police, and later prosecutors and courts, contribute to domestic violence by their laissez-faire attitudes toward what they view as essentially a personal problem. Further . . . police are socialized to regard females, in general, as subordinate." It is a matter of record that some policemen strike up a camaraderie with the husband in front of his victim.

The wifebeater is also a victim in that he gets subliminal encouragement from his culture to view aggressiveness as a good and proper stance for a male person. Dependence, "dumbness," and obedience are his expectations for a female person. The habitual wifebeater knows from experience that his wife is expected by courts, police, social agencies, clergy, and family to be "compassionate" toward her assailant—over and over again. Thus, his habit is reinforced, justified. Proving masculinity may require "frequent rehearsal of toughness," the National Commission on the Causes of Violence has found, as well as the exploitation of women, and quick, aggressive responses.[15]

One such wifebeater, an unconfident man addicted to "frequent rehearsals" to prove his masculinity, happens to be a man who is actually known to every American, although not for the crime of wifebeating. Dr. Arnold A. Hutschnecker* describes him as a "frail boy who did not belong anywhere, who could not give his ambition attainable goals in a world of reality. He had no conscious awareness of what it meant to feel secure, to be a man with self-confidence and self-esteem."

His wife testified that she and her husband had sexual relations "very seldom." She testified that "this man is very unhappy, and he cannot love." The psychiatrist observed that the wifebeater had tried to "repress a titanic inner fury" masked under an "impassive, rigid manner. And when his outer control finally broke under the pressures of marriage, children, economic responsibilities, failure to keep a job, and lack of money, he hurled violence at his wife. . . . He could possibly have become a homosexual but was perhaps too frightened and seemingly too much in need of a protective mother substitute."

This husband had beaten his wife even when she was pregnant or nursing a baby. His "reasons" were that she forgot to fill his bathtub, or served dinner five minutes late, or he did not like the dress she was wearing, or he did not like to see her smoking or wearing lipstick. The psychiatrist spoke of this particular wifebeater as a man who "could not love because he had not learned to love," who was "forever hungry, consuming, possessive." It was as if he were screaming to his mother, now substituted for by his wife, "You belong to me, to do with what I wish. You must love me even if I hate you, even if I wish you were dead, even if I kill you!"[16]

The wifebeater's name was Lee Harvey Oswald.

A trail of witnesses—friends, landlords, and his own

---

* Before he specialized in psychiatry, Dr. Hutschnecker achieved prominence as the doctor who treated Nixon medically.

mother—testified to his brutality toward his wife, Marina, only *after* the fact. No one had ever thought to stop him earlier, and so his habit had been reinforced.

A battered wife in affluent Montgomery County, Maryland, when asked why she thought her husband resorted to violence, said, "It was an integral part of his nature—his manliness. His ego couldn't stand opposition." Another wife responded that it was "deep feelings of inferiority aggravated by a somewhat Victorian attitude as to the wife's place in the family."

A third woman's reply sums up the entire premise of this book:

"The community seems to feel that male violence against women and children is acceptable or nonexistent. Why should he feel differently?"[17]

The perpetrator is the victim of a system that makes wifebeating easy for him and confirms his "right" to do it. In contrast to the psychopathological ones—who feel no guilt or shame at all about their behavior, and relish the imbalance of the justice system—many wifebeaters express an anguished wish that they did not *"have* to do it." They express a longing that there could be some way to control the uncontrollable, explosive violence. With few exceptions, however, the present system cannot be looked to for that control. (Some of the few rehabilitation programs for the wifebeater are listed in the Appendix.)

Of those victimized by the wifebeater, the most pathetic are the children, who grow up witnessing the torture of their mothers. Very few of them live through this conditioning without its taking a heavy toll. Some defend themselves psychologically by becoming apathetic and uncaring, feeling nothing for anyone, including themselves.

Some take on the battered personality themselves, fearing every authority figure, expecting bad treatment as a norm of life, trying to please and appease a threatening world. But some identify with the power and become superaggressive themselves, turning violence on strangers and loved ones alike, including their mothers.

A few escape by revolting against their parents' way of life—in itself a difficult and dangerous thing to do,

11

abandoning the mother or taking the risk of incurring the father's wrath. However, many of these emotionally battered children will be psychologically unable to prevent becoming the next generation of wifebeaters and battered wives.

Conjugal crime is a public concern, no longer simply a private relational matter. The well-being of people and institutions that never gave a thought to the problem is nevertheless affected by it. Employers, schools, neighbors; traffic safety, community safety, teen-age crime, increasing overall toleration of violence as an expected part of American life—all these are affected because conjugal crime continues.

Organized religion and religious-oriented organizations have not been in the forefront of the movement to help the victims of wifebeating and to prevent its recurrence. Those facilities, both in America and abroad, that have been established for this purpose, have not been sparked by churchly concerns. Only a handful of religious groups have belatedly—but enthusiastically—initiated programs for some help.

A resolution under consideration by the Consortium on Battered Women, St. Paul, Minnesota, described the more typical role of the traditional helpers of humanity: "Whereas, funded and established community service organizations such as the United Way, YWCA, and churches have been tardy or reluctant to turn their facilities and resources toward meeting the needs of women in crisis. . . ." (Each of these institutions has since, in some part of the world, aided in the solution, led by the YWCA.)

Typical of groups organized for active, effective amelioration is the Victims Information Bureau of Suffolk (VIBS) in Hauppauge, New York. This nonsectarian group provides services for victims of sexual assault and family disputants, specializing in battered spouses and their children. It evolved from a local NOW chapter's awareness of a need for a rape crisis center, and then expanded to what it is today.

VIBS's expressed goals are the goals of this book— to "initiate changes in the criminal justice system which will create a more positive approach toward the victim" and to "increase the public awareness of . . . battered spouses as victims of violent crimes and remove the stigma attached to victims of them . . . to change the image of the victims so that they are seen by the general public as victims and not as suspects themselves. . . ."

This book's goal is to increase awareness and to suggest alternatives to the life of violence in the home. It is essential to turn the spotlight of exposure and insight on this very complex "invisible" crime *now*, before another violence-addicted generation grows up.

Clearly, there is a need for this book. The time has come for it to be written and put into the hands of the silenced victims, their families, and the community. I know firsthand about the problem: I grew up with it. I was the unwilling witness to my father's habitual violence toward my mother. My father, ironically, was a member of one of those professions to which battered wives often first turn for help. He was a clergyman.

I grew up in fear of that wifebeater's power, despising what was going on inside the parsonage. It was made very clear that I must keep silent about my father's predilection. I lived through its incapacitating grip on daily life and its long-reaching aftereffects. My instinct was to scream for help from the very beginning, but there was no help then. His wifebeating was the family secret, the family *skeleton,* decreed by both mother and father never to be let out of the closet. Divorce was a sin—and so was exposing my father's conjugal crime. It was a family rule that I drop my ideas of changing things or of getting someone to rescue us.

Although I tried, I never was in a position to aid my battered mother effectively, and my outrage at the continuing injustice and the apparent do-nothingness of the community would not go away. As long as my parents lived, my belief—mistaken, I now realize—that somehow sanity and the Christian ethic would prevail, was never entirely extinguished. Since my parents are no longer living, I am now in a position to help other families trapped in this horror. I have interviewed numbers of other families, including wifebeaters themselves and their children. I have interviewed their therapists, police, attorneys, judges, elected officials. I have been a volunteer in this work, a consultant to local shelters starting up and a speaker before concerned groups. As an investigative reporter, I worked on a story for *The New York Times* on the subject.

And I have found the historical precedents for the toleration of wifebeating—a history, I discovered, that was as old, as hidden, as the crime itself, beginning in the days of the Old Testament.

The modern history of the movement against wifebeating is more encouraging. For a very new movement, it is moving fast, and I believe there is reason for confidence that the trend toward acceptance of conjugal crime can be reversed.

Until 1975 I had no idea that anyone at all knew or cared about the problem. My parents had been dead for several years, and my bitterness at my experience had diminished. I intended to put the skeleton from my family's closet out of my life forever, and to dissociate myself from the problem. I had wasted too much of my life being drawn into it and had decided to live the rest fully, without fear.

Then I accidentally heard about the first hotline for battered women on the East Coast, AWAIC (Abused Women's Aid in Crisis). I was napping with the radio on when I half heard Maria Roy, the social worker who founded AWAIC, speaking of her work on a talk show. At that time I was about to be graduated from my mid-life return to college, and planned to resume free-lancing for a while. I'd been out of income and away from my profession too long, in the pursuit of higher education. Now I was attuned, awake or asleep, to any potential magazine article idea.

That's how I viewed the news of AWAIC—only as a potential story idea, a hot new topic. It triggered no memories. (Not consciously, anyhow.) I roused myself from my slumber long enough to jot down the name and telephone number on something and, despite my apparent interest, soon went back to sleep.

It wasn't until a few days later that I recalled the incident. But where was that memo?

I tried the phone book. I tried Information, all boroughs. I tried the talk show. Too late. They were short-staffed; too much time had elapsed; no one knew.

My God, I thought, what if I were a battered wife? What if I desperately needed the information on courts and police procedure the hotline gave? How can it be anonymous? I began tracking it down through social agencies and psychological referral groups, police information, et cetera. No one had even heard of it. Some agencies asked me to call them back if I ever located such a thing. It sounded like a good idea.

Then my original note turned up.

When I called AWAIC, I sensed a great deal of guardedness on the other end of the line. The number was unlisted. The address was secret. These precautions were necessary because wifebeaters were known to retaliate against wives who tried to get help and those who tried to help them. I sensed that Ms. Roy was reluctant to give any face-to-face interviews in her quarters. All right, I would prove myself.

I had begun citing my professional credentials when I thought of my best credential: I told her about my father. She gave me the secret address.

In 1975 I approached six or seven editors of women's magazines with the hot new topic. Not one believed that the problem was widespread enough to merit the space. Surely *their* readers, being middle class, could not identify with the problem of under-educated, sociopathic people. So I increased my research (information was very hard to come by in those days), concentrating on statistics and examples from the middle class. I interviewed a reformed wifebeater. Despite the mounting evidence, the last editor I tried before I gave up told me flatly, "Only alcoholics and the lowest class of men do that: no one else." The need to deny was stronger than proof.

In the midst of all this, one textbook house did sense the coming trend and the need for knowledge-able ways of dealing with the problem. The publisher contracted for a professional reference work on the topic for the helping professions. I was asked to be a contributor to the book, *Battered Women*, edited by Maria Roy.[18]

The movement against wifebeating, as an organized, effective counterforce, started in England in 1971. A courageous woman named Erin Pizzey, feminist and maternal, opened a run-down house to which local women fled from violent husbands with their children. It was immediately filled to overflowing. Within a few years the work of that one woman led to a network of refuges throughout the entire United Kingdom and to a Parliamentary investigation of marital violence among all classes.

In 1972, Women's Advocates, Inc. in St. Paul, Minnesota, began a telephone information and referral service for women. The seven or eight women who were the advocates began taking battered women and their children into their homes and apartments because the community had no facilities for them.

In October 1974 Women's Advocates began operating the first refuge in America for battered wives and their children, open to any woman in need. Earlier, in 1973, Joann Gerardi, Ph.D., a clinical psychologist, and a Manhattan therapist named Carol Victor opened Growth & Life Center, Inc., a counseling service dealing with problems of separation and divorce. The Center soon observed that physical abuse was a factor in many wrecked marriages among its mostly middle-class clients and began setting aside some time for therapy-over-the-phone for wives who had to remain anonymous because their husbands were too prominent for them to risk the exposure. For years Ms. Victor was the only therapist on the eastern seaboard specializing in counseling for the entire battered family: the wife, the witnessing children, and those husbands who wanted to change and save their marriage.

A year later the first sociological studies in the complex matter of violence of the stronger against the weaker in the marital home were published: *Violence in the Family*, by Suzanne K. Steinmetz and Murray A. Straus; and *The Violent Home: A Study of Physical Aggression Between Husbands and Wives*, by Richard J. Gelles. All were university sociology professors. For several years these professional reference books were the only texts available. *Battered Wives* by Del Martin of NOW, was the first presentation of the problem that actually reached the reading public.

In January 1975 Maria Roy called the first New York State Conference on the Abused Wife, and shortly thereafter began operating the AWAIC hotline, unfunded, on a very limited basis.

In April 1975 two young women who were law students at the University of Michigan completed a detailed study of actual cases of wifebeating, including middle-class couples. In their report they told of the runaround experienced by such women from the legal and medical professions and the "helping professions" when they sought aid or escape or protection. They aptly entitled their landmark work "Catch-22 Revisited —A Preliminary Overview of Wife Beating in Michigan." Sue E. Eisenberg and Patricia A. Micklow presented their 140-page paper to the local chapter of NOW.

The Ann Arbor–Washtenaw County NOW members wasted no time in deciding to do something about the problem. Although conjugal crime was not a factor in their own marriages, they formed a task force to find what local social agencies dealt with the problem. None did. Members began to take into their homes individual emergency cases of battered women, fleeing with or without children. Counseling and information about options and procedures were provided.

Today the Wife Assault Task Force in Ann Arbor is a leader in designing training manuals for other groups interested in setting up similar programs. Funded now, it is equipped to supply emergency housing, support counseling, advocacy with law enforcement and social service agencies, and a twenty-four-hour hotline. The husbands of the victims they serve have run the gamut from the sociopathic personality to the "M.D. or Ph.D. who beats his wife because he cannot stand the frustration of defeat in his work . . . and many men, rich or poor, who think they have a right to beat their wives."[19]

In October 1975 the Eighth Annual Conference of NOW established a national Task Force on Battered

Women. Its mandate was to "raise consciousness about the problem, do research into the incidents and prevalence of battered women and exert pressure for the establishment of refuge houses throughout the country for battered women and their children." Across the country much of the recent community action against this social evil has been initiated because of local chapters' promptings.

These were the pioneers.

In early 1976 New York NOW formed a Task Force on Battered Wives. The coordinator was Susan Maurer, a social worker employed as a foster child advocate. The task force began, she said, as a result of reports from NOW's office managers saying that they were "receiving a lot of calls from women who had been physically abused by their husbands and did not know what to do about the situation. Many sounded middle class and most had not reported the assault. We wanted to meet to look into this problem area."

A panel of people working in the field of marital violence was called by Enid Keljik, the marriage and divorce coordinator, and, coincidentally, formerly a battered wife herself. The panel consisted of Maria Roy; Marjory D. Fields, a Brooklyn lawyer specializing in divorces for poor women; and two noted psychotherapists, Erika Freeman and Natalie Shainess, M.D.

Early in March I got Enid Keljik's name from Channel 13 as a knowledgeable source of information. We traded our thoughts and research on the telephone and she invited me to come as her guest to the initial task force meeting.

At the meeting there was a woman I'd met earlier at one of AWAIC's Outreach meetings, Eleanor Kremen, a professor at Adelphi University's School of Social Work, and a doctoral candidate at Columbia University's School of Social Work doing her dissertation on the subject of battered women.

Enid and Susan asked me to come to the next task force meeting, three weeks later. As the months went by, a number of women came and then drifted out of these meetings, but the four of us remained as a solid working unit. In the process I joined the chapter of NOW.

From now on I believe there will be more and more help available for each one of the victimized participants in the unfortunate life-style of the wifebeater's home. I believe this book can be a first step toward change, not only for the battered middle-class wife afraid to speak out, but also for her confused husband, afraid to admit he is caught up in anything so barbaric, so outside the presumed mores of his class, afraid to listen to his inner voice crying out for help. And I also hope it will allow the witnessing children, divided between struggling to make everything all right again and struggling to block the nightmare out completely, to try to make sense of life.

To the children I say: I know what it's like to feel that you can't talk about the terrible rituals mother and father participate in, feeling all alone and horribly "different." Or what it's like to get up the courage to speak up finally and then find no one believes you because "a nice kid like you couldn't have come from such a home." There are some ways to make these years more bearable, which I will outline later in this book.

To the battered wives I say: The therapists and experts in this field agree that it takes a lot to get most of the middle-class victims to make a move because they are so immobilized by terror, habit, and the excruciating double-binds of the situation. I hope this book will spark the move, after seeing the problem from so many viewpoints, and especially after seeing how futile the "reasons" for remaining a victim are. And for those wives who had been trying to escape and were thwarted by the justice system, the later chapters will show that at last, rescue is possible.

And to the husbands: If you are reading these pages, it must mean your consciousness is ready for a change and for growth toward a more fulfilling way of life. The experts say that deep down there is horror and helplessness at the lack of control, at being locked into only one way of communicating the emotions of the frustrations felt *at life,* not really at the marriage partner. It is possible to finally understand, put it all together, see other priorities and values, and move onward. There is a way out, and I hope this book will help to point the way.

And to the public, the decision makers, the legal, medical, and religious communities, the helping professions: It's time to end denial. It's time to face the awareness of reality that surely must be there underneath the denying. It's past time for the emphasis of attitudes and law to shift from protecting the assaulter toward protecting the victim and preventing future victimizations.

It's beginning to happen in cases of rape. And in cases of child abuse, ten years ago the problem was the one public consciousness could not face. Yet little by little, people who *knew* got the word out that the unspeakable problem was very real, and then help did indeed come into existence. Today, doctors no longer have to keep their suspicions quiet, and every state has laws allowing investigation into child-abusing homes.

The same expansion of public consciousness can happen for the problem of conjugal crime.

What Kind of Man
Would Beat His Wife?

"You Mean I Can't Beat My Own Wife?"

Two examples of wifebeaters from cultures very different from our own will, paradoxically, depict quite clearly some attitudes shared by certain Americans. The first is a segment of the divorce trial of a wifebeater in revolutionary China, 1960:

WOMAN'S ASSESSOR: Was it because you had different opinions that you fought with your wife?
MAN: No, but because in the past, before Liberation, I often saw my father beat my mother and I was brought up to think that man should be superior.
JUDGE: When did your father beat your mother?
MAN: In the old society.
JUDGE: And what does the present law say?
MAN: That men and women are equal. But I still think the wife should obey the husband.
JUDGE: But don't you know the law?
MAN: I don't think it matters if a man beats his wife —but he mustn't beat others. In the family, that's all right.
JUDGE: What law allows the husband to beat the wife?
MAN: No law.[1]

The second is a news item in a feminist pamphlet:

LETTER OF THE LAW: The recent Iranian reform law forbidding wifebeating can't be circumvented that easily. Heydar Quassemi tried to keep up domestic tradition while staying within the letter of the law by relegating his "duties" to his trained monkey, Makmal the Third. Quassemi was arrested on his wife's complaint and explained in court, "For upward of seventeen years I have given my wife a good beating on the last Tuesday of every month. When the new law against this ancient rite was passed I taught Makmal to do the job instead. It was not my intention that he should knock out my wife's tooth, but you cannot get everything right the first time. . . ." Quassemi was sentenced to three months in prison. The judge permitted him to take Makmal along.[2]

The Chinese and the Iranian wifebeaters indicate three attitudes in common: (1) they feel their behavior is acceptable and/or justified; (2) they do not quite know why they did it, other than that it is a continuation of a ritual; (3) they do not feel guilty or ashamed; they appear mystified that the law should object.

These three attitudes are among the most frequently encountered from American wifebeaters who refuse to receive psychotherapy because of their behavior. Attorneys and police hear over and over the astonished, indignant response: "You mean I can't beat my own wife?"

Hal Steiger, a Minneapolis Gestalt therapist working on the problem of wife abuse, told me, "There are two kinds of wifebeaters, treatable and intractable. The intractable type doesn't give a damn. Violence is part of his life-style, his repertoire of usual behavior. He is generally abusive. He doesn't seek psychological treatment, or if he happens to be in it, he doesn't respond. It makes sense criminally to prosecute this type.

"The treatable wifebeater is heavily invested in control of all his emotional life—sadness, joy, anger. He must stay in charge. Much energy is invested in not letting go. When he does pop finally, it's with the socially approved 'masculine' way of aggression or violence, versus the 'feminine' way of being hysterical and falling apart. He has much shame and remorse, but wants to forget as soon as possible. Violence may happen again. Or never again. If his wife threatens to leave because of the violence, it might help to get him into treatment—in your average middle-class family. With the first type, it only brings on more violence."

Shame versus Guilt

Mary Pat Brygger, a Minneapolis family counselor working with couples in the battering pattern, observes the difference in the shame-based man and the guilt-bound man. "Shame is a deeper feeling than guilt, more disabling. Shame has to do with you-the-person. Guilt is about behavior.

"When the guilt-bound man does something wrong, his reaction is, 'This is what I'll do to change it. I feel really bad about it, so I'll try to repair.'

"The shame-based man, however, feels so bad about himself as a person doing wrong that he gets into denial of the behavior and responsibility. He may even apologize, but he is disabled from doing anything about it because he feels so terrible as a person."

The first part of this chapter will deal with those wifebeaters who refuse to have anything to do with counseling. They are in the majority. (Until recently, there was almost no counselor or agency equipped to work with wifebeaters.) Therefore, the portrait of the kind of man who beats his wife tends to cover material that can be gleaned not firsthand, but from those involved as victim or helper of the victim. Most of the early studies were unable to reach many wife-beaters directly, and even if they did, could not probe the actual feelings of the perpetrators, only their behavior. In the latter part of the chapter I have attempted to touch directly on what it feels like to *be* a wifebeater, through my interviews with wifebeaters or with counselors specializing in this phenomenon. Most of the perpetrators were from the business and professional classes.

Only a small percentage of wifebeaters will talk about their problems. Very few have much to reveal even if they are questioned. One woman, for example, tried to open the lines of communication with her occasion-ally violent husband before another episode took place.

23

She asked him directly: "What do I do that makes you do this to me?

"He said he didn't know," she reported. "He's really sorry. He said, 'Do you think husbands like to beat their wives? Do you think husbands are proud of that? . . . That's something I have to do, because I feel so helpless . . . in other things that are happening in my life.' "[3]

Sociologist Richard Gelles found that ". . . those offenders we talked to struggled hard to justify their actions but often simply confessed that they hit their spouse . . . because they could not help themselves or that they knew of no other way to handle the situation."[4]

The Wifebeater Who Denies It

Many middle-class men who are violent at home simply do not see themselves as wifebeaters at all—not consciously, at least. Many have gone so far as to deny *to their wives* that anything happened.

A retired manufacturer had become violent for the first time in his marriage soon after the children left home. Following an assault he'd go off and stay in their city apartment for days and then return as if nothing were amiss. He expected to be greeted lovingly. On one violent occasion he grabbed at his wife's hair, yanking it as if to scalp her.

Never before had it occurred to her to fight back or to try to escape. This time she tore out of his grasp and fled upstairs to a bedroom, trying to barricade the door. As he broke through, she flung open the window, screaming to the people below for help. Instantly he stopped, turned around, and went downstairs and put on some music. When a neighbor hesitatingly asked if anything were wrong, he replied with a conspiratorial grin, "Oh well, you know how some women get during the change of life. . . ."

Later, when she confronted her husband with, "Look what you've done; we can't go on like this," he responded reprovingly: "I don't know what you're talking about. You're driving me crazy lately. Come on, admit it, you're trying to get me to buy you a new fur coat."[5]

This man would certainly not accept psychotherapy. He and others like him are accustomed to wifely helplessness, passivity, trying to please, "taking it." On some gut level they may wish they "did not have to do it," but nothing challenges them to stop. If they meet no resistance to physical abuse—from a terrified wife or an accepting social system—they usually become so comfortable with conjugal crime that it becomes a pattern.

He Looks Like Such a Nice Guy

Despite the pattern of violence, the middle-class wifebeater wants his world to approve of him. And it often does.

Erin Pizzey, who founded the British Women's Aid refuges, uses the term *plausible* to describe this type of wifebeater. *Plausible* is derived from the Latin for "deserving applause." Its definitions include: "that which has the appearance of truth but might be deceptive; striking the superficial judgment favorably."

A number of battered wives have told me that the image the husband presents outside the home is in total contrast to his uncontrolled violence behind closed doors. The public pose is a carefully cultivated act, indeed deserving applause, perfected so as to make any possible charges easier to deny. Very often that charm —or courtship behavior—is also directed to the wife, during the guilty–anxious or nonguilty calm period that may follow the worst beatings. And many a wife is thereby kept from taking any action.

The wifebeater from the business and professional worlds, in particular, is seldom a person from whom you would run in panic on meeting. He is not likely to injure *you*. As one such man told me defensively, "I don't go around hurting people." No, he only hurts his wife. He usually does not feel like a criminal; in fact, he often feels he is within his rights as a husband. His hero is frequently the old-fashioned stereotype of a patriarchal man, whose very wish is law, and he believes the ideal woman should agree with this concept.

A woman married to a psychologist of this description determined to make some kind of start toward a normal life. Her first step was to confide in a relative, an aunt she judged was strong and secure enough to give her moral support if not actual practical support in her attempts to free herself.

However, the aunt treated her like a silly, over-imaginative child: "But, my dear," she chided, "surely you must be exaggerating. I adore your husband. He is so charming. . . ."

Says therapist Carol Victor, the co-founder of New York's Growth & Life Center, Inc.: "The wifebeater needs to understand his anger. He doesn't want people to find out that he's not a nice guy, that the bad he is trying to beat out of her is really inside him. He is often rigid and uncompromising, really believing that his wife should be punished for violating *his* moral standards; also for the previous wrongs he suffered at the hands of women—real or imagined."

The Wifebeater as Oppressed Personality

The wifebeater shares certain characteristics with those husbands manifesting other aberrant behavior, such as incest or child abuse: low self-esteem, lack of ability to be open about his feelings, and very little understanding of what his real feelings are. Why does he turn to this particular crime and not another? Because it has been sanctioned by public attitude and laws are not enforced. His wife is the most accessible target, and he knows society won't interfere. To make doubly sure, however, he frequently keeps her isolated from society—as well as from friends, neighbors, and even family. This is a man who feels powerless, inarticulate (in communicating emotions and real feelings, that is—he might otherwise be very glib) and somehow inadequate. He may hold a good position in life. He may be at ease in business or among men friends. But these benefits are only relative. He himself feels victimized and oppressed—oppressed by the *existence* of his wife, if not by the specifics of her existence—and definitely oppressed by his *life*. He has in wifebeating his one opportunity to be an oppressor instead of the oppressed. Violence is the expression of the man's impotence.

For this type of man, life has not measured up to expectations. The realities and responsibilities of parenthood are more than he bargained for. His marriage has not measured up to his fantasies, either. His wife "ought to" be this and this, do that and that: but she does not seem to realize her duty. She lets him down. If he could only knock some sense into her, make her understand. . . .

The wifebeater often feels that nobody really cared about him in his childhood and adolescence. And his marriage is not providing the caring he needs now. Self-pity is always just beneath the surface.

A midwestern psychiatric social worker describes such a man:

> Mr. B. had come in for help because he wanted to kill his wife, and he was afraid he would. He had already tried to choke her. His physical abuse had begun ten years ago, three days after the wedding, when he interpreted some joking remarks Mrs. B. made to her sister as ridiculing him. This client, like many others, had a terrible need for emotional support and dependency that was not easily verbalized.
>
> The therapist in this case was able to respond to her client's need and express concern and empathic recognition of his distress. She was able to reinforce "the rational aspect of the functioning adult toward self-understanding and self-control."

This was one time when the wifebeater could and did change: He brought his wife in for counseling also, and the case was terminated as "each partner was progressing toward greater self-esteem and competence."[6]

The Macho Man as Little Boy

Sociologist John E. O'Brien, of Portland State University, Oregon, touched on the lack of maturity and inner sureness among wifebeaters. He found them

27

through his study of 150 individuals involved in a divorce action. The violent husbands made up one out of six in the entire group from an anonymous "midwestern standard metropolitan area . . . dominated by a state government–state university complex . . . and devoid of any sizeable number of poor families and of black families."

Represented were 24 percent upper middle class, 29 percent lower middle class, and 47 percent working class (defined as regularly employed blue-collar workers, paid hourly, with a high school diploma or its equivalent). Both men and women were interviewed.

O'Brien found that the wifebeaters were "characteristically underachievers in the work-earner role . . . deficient in certain status characteristics" (their wives often had better education and job level).

According to the O'Brien model, in any social system violence is directed by the superior status group toward the inferior. "The husband-father role has a higher ascribed status than do the wife-mother or child roles . . . traditionally supported by his superior competence in handling the world at large, and specifically in the work or earner role." Thus the sociologist theorizes that the wifebeater is trying to reaffirm his superior ascribed sex-role status.

He especially notes the "high prevalence of violence in . . . nonpoor, nonghetto families"—a statistic counter to the popular notion of violence being associated with poverty. He theorizes that "violence in the family, as with violence in the larger society, most often represents a response to certain status imbalances in the social structure."[7]

This 1969 study may have been one of the first to touch on a characteristic that was discerned later by counselors specializing in this work: It is the concept of the violent husband as little boy, wanting to be grown up and superior, as he'd been taught he should be, yet was not in fact; requiring those around him to join his pretense if he were to survive emotionally and his family survive physically.

The wifebeater doesn't know what he wants. He doesn't see himself very clearly, and his wife doesn't want to believe what she sees: Underneath his super-

28

macho exterior, her husband is a dependent little boy who never grew up—except in brute strength. In fact, in counseling the husbands in her joint therapy groups, Minneapolis therapist Mary Pat Brygger has found that "the husband is more dependent on the wife than the wife is on the husband."

The Wifebeater Needs His Wife as Part of Himself

Other therapists have also discovered unexpected *mutual* dependency. There is a certain *ego-merging*, according to Margaret Allen Elbow, executive director of the Family Service Association of Lubbock, Texas, who has worked with many problems of battery:

"Some people tend to fuse their personalities with those of others. They discern little difference in their own thoughts, feelings, hopes, dreams, fears, and so forth, and those of a person with whom they are intimate. If the other person pulls away by leaving or asserting self as separate, he (the wifebeater) feels a loss of part of himself. This concept is not unique, but as applied to family violence [including child abuse], I believe it is."

The man manifests a real need to control his wife, and sometimes his children also, or he becomes uncomfortable, "almost as if he would lose control of himself." He sees his wife as a part of himself.

Further, it may be that the wifebeater *needs* the woman to beat so that he won't assault those who really provoke him in his world of job and social contact. I think this may be true especially in middle-class families, where violence on the job would be unthinkable. Perhaps on some level the super-caretaking wife may sense this need and know she is meeting it.

British psychiatrist Peter D. Scott commented on mutual need in the "frequently observed return of a battering couple to one another." He says that rather than the sadomasochism it may suggest, it is probably "other conditions which stimulate the returning, especially dependency, fears of loneliness, and not knowing that there is a better form of relationship."

Scott also addressed himself to the concept of marital

partners identifying with one another. "Some individuals have difficulty in effecting this identification because they cannot trust." In the worst cases, they haven't really established their own independent identity as yet. "If their own self-image is very unfavorable, as happens when individuals are rejected or ill-treated in the formative years of life, then the partner is likely to be disapproved of in like fashion and will perforce have to share the anger felt by the spouse for him- or herself."

Scott sees the problem of marital battering as "a failure in adaptation." The man just has not acquired the necessary social lesson that beating up his wife is wrong.[8]

Detailed Studies

Two research projects, one British and one American, add significant details to the dearth of actual statistics on just who the wifebeater is and how he operates. John J. Gayford, a British psychiatrist, has interviewed the first one hundred women sheltered in Erin Pizzey's refuges, and noted what they reported about their husbands.[9] They were predominantly lower class, since women of higher classes are less likely to agree to be part of mass research. In his three-year independent study, he found that all one hundred men had in common a "loss of control" once the violence got under way. All of them used fists, many adding kicks with heavy shoes. Almost half also used weapons such as belt buckles, knives, razors, and broken bottles.

As children, over half the husbands had witnessed their fathers assaulting their mothers. Fewer than a quarter of them had what could be called good relationships with their parents. Seventy-four percent had a drinking problem.

Sex and Violence

Sixty-six percent of the men were markedly jealous, although 83 percent of the wives insisted they were faithful. Forty-five percent of the men had extramarital affairs themselves.

Fifteen percent seemed to experience sexual arousal from the violence—since they demanded sexual intercourse immediately following the assault. Dr. Gayford theorizes that possibly the men were actually feeling guilty and trying to kiss and make up. Not everyone would agree with Gayford's motivation theory, however. It is neither love nor guilt that is operant. In the experiences of battered women I have talked with, that sequence of behavior is labeled, in no uncertain terms, *rape*. And the woman is given no opportunity to use birth control.

The husbands in this study did not like to be left, during or after the violence. When their wives fled, wifebeaters either promised to reform, begging their wives to come back to them, or threatened them with further violence if they did not obey.

It should be noted that 60 percent of the wifebeaters in the Gayford study had impregnated their wives before marriage. They may not have freely chosen to be married. Half of these men had already spent some time in prison.

American Marriages Under Scrutiny

A study conducted in the midwestern United States is somewhat more representative of the middle-class problem. Two law students, now in practice, then at the University of Michigan, researched the frustrating conditions a battered wife met with in trying to get help in the state of Michigan.[10] Although Sue Eisenberg and Pat Micklow had to rely on those victims who were willing to talk despite their terror, they did manage to locate a small sampling of middle-class couples out of the usually available lower-class population.

In the study of twenty cases, 25 percent of the husbands represented white-collar professionals, including two plant managers, an attorney, an engineer, and a corporation president earning $40,000 a year. The average educational attainment of the assailants was 13.2 years, a little more than a year of college.

Of the total group, four had been dishonorably discharged from the service, and three had learned "how to inflict nonvisible injuries during training."* In half the cases, there was no violent physical behavior reported between the parents of the assailants.

Despite the men's knowledge of inflicting nonvisible injuries, most of the wifebeaters in this study attacked the head most frequently, and then the face. Some especially wanted to humiliate their victims so "always went for the face first."

About a third of the husbands chose the abdominal area for blows during pregnancy. More than half didn't stop until they had punched and kicked all parts of the victim's body.

The weapons used, besides fists and feet, were guns, knives, a broom, a leather belt, a brush, a pillow (to smother), a hot iron, lighted cigarettes, and a piece of railroad track.

In addition, these husbands employed verbal threats of killing and threats to kill the children also. One man whose assaults resulted in his wife's need for medical treatment, forced her to cancel the doctor appointment.

THE PATTERNS OF VIOLENCE

Wifebeaters can be incredibly dedicated to their violence. In the Eisenberg-Micklow study, one husband initiated battering on the first day of his marriage. Two demanded their wives send the police away from the door or they would kill them. It was common to use further violence upon hearing that a complaint had been made.

These men made certain their wives would not escape. Five of them injured their wives so effectively they were in no condition to leave. Four "locked their wives out without car keys, money, wallet or coat."

---

* Inflicting nonvisible injuries (at least nonfacial ones) seems to be a specialty of many of the middle-class wifebeaters coming to my attention. No matter how frenzied these husbands may have become, they seemed to remember their social conditioning—it is not nice for your wife to be walking around with a black eye or bruised face.

The *threat* of disfigurement, however, was also common. When it was carried out, it seemed to be an intentional act rather than a part of generally out-of-control behavior.

The assaults lasted anywhere from five to ten minutes to over an hour. The frequency range included a *daily* habit, once every two or three days, weekly, monthly, once every two months, four times a year, twice a year, once every two to five years.[11]

Why Did They Do It?

The reasons were not very complex. They wanted dinner ready when they came home, and it was not. The house was not clean enough. One wife did not "think before she spoke." One husband was "tired and cross." Two assailants found the wife asleep when his impulse to attack occurred.

Who Is He Really Hitting?

The place of alcohol in the dynamics of the wife-beater is a curious one. Is it the trigger of violence? Or is it the excuse? Drinking may be the trigger that unleashes the pent up violence normally held in check. It may be, conversely, a cover-up for intended actions which are bound to take place as soon as some blame can be invented.

Richard Gelles, the pioneering sociologist in this field of conjugal crime, has observed that both husbands and wives clung to the fact that the man was drunk as a convenient means of forgiving or overlooking the violent act. A wife could claim that her loving husband would never harm her when sober, but when drunk he simply did not know what he was doing. A husband could discover that he seemed to "black out" and had no memory of committing the beating. Thus, he was able to enjoy a "time out" from taking responsibility for his behavior.[12]

"'I was drunk' became my husband's handy, all-purpose excuse," a former battered wife told me bitterly. "It meant he didn't have to apologize. He needn't bother acting contrite. He didn't have to change anything. Maybe he'd bring me some flowers, but then he'd go on his merry way. We couldn't even sit down and discuss how I felt. What he did to me just didn't count because he was drunk."

33

Other husbands who woke to a hangover and evidence of the previous night's violence used the occasion for extravagant expressions of horror (possibly even genuine) and extravagant begging of forgiveness and vowing to be different. I know of no cases, however, where these truces lasted.

I find myself that there is a widespread assumption that alcohol (and/or certain ethnic cultural conditioning) is the exclusive cause of marital violence. It also shows up in the studies with some frequency. However, there are a number of cases where the husband is not drinking during violence or he never drinks at all. I have found that much conjugal crime occurs unprompted by alcohol. The sober wifebeater "attacks in cold blood," as one victim expressed it to me, and it is therefore much crueler.

Who Is He Really Hitting

It may be that the wifebeater, drunk or sober, does not consciously know whom he is really trying to demolish. Although it is small comfort to the wife who receives the injuries, she herself may not be the one the perpetrator most deeply wants to destroy.

Psychiatrist Bernard Chodorkoff,[13] who was a consultant to the National Commission on Causes and Prevention of Violence, says that sometimes the actual victim assaulted is not the original trigger of the internal psychic state leading to the assault. There are three possible mental representations in the mind of the assaulter:

1. the primary target
2. the fantasy target
3. the actual victim

The *primary* target may be a parental figure. (It has already been established that wifebeaters feel they were not sufficiently loved in childhood.) The *fantasy* target is an imaginary figure who may seem to be critical of him or castrating or dominating him. The *victim* is, of course, the individual selected by the assailant upon whom he discharges feelings of rage projected from the primary and fantasy targets. A weak and dependent wife, with few resources for escape or retribution, makes the most likely candidate. She is an always available, built-in target.

The Momentum of Violence

Battering husbands have been described as "angry, resentful, suspicious, competitive, moody, tense. They have an aura of helplessness, fear, inadequacy, insecurity. Alcoholism, jealousy, unemployment and frustration are often cited as contributing to a husband's violent outbursts."[14]

Life can be frustrating for anyone. Every human being has known times of misery and frustration. At such times it might feel good to lash out at the world, if not at a particular person, but for most people there exist certain "civilizing" interfering emotional responses that inhibit them from expressing themselves with violence.

However, once an act of violence is carried out, these inhibitions decrease, leading to further acts. As feelings of rage develop into violent behavior, a "scarring of the ego" occurs, according to Dr. Chodorkoff, and treatment becomes more and more difficult.

British psychiatrist P. D. Scott has also found similar effects of escalation: "Once the [wifebeating] conflict has acquired sufficient momentum, nothing will stop it, even occasionally the presence of a stranger actually trying to stop the violence, or even if the police had been present a few minutes earlier and had confiscated a weapon. The police may be most effective in the milder cases in which there is little real risk. Some individuals may only be further enraged by the presence of the police, who may themselves be attacked."[15]

Dr. Chodorkoff differentiates between violence and the lesser state of aggression. The emotions stimulating violence are *rage* and *hate*—both more intense than *anger*. Violence is more explosive than aggression. It is possible to deal with aggression, which can be planned, rational, deliberate, and goal-oriented. (In counseling, a short-term goal is to deescalate violent tendencies to a state of aggression; then at least a little communication is possible.) After an act of violence, the inflicter returns to his original psychological state —not necessarily a violent one, according to the psychiatrist, but a psychopathological one.

The basic components of violence, as outlined by Dr. Chodorkoff, are psychological states that increasingly lead to violence. These feelings are:

1. a sense of helplessness
2. a sense of hopelessness
3. threatened loss of self-esteem
4. fear and desire to hurt which is unmodulated by feelings of trust and love
5. anomie (a breakdown or absence of social norms and values)

The Unprovoked Attack

Dr. Chodorkoff's approach leads me to a tentative theory about the unprovoked attack. Beaten wives often cannot imagine what they did to incense the man: and wifebeaters themselves often have a pathetic lack of understanding of their own motivations.

One of the most anguished questions I have heard comes from wives of men with good education, with good status and position, and who are often active in their religion and community: *"Why does he do this when he knows better?"*

Perhaps it is possible that doubts about masculinity and/or sexuality are more frequent than generally realized. I suggest that a certain type of man might put those doubts to rest by feeling "potency" in violence, blaming his wife for his loss. And he will find many occasions to put this into practice.

When I suggested this theory to some formerly battered wives, a number of them recalled—often with surprise—that "he *had* lost interest, come to think of it," or "he *did* complain his youth was going," or "sex seemed to make him angry."

Further, I suggest that the confirmed wifebeater is adroit at interpreting the smallest response to a nonviolent wrongdoing of his as incitement to violence. Obsessively compulsive in triggering himself, he may even interpret his subsequent behavior as "defending himself."

To illustrate this sequence, let us take a hypothetical middle-class family. The unprovoked husband does something that he knows, on some level, is wrong: it could be withholding food money or the children's school expenses, refusing to let the wife go out of the house, bringing a girl friend into the house, coming home from work after midnight without phoning, or coming home late and inebriated from an entertainment he did not share with his wife. (These were examples recalled by interviewed wives.)

The wife reacts. She may say nothing, but her emotions—hurt, anger, bewilderment, blinked-back tears, indignation, fear, anxiety or disgust—show in facial or body language. What he wants is no reaction at all. Just simple acceptance, compliance. Her reactions will trigger his guilt into defensive acting out. Yet if she hides her reaction, he may interpret this as "not caring."

So he starts "retaliating." Perhaps it is with verbal abuse at first. But since she can never live up to his nonreactive ideal of a wife, he punishes her for her failure. From his viewpoint, she has it coming to her.

"She Can't Do This to Me"

Some husbands are strongly defensive about their concept of married life, covering up their self-pity and denial of wrong-doing by angrily blaming the woman. The wife-battering executive who lived in a $140,000 house, for instance, wanted very much to keep that house. He attacked his wife in a drunken rage, threatening to kill her. As she was recovering from the resultant surgery, she filed for divorce. He denied his wife's charges in a sworn affidavit. He countercharged that she had thrown an orange juice can at him. Further, he said she had accused him of "adultery with every imaginable airline stewardess between Washington and New York." He charged that she had repeatedly provoked him into arguments and fights "which she has threatened to use as a basis for taking my house away from me."[16]

I discussed this defensiveness with an attorney for

battered wives, Richard Weiner. He made it a point to try to have a talk with the husband first before proceeding with separation or divorce papers. He told me, "There's a lot of denial. I've never heard a husband say, 'I hit her and I'm sorry.' If he does admit his actions, it's a justification: 'I had to, to quiet her.' The assaulting husband's perception is completely different from the wife's—or that of a third party. In my experience, there's never been a sensitivity to the fact that the woman he's in love with and brutalizing is also a human being like himself with sensitivities, too. In all my cases, the husband's attitude has been, 'She's my woman. I love her. *She can't do this to me.*' "

What Happens If His Wife Tries to Leave

The wife's threat to divorce or legally separate may cause a sudden change in the wifebeater's personality and tactics. He may promise, and probably feel at the moment, that he will "do anything" to keep her or have the children with him. The attorney spoke of another brutal man whose wife left, after she found a secret place to stay:

"On his knees, with tears in his eyes, he begged me to ask his wife to let him see the children."

Typically, if the middle-class husband thinks he is losing, he will promise to go into counseling if only the battered wife will come back to him. And typically, if she returns before the promise is actually carried out, and for a significant number of sessions, the old patterns of conjugal crime resume. Even with effective therapy, an immediate reforming of long-ingrained behavior rarely happens.

A more frequent consequence of a wife's plans to leave, however, is the husband's swearing to kill or maim her or the children should she dare to try to escape or expose him. When she has no place to go, or her determination is shaky, or she has no strong support system, and he knows it, she invariably will suffer more for threatening to leave. (See chapter 9 for advice on how to handle this situation.)

He *demands* her love, interpreted, as he sees it, by her remaining with him. He makes no rational connection between his behavior and her reactions to it. However, if she does return before a counselor has succeeded in getting him to face his anger, his real cause of stress (it's not his wife), and acknowledge his behavior and how he feels about it, then case after case shows that he devalues her for letting him get away with near murder. He usually becomes more violent than before, blaming her for not stopping him effectively.

Violent Men from Nonviolent Homes

The academic studies show that many wifebeaters are themselves the children of violent fathers and are conditioned to the pattern of marital violence as the norm. However, much of this research did utilize a heavy population of lower socioeconomic couples. I have found, on the other hand, in talking with middle-class couples and their therapists and friends that there is frequently no violence in the husband's background.

Some of these white-collar, entrepreneurial, or professional men from nonviolent homes are so ashamed that they can hardly talk about it. "They are surprised they did it," one therapist told me. "They feel as if another person comes out in them, a monster. The violence is a burst they can't control and they want help." Several of this group have been helped.

I interviewed two men in this category. I had asked several therapists if any client would consent to an interview, promising I would not use real names or identification. Wally was eager to talk with me because he felt he had a good case against his wife, and he wanted "the man's side told." Leonard was eager to talk with me because he was proud that he had ceased his violence and wanted to "help other husbands like me."

WALLY

Wally's therapy was assertiveness training, with the goal of learning to articulate his feelings rather than repress them until they exploded in violence. The problem still existed when I met with him.

"My wife and I have been living apart for two

months," Wally said. "We still see each other. We'd planned to try a vacation together this week, as a reconciliation—and then I beat her up again. So that's off."

Wally looked bewildered and dismayed. I could feel his pain and distress. His manner with me was consistently shy, polite, deferential, almost humble. He was cooperative with questions, trying to search out honest answers. Although I have condensed it here, he continually stressed how wronged he felt by his wife's choice of leisure time with her girl friends.

"After I hit her, Lucy said she'd call the cops. I laughed at her. I didn't care. The cops would find me back home in bed."

Lucy had more faith than he that the problem would work out. She encouraged Wally to visit, on a kind of dating basis. It was she who found a therapist for him, a man she had seen herself for crisis counseling.

"I'd like to continue our marriage, but my wife has to change first. There wasn't any violence for our first ten years. Lucy always wants to go out with her girl friends. It used to be Bingo. She'd ask me if she could go. I didn't want her to do that either, but I was nonassertive. I never told her how I felt, I just gave her the money. Now she likes to go out with her girl friends for a few beers. Now I know . . . I think I do . . . that she doesn't *pick up men* there—the bunch of them are just talking and having a few laughs—but I feel threatened. Then I rationalize that she's been so unsuccessful in most of her life—in her job and her looks—she needs the success of being popular there. Yes, she comes home, but I get fogged up with rage and I hit her."

They both seem to spend a lot of their leisure time in neighborhood pubs, together or separately. Wally —attractive, trim, and suntanned, the owner of a sporting goods store—was apparently well liked by the crowd, although he found it difficult to get his viewpoints across. He was "good old Wally," and wished he could be more forceful.

"Once Lucy called the bar where I was that night and said she'd be home later, but refused to say where she was. A week later I got home from work and found a message to meet her in a certain place. Although she did tell me this time where she was, I felt all fogged up, in a rage. I don't know why. Lack of trust, I guess. I went there, grabbed her by the hair. She screamed. I pulled her out to the street. I don't know if I hit her. She drove off with her girl friend to spend the night. She phoned me later. I went over and . . . I don't remember hitting her, but our friends stopped it."

None of the onlookers inside or the bystanders in the street had intervened. Wally said alcohol was not greatly involved, "just a few beers."

"Last year she left me for a week. She met a guy, but she came home when he didn't want her. It was the first time she did that. She hasn't again."

Wally and Lucy don't discuss his violence with each other—"not during the calm times. It isn't necessary. But it comes up during arguments over raising the kids. She doesn't express her feelings to me, what she goes through. She promised to stop going out with her girl friends for a while."

He doesn't speak of the problem with anyone but his therapist, a jovial, warm, sensitive man. Wally is sure the people who mean a lot to him do not know. "If my mother knew, she'd be hurt. I'd be embarrassed, I wouldn't like her to know. She was good to me as a child."

His own three children know since they have witnessed some of the violence. Now two children live in the mother's new apartment, and one stays at home with Wally. The junior high school–age daughter has tried to intervene. "It settles me down. I stop." When I told him many wifebeaters will hit the child for interfering, he was aghast. "I'd never do that. I'm not a monster." What has the effect on the children been? "There isn't any ill effect. I don't notice *any* effect —unless I've put it in my unconscious. Maybe my daughter shares my 'getting shit on' feeling when mommy goes out with the girls. Maybe deep down she thinks it's justifiable vengeance."

Wally's memory of how he feels during a violent episode, and what it is all about, is a mixture of denial, anger, and sharp chagrin. What he feels during his rages, he thinks, is "justifiable vengeance. Hurt by the

41

threat to our marriage. I remember only the hairpulling, not beating."

So far, he has been able to stop himself before Lucy is seriously injured. "I stop when I know I've hurt her. When I recognize a degree of powerlessness on her part, that I gained a certain degree of control over her. Or that I realize it's not going to produce the control I want. I don't know what stops it. Maybe it's that she doesn't fight back. But her reactions frighten me. Screaming, pleading but not begging, all anger and rage. She threatens she'll walk out. Her eyes blaze with hate. It's frightening, takes me hours to get over it. I'm embarrassed. I hate myself. I'm more angry at myself than with her. I pride myself on being in control of my emotions. Hitting is just self-destructive to what I want to occur.

"She wants us back together now, if the violence is over. She says she's lonely. We have a fairly good sexual relationship. That's one area where there's no bullshit. I went over to her apartment the other night; we went to bed. When I got up at 3:00 A.M. to go home, she asked me to stay. But I'm not going to get sucked into that until we straighten things out. She gets lonely and depressed and then she phones me. I'm not going to get trapped again, too dependent on her whims and fantasies, her flighty moods.

"One thing I got out of this therapy is self-awareness and my values clarified. I know I don't want a power struggle. I hate to use my physical power to get control. I hate games."

LEONARD

Leonard's wife did not go out with girl friends—she had none. She stayed in their extravagant suburban home with their children who were in nursery school, kindergarten, and first grade. Leonard is a partner in a small manufacturing company, very much involved in his work—"my main hobby." His other hobbies are tennis and "high living."

When Leonard first came into therapy, he could not control his rages of kicking, choking, and spanking his wife, although he hated himself for it. His children ran and hid from him, and it deeply grieved him.

He spoke of his helplessness to know why he attacked his wife, and why, before therapy, he could not stop. "Leena would say something and I'd get angry. And before I knew it. . . . It was agony. I don't know what got into me. I'm not like that. I needed help. No one in my family ever did anything like that. I'm not a bad person. I don't go around mugging old ladies.

"People like me have got to help. If a dog is sick, you don't kick it, you get help for it."

Did his wife ever phone for help, call the police or their minister? Leonard was outraged at this thought. "Never!" He pounded the table. "I would never let a cop or a preacher into my home. That's not the way to do it. A man who beats up his wife is *sick*. That would only make it worse for him. Someone should *help* him."

When he first went into counseling with a specialist in conjugal crime, Leonard had his doubts about staying. "Then I realized I could trust her. Right away she made it clear that everyone gets angry, very angry. She told me how she almost broke the phone one time, slamming it. She treated me like a decent person who's got a terrible problem, but not a monster."

When I asked Leonard how he felt during his violence, the question shocked him. "I never thought about it. I don't know. I didn't think about it then, either. All I know is that I felt terrible afterward." I mentioned the statistics that some men found violence a turn-on and wanted sex immediately. Again, he was shocked. "Not me! Never! My wife didn't want to have anything to do with me for days after, and I don't blame her. I couldn't think of sex at such a time. I'm not weird."

The violence decreased gradually. Several times both Leonard and Leena thought it was over for good, and then he'd lash out again. What made it stop finally? "My therapist asked me how I'd feel if my little daughter married someone like me. What? I'd kill the rotten bastard who laid a hand on a helpless girl! Well, it brought the truth home to me."

Leonard said his relationship with his children was

43

all right now. "They were too young, they won't remember. They are not afraid of me anymore.

"I can't stand people to be afraid of me. I'm not a dangerous person. I'm not evil. An interviewer for one of the local television news programs talked to me for a segment on wifebeating and I could see she was afraid of me. And they never aired the show at all. Here I wanted to be helpful to other guys in my position, and yet she acted as though I wasn't a human being. I can't stand that. I see you are not afraid of me, you're treating me like a decent human being. I appreciate that.

"I'd like other husbands to know that wifebeating is a symptom of a larger personal problem. Don't look for the blame in the wife, look to yourself. My problem was terrible insecurity, that's where my anger was coming from. That symptom has been gone for almost a year. In therapy, now, we are going on to other things. My life has more meaning. My business is improving. I've always loved competition, a tough fight with winning out over competitors, and now I'm more effective with it.

"I'll always be ashamed of what I did to my wife, always have to work on it. But it's over. Leena should not have put up with me. She didn't realize she should be treated with respect, and I didn't want her to be on that low a level. She had no self-reliance, no dignity. At least she is beginning to follow some of her own interests and doing very well. I'm proud of her. I like to see her stand on her own two feet. She's got abilities and at last she's doing something with her own life. Therapy changed us both. I wish we hadn't waited so long, but therapy saved my marriage."

In common with many wifebeaters, both these men felt powerless to stop their violence without therapy and looked to the wife to somehow make them stop. Both found it too painful to acknowledge the lasting effect on the children. On the other hand, both Leonard and Wally were exceptions to the overall statistics on wifebeaters. One, in the very fact they would be willing to sit through embarrassing personal questions. Other wifebeaters I'd talk with would refuse to continue if vulnerable points were touched. Secondly, they acknowledged they had a problem beyond their control, suffered mental agony over it, and were willing to seek therapeutic help; and thirdly, these men were less vicious and more aware than many, comparatively more in touch with their feelings. Their motivation to change was strong.

What Being a Wifebeater Feels Like

So new is the awareness of this conjugal crime among all socioeconomic classes that the few published studies have not been able to cover all significant aspects of the problem. In particular, there is little literature of academic research gleaned directly from the perpetrators themselves.

Therefore, I gathered up my own notes, interviews, and impressions, and created a questionnaire to try to probe more of the "cultural norm" of the average wifebeater's mentality.

The Family Service of Detroit and Wayne County, Emergency Counseling Division, was the first, and at the time the only, large funded agency actually devoting itself to greater professional understanding of the little-known dynamics of the perpetrator as well as the victim of conjugal crime. When I contacted the agency, it was working on a statistical analysis of the problem. Although the answers were derived "only from clinical impressions," and not structured data, Margaret Ball, ASCW, was able to provide some fascinating, insightful responses to my questions.[17]

I. The wifebeater generally wants the battered wife not to leave him. Why?

(a) Battering is his pleasure. *(b)* She provides a familiar, comfortable life-style. *(c)* He wants her housekeeping services. *(d)* He wants her sexual availability. *(e)* He doesn't want to be deprived of his "possession" any more than of his TV set.

Response: Many alternative answers are possible—even in the same person. The husband who beats his wife may also value her, sometimes as a possession, and one way for him to validate his strength and worth, other than as a mate with any kind of equal worth. But in other men, there is a more genuine, mature caring alongside puzzling bursts of rage and abuse. People are complicated!

II. Although he will get little or no punishment, perhaps even condonation from law and society, the wife-beater usually does not want his wife to tell (often on pain of worse battering) and seldom will talk about his behavior himself. Why?

(a) He "knows" his behavior is wrong, and once known, he'd have to face it consciously. *(b)* He is afraid of loss of face, or public censure, or possible punishment or retaliation. *(c)* It's his chosen life-style and he wants no interference. *(d)* He "knows" he's right/justified, but feels no one else would "understand."

Response: "A" comes closest, I believe. The abusive husband is not truly proud of his violent behavior and knows at some level it is inappropriate.

III. Animals in combat respect the "cry uncle" admission from the loser and stop fighting; the winner does not continue demolishing the weaker. Yet wifebeaters tend not to stop after they've struck the first (sufficient) blow, but continue on into overkill. Why?

(a) Momentum/inertia—once started, he "cannot" stop, similar to the alcoholic. *(b)* At that moment he despises her and really prefers to demolish her, as opposed to simply "expressing his point." *(c)* He sees her as a nonperson (similar to soldiers re the enemy) and a victim-therefore-guilty, so she becomes increasingly to deserve battering. *(d)* The barbaric act puts him out of control and beyond reason. *(e)* By that time he does not know how to stop, cannot turn back—despite some possible wish not to go so far.

Response: Again, there are many triggers for the behavior. Abusive behavior stems from anger and frustration. If it is strongly violent, and the abuser loses control of his judgment and behavior, then it is very likely his rage comes from deep within and is related to old hurts and insults from childhood—not really from the present situation or person. In that sense, the present triggers the past. Current stresses in the family or in other areas of life are also precipitants. And violence as one method of interacting is "taught" (by example) in families and passed on to the next generation.

IV. How does he feel *during* the wifebeating?

(a) Powerful and enjoying it. *(b)* Sexually stimulated, akin to committing rape. *(c)* Nonimpotent at last. *(d)* Able to substitute it for sex. *(e)* Losing of sense-of-miserable-self, and therefore experiencing the incident as "mentally healthful" and, for him, worth repeating.

Response: My guess is sense of release (of tension), relief (from old pain), and justification or justified revenge. This may not fit the reality situation or object, but a former, early one, or a fantasied one representing and disguising a parent. Self-esteem may be temporarily heightened, as also a sense of power.

V. How does he feel *afterward?*

(a) Proud/victorious/triumphant. *(b)* Ashamed/guilty. *(c)* Sorry for wife. *(d)* Penitent (I've found this, but seldom lasting). *(e)* Feeling too much like Harry Stack Sullivan's "Bad Me" or "Not Me" to deal with it.

Response: Confused, anxious, guilty. Any "pride" is a cover for above. Denial and avoidance occur, especially since he doesn't really understand or like his actions.

Will He Beat Future Wives?

There are additional questions that will require years of follow-up before conclusive answers emerge: Does the middle-class wifebeater repeat his pattern of easily triggered marital violence in future relationships with other women? Or was there something about that particular woman or that particular combination of human dynamics that fueled behavior not likely to occur otherwise?

An individual middle-class wifebeater—who is accepted as a nice guy in his community—will accuse his mate of being "the only woman in the world who could set me off this way." And his wife, being so isolated—what can she say? As far as each one of the hundreds of thousands of silent battered wives knows, she *is* the only one in the world undergoing such a marriage, and she agonizes over why it is so.

Of course, there are some women who have been successful in refusing to put up with a second beating. Numbers of self-confident women have stated that early in the marriage their spouses had "tried something once." These wives then made it very clear that physical abuse would not be tolerated. Thereafter these marriages continued nonviolently, or if they did break up, it was for other reasons.

What kind of woman would a *confirmed* wifebeater marry the second time around? Would he seek out a woman who would never put up with violence? Could she sense his real nature despite his "plausibility"? (Chapter 9 gives some clues to predicting a potential wifebeater.) Would his record stand as having once been married to the only woman in the world with whom he became violent?

I know of a few cases where a divorced wifebeater underwent a major personality change *before the second marriage took place,* thereafter rejecting not only marital violence but other unhealthy behavior and attitudes as well. For example, a university professor described to me very frankly how he felt during wifebeating in his younger days, before he became the nonviolent man he is today: "I felt wonderful. Like Marlon Brando. It was a big macho thing. I would go to the bar and brag to the guys, 'I sure put my shoe up her ass.' But it's a power play I dropped after I became more sure of myself."

On the other hand, there is greater evidence, from cases told to me where the man's behavior after a divorce is known, that there does seem to be a continuation of former patterns.

The most dramatic example is the case of three marriages out of four. The man had been married four times, according to his daughter, and habitually assaulted each of the first three wives. In the final marriage, he "felt too old to bother."

Another man had a wife whom he beat and, concurrently, a girl friend whom he did not beat. When the girl friend eventually became the man's new spouse, she became his second battered wife.

And then there was the case of the young graduate student who gave up school and career to settle down with a charming, well-to-do older man. The man's former wife came to the girl's mother to warn her about probably impending violence.

The mother was concerned. The girl dismissed the warning as mere "jealousy." Before the first year of their marriage was out, however, the bride had fled back to her parents, terrified of the wifebeater, suing for divorce, and so eager to be free of him that she left him all the furniture and wedding presents.

What kind of woman finds herself in such a predicament? Does she have a masochistic streak? Poor judgment? Or bad luck? A provoking nature? Could she have foreseen what her love would be like as a husband? Could she have prevented the consequences? The next chapter will take up the question, What kind of woman becomes a battered wife?

3

What Kind of Woman
Becomes a Battered Wife?

It Could Be Anybody

There is little similarity or consistent pattern in the psychic makeup of women who have experienced *one occasion* of assault. Almost anyone could feel, "There but for the grace of God, go I." The National Institute of Mental Health suggests the number is as high as 50 or 60 percent of all American marriages.

But one occasion does not create the battered wife syndrome. It is what happens afterward that does. What will the woman do about it? Will she fight back in an effective way? Will she make sure it never happens again?

Or will her reaction take the form of walking on tiptoe, devoting herself to not precipitating another incident? If she lets her husband know in no uncertain terms that he's in big trouble if he ever thinks of resorting to violence again, will she really be able to make her ultimatum stick?

Or will she be so overwhelmed with humiliation, shock, and fear that she will find it more comfortable to pretend—to herself, to him, and to others—that it never happened? The middle-class battered wife's response to her fear tends to be withdrawal, silence, and denial. Fighting back would be foreign to the way she was brought up. Exposing her husband-assailant would be foreign to her also.

Meanwhile, her husband is learning, whether consciously or not, that hitting his wife was somehow acceptable the last time; she did nothing about it. Thus a pattern is set. All the evidence is that when the first or second assault is not firmly dealt with, there will be more. And the assaults will become more frequent and more severe.

Women who have stayed in a violent marriage long enough to bear the label battered wife may have a family history of the conjugal crime, but not necessarily. When a wife—or the man she marries—comes from a background of parental violence, and she did not make her feelings about it very clear, a repetition in her own marriage may not come as a total surprise. If the couple did not communicate openly about expectations and goals of marriage beforehand, childhood conditioning may play a part in the acting out of marital roles.

The Woman from a "Good" Family

While it is true that some women do participate in or initiate violence, this is not the usual middle-class pattern. For these women wifebeating comes as a stupefying shock. The victims may exemplify society's old image of ideal womanhood—submissive, religious, nonassertive, accepting of whatever the husband's life brings. They may exercise no independence of income, ideas, or movement, be anxious about housekeeping, and develop devotion to home and family to the exclusion of outside friends and interests. The husband comes first for these women, who perceive themselves as having little control over many areas of their own lives.

They are meek. Their reaction to their predicament —often mistaken by others for masochism—is cowering and submission, not retaliation or action. They are the ones whose marriages are lived out in fear, trying to please and appease, terrified of inadvertently making the wrong move. All their energies go into making the relationship survive with as little violence as possible.

Marriage is important to them. Outward appearances are important, too, especially to those middle-class wives who have endured years and years of silence, covering up for their husbands. They feel an unspecific guilt that they must have made some sort of mistake in order to be in their predicament. So, they keep trying to identify and rectify it. Or they become numb, resigned, incapable of independent thinking. Their world is limited by their cocoon of fear. They become accomplices in their own downfall, as they lie about the cause of their obvious injuries, returning to the injurer as if they loved him and were loved in return, defending him when anyone begins to suspect the truth.

For such women, keeping the image of a socially and religiously acceptable marriage takes priority over the possible consequences of exposure. Their husbands agree.

The pattern of not getting any relief has set in, along with the pattern of wifebeating. Has she no self-respect? Doesn't she care about what is going on? Of course she does. She grew up to believe that marriage and husband were what life was about, and that it was up to her to make her marriage work. She wants "everything to be all right again." But since that now seems impossible, she cannot think of other alternatives.

Further, if her husband goes through a period of trying to win her back—typical of some wifebeaters when they fear they've gone too far and may lose the woman—she becomes confused. She longs to believe this new wooing behavior will last.

The Battered Personality

Carol Victor, a therapist who has had success in helping battered marriages become viable again, explains the woman's role in the problem: "The battered wife is not blameless. Whatever is happening, it is satisfying some unhealthy need that should be clarified —perhaps a need from childhood to believe that she cannot do much of anything, or that she needs to be kept under control. At the thought of removing herself from the violent marriage, she thinks, 'I know what I've *got;* I'm scared of what I *might* get.' Why is she comfortable with this behavior? It's part of the battered personality. It's what she's been subjected to all her life.

"And I'm not necessarily talking about women one would think of as *pathetic*. Many of my clients don't fit the stereotype at all. Many are outstandingly attractive and well dressed. Many are successful in business or professions. They are not ready to leave the marriage. They are not ready to identify themselves as 'battered women.' Not ready to go into group therapy. They tell me, 'I'm not like those other women.' "

Some women feel disgust, a sense that "this is so lower class." But wifebeating happens in the best of families. In Carol Victor's survey of eighty clients with the problem of wifebeating, all socioeconomic educational classes were represented.

Four of the battered wives had completed graduate school, six had completed college, seventeen had attended college. Nine of the wifebeaters had completed graduate school (several were Ph.D.s and M.D.s) and nine had completed college.

Occupations of the women included one or more of the following: social worker, psychologist, librarian, teacher, artist, nurse, designer, manager, medical technician, computer programmer, law enforcement officer, banker, secretary, accountant. There was also a waitress. Occupations of the men included one or more of the following: physician, self-employed businessman, draftsman, engineer, teacher, pharmacist, medical technician, librarian, police, career military man, and computer programmer. There was also a sanitation worker.[1]

How Husband and Wife Interact

Though her economic background might indicate a measure of independence, in personality the battered wife may be everything a stereotypic male chauvinist could desire. "She looks up to the male as superior, and looks down on all women, including herself, as inferior," says Mary Pat Brygger, a Minneapolis therapist who runs a group for battered wives and specializes in treating couples from these marriages jointly. She says that the wifebeater, who has an overwhelming sense of frustration and inadequacy, "consumes a great amount of energy living up to the old-fashioned masculine stereotype, and then finds it too difficult. . . . She can't take care of herself and yet he can't take care of her either The wife's dependence on this man finally becomes too much for him. He expects himself

53

—and his wife expects him—to have all the answers, to be the strong one.

"His sense of inadequacy is increased," continues Brygger, "because he cannot fulfill the fantasy. The woman is being what she has been conditioned to be, what she thought her husband wanted—and what he thought he wanted. It doesn't work. He can't express his frustration in words. He expresses himself in violence."[2]

The men's liberation movement has similar views on this subject. Mel Grey, of the Men's Awareness Network in St. Paul, adds: "Men are taught to conceal their vulnerability and emotions. They are thrust into the role of breadwinner and protector, and the resulting pressure can lead to resentment over all that responsibility, with the woman oftentimes feeling the brunt of resentment if expressed.

"The woman, on the other hand, is seen as a weak, emotional, and dependent person who lacks status (e.g., gives up her name, ceases to earn money, etc.). She 'nags' because she is not pleased with this role, and the man is oftentimes the only person to whom she can express her frustrations. Portrayed by the media as dumb and/or indecisive, objectified in advertising as unable to control the 'ring around the collar,' what does it matter if she is beaten?"[3]

How Does It Feel to Be Beaten?

What is the woman feeling as she lies there, where she was hurled, not crying out or threatening or escaping or attempting to fight back? She is too overwhelmed to think or feel. But soon the physical pain surfaces; then the emotional pain.

In the past, her husband was the natural one to turn to in time of pain or bewilderment. But to whom can she turn now? She may have thought she was a model wife. What could have gone wrong?

Carol Victor asked her clients what their feelings were toward their husbands and toward themselves during and after the beatings, thereby opening an area I have not found explored in any of the literature. The responses show the sense of total inadequacy the woman feels, the total victimization. Not one was able to think how to save herself, or even *of* saving herself (except in a fantasy of murder), the shock was so great.

Many wives were so out of touch with their feelings that they hardly considered themselves as *persons,* important enough to think, to have reasonable responses to being persecuted. To the question, "What were your feelings toward yourself during and after the beatings?" one quarter of the women replied: "I don't know." The next highest response was "degraded." Others said, "I don't deserve it." Still others directed negative feelings of "anger, guilt, frustration, and hate" toward themselves.

One, whose husband was "so sweet before the judge" that she was unable to get justice, said, "I wanted to kill him. I guess I loved him. Fear made me stay. No matter what he did to me, I always felt sorry after. I don't fight back anymore, he had gotten me so worn out. What is there to life? There's got to be more. The only way I'll be free of him is if I were dead."

The torment is mental as well as physical. "My body is in pain; but my psyche is worse." Another woman said, "I am afraid. I don't understand why he is doing this. I think I must really be crazy. No one believes me." This woman, like so many, had a well-educated husband who was perceived by friends, acquaintances, and her own family as "very charming." These listeners were only uncomfortable and skeptical when she tried to explain what her marriage was like.

Many seemed determined to take the guilt upon themselves: "I'm sure I do provoke him. There's something I'm not doing right, even if it's being too submissive. I'm really worried about him. He doesn't deserve this. Somehow I must have brought him into it." Another said, "I can't hate him, there's something wrong. I have to make up my mind, either I live with him or make a clean sweep. The kids are getting too hurt by all this."

One woman said, "I can't think when he's doing that," but a few were strong enough to reach out for self-preservation. "All I think of is, 'God help me to think my way clear. There must be a way out.' " Only one wished "someone would come to my rescue."

A likely reaction to abuse by a husband would be anger. But many of these women have trouble expressing their anger. Having become such nonpersons in their own eyes, they often turn the anger at the assailant inward. The result is feelings of guilt and self-blame. Or, sometimes, the woman may displace the anger, beyond her control and rationality, to someone else close at hand. This is what is going on when—as occasional police accounts attest—the battered wife turns to the police coming to intervene or on hospital personnel or on the social worker or even her own children. (This is exactly what her husband has done when his business world angered him. He cannot beat up his boss, but he can displace his anger at someone at home.)

Battered wives tend to be isolated—from other women, from friends, and from the community. Mary Pat Brygger notes, "Without exception, the women in my battered wives group had less respect and liking for women than for men, until therapy had progressed for some time. They devalued women and themselves. They tended to see men as rescuers—rescuing them from an unpleasant job, from parents, from another wifebeating man, from loneliness. But then the rescuer turns out to be the persecutor.

"A battered woman tends then to isolate herself—with the help of the husband himself. He doesn't want her to give time to friends, neighbors, relatives, outside activities. Some even object to her going to church. He wants all the attention himself. So she begins to rely on him for *all* her needs—needs previously met in other ways—which he then discovers is too heavy a responsibility. He doesn't like the role after all. He beats her. Except for a kind of *coffee klatsch* relationship, whether she is working outside the home or not, she isolates herself from other women emotionally, not perceiving them as sources of strength or friendship."

Even for the woman who does manage to separate from her husband, her dependency on him may be a strong pull back to the marriage.

One woman returned to a shelter after each of several ill-fated "reconciliations" with her violent husband. She explained: "If you don't have friends on the outside, and your priest and doctor and the courts have all let you down, the familiar world at home is, well, at least familiar. It becomes the only world you've got."

Among Carol Victor's clients, 60 percent were not "allowed to initiate and maintain relationships with friends and family." Some were allowed only *his* friends. Some could have friends "in the home only, not outside." Clearly, the kind of woman who becomes a battered wife is either not outraged by this form of dictatorship over her private life or else perceives herself as powerless to change it. The noose tightens as she begins to lose her potential allies and rescuers.

Loss of Control

The battered wife has been at the mercy of someone else's mood fluctuations and predictable or unpredictable temper to the point where she feels she has no control over her own life. No one seems to care about *her* moods. Indeed, she has to deny them, stifle them.

Living this kind of life results in generalized fear and emotional paralysis. If, in addition, her efforts to find help from the traditional channels (see chapter 4), meet with a series of runarounds—the usual procedure—her image of herself as "helpless," "hopeless," and "unworthy of the world's cooperation" is verified. The locus of control is not within herself. It seems as if whatever happens is *done to her*. She is only a pawn manipulated by her husband and the indifferent world. The concept of making a decision on her own is only ludicrous. Experience has proved it wouldn't make any difference to anybody and could not be followed through in any case.

Adding to her difficulties is the fact that no matter how high the income bracket of her husband, the wife-beater's wife seldom has access to money, even if sometimes she herself has a job. She may have closets full of furs and new clothes, an expensive home, charge accounts in the best stores, but she would be hard-pressed to accumulate the cash, even for one secret visit to a psychiatrist. The husband controls the purse strings and demands an accounting of any unfamiliar expense.

Reaching Out for Counseling

It takes a lot of gumption for a woman who has been so beaten down, psychologically and physically, to take a positive step of self-affirmation and hope and seek counseling. That takes energy, and she has little left. Any important decision takes clear-headed thinking, some self-confidence, knowledge of options, availability of advisors, time and privacy, to sort out the facts, and she may feel denied all of these. It's hard to concede that something is so terribly wrong, so *uncivilized*. Also, the very act of seeking help may be dangerous; if her husband-assailant finds out, he may harm her further. Finally, she may have doubts about her own ability to use the information and insight offered to her in counseling.

Most battered women have not sought psychological help. But of those who do, most do not appear for counseling when they are first assaulted. Usually there is a long history of beatings. Perhaps the most recent attack was the last straw, breaking through to awareness of the despair which had been masked by denial and false hope. Or perhaps the husband's violence has begun to expand to include the children, and a concern is felt for them that the woman did not feel for herself. Or perhaps she is not in a state of crisis at all, but motivated by accumulated despair, at last ready to give up on the violent relationship and to begin trying to salvage her own life and the lives of the children.

The woman comes to counseling with many anxieties. Since she feels she has failed miserably at the most important thing in her life, she worries about how she can possibly communicate with the therapist. Feeling guilt and bewilderment about how she ever got into her predicament, and why she couldn't better it and why she then stayed, she fears the counselor will judge her as she judges herself. She may feel embarrassed at being designated a battered wife.

Another type of client, usually a younger woman, comes in anger and frustration. All her attempts to use the societally provided means of help have backfired. Police and the courts have done nothing for her. She has a healthy indignation along with her paralyzing fear. This woman has more of a chance because she has not yet been conditioned to accept her fate.[4]

Until the last several years—when public exposure of the problem made a middle-class woman realize she was not the only one of her kind with an "unspeakable" marriage difficulty—very few traditionally trained therapists encountered this problem in their practices for the simple reason that women couldn't bring themselves to talk about it. They might enter therapy for "nervousness" or "depression" or "fears" or "suicidal tendencies" or "inability to cope with life." Or even because the marriage was "not very happy." But the element of violence by husbands was omitted.

When I first undertook my research I began asking friends and acquaintances in the helping professions for some case histories. Incredibly, I was often told they had not found the problem in their practices, or not very often. As public consciousness began to be raised, some of these same M.D.'s, Ph.D.'s, counselors, and psychiatric social workers began to find longtime patients finally revealing that previously hidden trouble. If a therapist is not aware of the existence of marital violence as a phenomenon, he is not likely to see the clues. Or if he is one of those who do not view wife-beating as much of a problem, or who believe that "reconciliation" is the goal of all marital counseling, no matter how dangerous to the wife—then it won't receive high priority either.

The battered woman who, year after year has waited, hoping the assailant in her home would change, becomes burdened with many complex side effects beyond the obvious problem of physical injuries. The longer she waits, the harder it becomes to break out of the fear-filled universe she inhabits. Her problems color all of her chaotic life.

Why She Stays

Divorce may be against her religion. It is, for many wifebeaters' wives. Separation may seem a lonelier alternative than she can bear, involving more responsibilities than she knows how to handle. Because of her extreme dependence on her husband—for making decisions, for handling financial matters, for dealing with landlords or repair people or banks, for friends and social life—she feels about as capable of living alone as a ten-year-old.

In addition, for the woman who has remained loyal to the marriage year after year, a vicious circle begins about who is "right" and who is "guilty." In Hans Toch's studies of the psychology of violence,[5] he found that if only one person is violence-prone, then it is he who shapes the incident. He must *feel* provoked.

In a marriage where the violence-prone person is the physically stronger, the weaker person may well become conditioned by the assailant's "reasoning." She may come to believe that whatever she did—even if she is not sure what it is—must have been provoking, and violence was her husband's logical reaction. She constantly asks herself: "Was I wrong? Was I so bad? Wasn't I right? Could I have done anything different? What else could I have done?"

Provocation

The question of provocation and wrongdoing is one that is raised constantly—not only by wives and husbands but also by judges and uninvolved listeners. Is the kind of woman who becomes a battered woman one with a provoking disposition?

Provocation often exists only in the mind of the provoked. The same situation that will trigger a violence-prone husband may elicit little or no response in a more self-confident man. Wifebeaters, for example, are frequently consumed by fantasies of jealousy. It is not unusual for such a man to take offense at a simple "hello" to a neighbor, whereas a more secure man will —if he has any reaction at all—be pleased his wife is friendly to the people in his world.

In some of the first marital violence research, begun in the early 1970s, the question of provocation was examined. A young graduate student in sociology at the University of New Hampshire, Richard J. Gelles,[6] interviewed eighty families in a predominantly working-class community. Some of the names were given to him by a social agency as having had domestic violence in their past. The control group was made up of neighbors whose history was unknown. Yet 34 percent of those turned out also to have had at least one incident of violence in their marriages.

Gelles observed that "certain verbal assaults made by the victim, if directed at vulnerable aspects of the offender's self-concept, are likely to produce violent reactions. Moreover . . . the victim is able to direct these verbal salvos at the partner's vulnerable points because the intimacy and emotional closeness of marriage exposes each other's weaknesses."

Gelles found that "characteristic incidents . . . occur in family interaction that often lead to violence." Among these were "interfering with one partner's attempt to punish the children, nagging, arguments over drinking and gambling, using vile names, verbal criticisms of sexual performance, and escalating family arguments by bringing past and present conflicts into a fight." Are these provocations? To unpleasantness, yes. To a dispute, yes. But to violence?

Gelles found that it was almost impossible in family interaction for a wife or a husband not to nag each other. One of his interviewed wives expressed the hopelessness of it all with, "You got to live in dead silence and then you don't have no fights." One type of battered wife is a woman who has not been able to maintain the "dead silence," even when she knows her husband is an easily triggered, insecure man.

In Gelles's subjects, the nagging or verbal blasts were frequently caused by and directed toward social, psychological, or emotional "defects" in the partner. Drinking or gambling were high on the list. Deficient sexual performance and sexual appetites were included, as well as resentment at "male chauvinist attitudes" or dissatisfactions with being a "harried housewife." The provocations were often multidimensional complaints such as "upset over their husbands' drinking [and] anger over having to get up and cook for them and then have sex. They were extremely angry that

61

their husbands had wasted the family income on liquor and gambling."

On the question of nagging, a typical scenario goes something like this: The wife asks for money for groceries or children's school expenses. The husband says, "Yes, soon," but doesn't give it to her. Or says, "Later." Or objects. In any case, he doesn't do it. She asks again. He repeats the former response. She becomes frantic or irritable or vituperative or super-careful to avoid the "upset" that is likely to come. But she asks again. That, according to some wifebeaters, constitutes nagging, or verbal attack—an offense punishable by physical assault. The need is still not met. After the beating, the woman still must find a way to take care of the children's school expenses.

Two of the wifebeaters I've interviewed, one a professor and one a social worker, protested, "But her verbal attacks on me feel worse than a beating."

Gelles cites examples of the "fallacy . . . that the wife is totally to blame and that she is a nagging shrew. In addition to admitting that they were nags, wives also explained that there was often a reason for their nagging." One, for example, was "hit in the eye by her husband after she kept asking him to help shovel the snow."

BATTERED HUSBANDS

Certainly there are women who *are* provoking or malicious. Some habitually resort to violence themselves. In fact, a question I've been asked frequently by men during my research has been: "But what about battered *husbands?* There must be some of those."

The answer is, "Yes, there is at least one I know of." He is in England, and wrote an anonymous letter to the Parliament's Select Committee on Violence in Marriage:

2nd May, 1975

Dear Sir,
    Press reports suggest that the problem of violence in marriage is confined to the "battered wives"

62

problem. It seems to be overlooked that many husbands must suffer from the violence of their wives.

My wife is extremely violent at times. During these periods she is very strong and hits me and kicks me, or belabours me with whatever comes to hand—a plank of wood or perhaps a broomstick. On one occasion she hit my ear so hard that the eardrum was perforated. On another occasion she came at me with a kitchen knife. I put up my hand to fend her off and she cut my right finger to the bone, necessitating four stitches and it is now permanently painful.

A psychiatrist has said that she is emotionally immature, and that her reactions to life are those of a child, i.e., if something displeases her she throws a tantrum or lies on the floor kicking. He said that at age sixty-three she is unlikely to change.

There must be many husbands who have to suffer this wifely violence, and I hope your committee will not overlook this aspect of the problem of violence in marriage.

For obvious reason I am unable to give you my name or address.[7]

During the course of their study, Eisenberg and Micklow also were frequently asked, "What about battered husbands?" Their answer was: ". . . This tends to be an almost insignificant minority . . . no statistical data is available. Experts agree that males would encounter severe cultural reactions in the event that they sought help and protection for such an assault."[8]

Woman as Caretaker

What kind of woman becomes a battered wife? She is one who is willing to mother the emotionally immature man, sacrifice for him, spoil him, and not expose him, no matter how unrealistic his demands. There is another type—a woman who is not willing to stay but is prevented from leaving. The first type, however, when complaining of her husband's irresponsibility, does not go on to say that her response is, "Why don't you grow up!" Instead the typical response is an attempt to "make him feel like a man," a quality that neither husband nor wife feels is a strong part of his character. Many such women feel that they are expected to act more like mothers than wives. "He's like a little boy demanding his mother treat him like a king so he'll *feel* like a king," ran one complaint. Such a woman can work at the fiction but her husband knows, and she knows, that he is pretending. How ironic that this particular "little boy" holds the power of life or death, safety or maiming, in his irresponsible hands.

Surprisingly, once they have gotten away from their husbands, many battered wives are sympathetic and forgiving toward the man. Some are indulgent, even maternal, toward the wifebeater they left behind.

One wife told me she'd been unable to get a divorce until her husband met another woman and wanted his freedom. The new wife had her own fortune and controlled the money and the man. There was no wifebeating in this second marriage.

Years later, he apologized to his first wife for his former brutality. She became friends with him, and his confidante. When she observed that no one even put flowers on his grave, she did so although it was an expense she could hardly afford. Safely out of the violent marriage, she was able to forgive him completely.

RESPOND is an organization in Somerville, Massachusetts, where battered wives meet to share their common experiences. One woman in this group commented, "The pressures on a man are terrible. He's got to be a super breadwinner, a super lover. A woman is often in the dual role of wife and mother, and a mother always forgives—and forgives and forgives."

An older woman exhibited that maternal kind of sympathy that is sometimes at the very core of the battered woman's personality: "A lot of the husbands really do love their wives, but they have so much hate inside themselves. Sometimes they really want to hurt themselves, but they can't beat themselves, so they beat us. We are their wives. We are the closest people to them."[9]

What Is This Thing Called Love?

Love is a word that crops up over and over again. A habitual wifebeater will tell the attorney after his wife has filed for separate maintenance, "But she's my wife. I *love* her. She can't do this to me." A long-battered wife, debating whether to file for a measure of freedom from endless injuries, will tell the counselor, "I don't know what to do. I *love* him."

What does love mean? What does it mean to these people? To the husbands it usually means a form of possession, although it is sometimes interspersed with genuine caring between the brutalities. Family advocate Mary Pat Brygger suggested that after years of a violent marriage "love" comes to mean, to the battered wife, "Mutual dependency. Past commitment. Shame and guilt that she's not better. She doesn't know that 'love' can be better. Husbands and wives are *supposed* to love, so she does. The worse things get, the less she believes it can ever be better. The more severe the problem, the harder it is to leave, because she has fewer emotional resources. It makes sense to her to say she still loves him."

For many people, even in satisfactory, nonviolent marriages, the sequence from single to married begins with a strong impulse to be mated and get in on all the expectations of benefits the individual fantasies bring to such a relationship. The chosen one is governed by proximity and availability. The relationship is cemented with what is called love. Each spouse then embarks on trying—with varying degrees of willingness, success, and insight—to adapt to the imbalance of expectations and actuality. In varying degrees each expects individual needs to be met in the process, all in the name of love.

Among the women in Carol Victor's study there was much confusion over love and hatred. Women would try not to blame the husband-assailant but to minimize or forgive his behavior. One woman with a more positive image of herself sought counseling because "I really want to be me again. . . . In the beatings I felt like somebody poured mud over me. I hate him as much as I can love him." One was "sorry for him." Another said, "I would hate him, but I loved him at the same time."

The Stereotype of Masochism

There are two common misconceptions associated with the woman who has a violent mate. One is that she somehow enjoys being beaten. The other is that the violence is somehow related to sexual stimulation. No therapists I interviewed, and no battered wives, could confirm this. Many women grow up *conditioned* to accept, as part of wifely duty, whatever behavior a husband manifests. The closest to enjoyment was mere noncomplaint: An occasional woman felt guilty. She must have deserved it for some misstep on her part and therefore would not allow herself to complain. Again this was part of her traditional conditioning. Early researchers found this free-floating guilt as well. But none of the women indicated they *liked* being harmed. Categorizing women in general, or battered wives in particular, as masochists is not so different from accusing victims of rape of taking pleasure in the event.

The false idea that violence serves as a sexual stimulant seems to be a male fantasy. It is not *women* who write the pornographic scripts. It's an extremely rare woman indeed who would welcome sexual advances from a man who had forced on her blackened eyes, fractured bones, fingers bruised from being stomped on, loosened teeth, torn and swollen lips, displaced vital organs, internal bleeding, external bleeding, disfigurement, and pain.

In Carol Victor's survey of eighty clients coming to the Growth Life Center, no battered wives desired sexual relations with their husbands after being beaten, although eighteen husbands did; and nineteen husbands had attacked because their wives had not wanted sex. For some wifebeaters, violence is akin to foreplay, and it makes no difference that the partner does not experience it that way. For these men, the assault is followed by rape, although they sometimes disguise taboo feel-

66

ings and actions with euphemisms such as "courtship," or "kiss and make up," or "I'm sorry, I love you."

Brygger quoted a client who complained, "My husband's overtures—which he called 'courting me'—for immediate sex after beating were only part of a further demand, a further abuse. It made the degradation even worse. If I resisted—and my gut feeling was never anything else—it signalled further abuse."

If the brutal man can convince himself that cruelty is somehow acceptable to his victim, he can like himself better. One typical deception involves a "command performance" sexual act following the violence, despite the wife's pain, repugnance, and lack of choice. With that, he tells himself—and sometimes her, even others—that her "compliance" proves she forgives him or doesn't mind or likes it. The debased, trapped victim cannot win.

Research has been done on the subject of masochism and sadism in conjugal crime. The conclusions of a committee of the Royal College of Psychiatrists in England, compiled by its chairman, Dr. Peter D. Scott, have provided the clearest insight of any research I've encountered. Scott cautions against assuming that a woman is masochistic* and suggests instead that one look at the "alternative explanations . . . covert threats to her or the children, inability to find alternative housing or support, isolation. . . . Where there are no bars to escape, and the wife, especially a childless wife, persistently returns to a battering husband, then it is

* The term *masochism* is one that gets tossed around handily by the man-in-the-street, especially in the context of wifebattery. It is sometimes used in the context of enduring much misfortune without finding a way out. The proper definition from a well-respected dictionary (*A Comprehensive Dictionary of Psychological and Psychoanalytical Terms*) is as follows:
1. a sexual anomaly characterized by erotic or sexual excitement and/or satisfaction from being subjected to pain, whether by oneself or another. In many cases, orgasm ensues. The pain may become the sole condition of sexual satisfaction, or a necessary preliminary to other forms of sexual activity. 2. The deriving of pleasure from being offended, mistreated, scolded, dominated, embarrassed, etc.; the tendency to court such mistreatment. 3. (*psychoan.*) the turning of any sort of destructive tendencies inward upon oneself.

reasonable to look for a masochistic element; [however,] it must be remembered that the expectations of marriage in some women who are themselves from violent families may be very low, and the hope of renewed affection in an aging or lonely woman may yet be strong. . . .

"The sadistic* element in the husband is much more clearly recognizable. . . . Sadism is not the same as bullying or callous cruelty. . . . Masochists like being hurt, but they like to submit voluntarily and to retain some control of the situation—they avoid punishment like the rest of us.

"It is expected that future research will demonstrate that frank masochism or sadism in either marital partner is *not* a central feature of . . . wife battering."[10]

I would add that if there *is* a masochistic component among battered wives, it is unconscious and of non-sexual nature—reinforced by society's antagonisms to their plight.

Sex and Violence

The woman who lives with marital violence often has no choice about her sex life. The problem of unwanted pregnancies is quite evident. A woman at the Massachusetts RESPOND rap group spoke of the beatings as being part of her husband's drinking problem. He would express shock the next morning to see the cuts and bruises he'd inflicted. "With alcohol,

---

*Sadism is defined by *A Comprehensive Dictionary of Psychological and Psychoanalytical Terms* as follows:
1. the tendency to associate sexual satisfaction with the infliction of pain upon another. In some cases the infliction of pain itself yields satisfaction; in others it is a necessary preliminary to other forms of sexual activity. [The Growth & Life Center studies mentioned earlier in this chapter of women whose husbands demanded sexual intercourse after beating would seem to indicate this element of sadism.—author.] 2. Loosely and generally, love of being cruel; the compulsive tendency to vent aggression and destructiveness upon another person. Vindictiveness, exploitation, humiliation, or frustration of another may substitute for or be added to, the infliction of physical pain on another. Overt sexual satisfaction may or may not accompany these behaviors.

there's always a lot of kids, because there's a lot of kissing and making up. I've got eight."

Another woman did not take the relationship of sex and violence so lightly. "They say you can't be raped by your husband," she stated, "but you can. That's what made up my mind to leave."[11]

Three wives in Gelles's study "discussed at length the verbal and physical battles that ensued after their husbands attacked them privately and publicly for being 'cold.'" One woman, who was slapped and pushed by her husband on occasions when he complained that she was frigid, spoke of the public revealing of their bedroom life by the husband: "He used to tell everybody I was cold. Of course he never bothered to explain that the reason I was, was because he was always drinking, and I can't stand drinking. Or that he was out all night long and then when he came home he expected me to welcome him with open arms." There were three other wives in Gelles's study whose husbands "just didn't like sex. Whatever the reason, the husband's apparent impotence was a major factor involved in these occurrences of violence."

In a number of battering marriages, the existence or nonexistence of a sexual life, whether pleasing or boring or disgusting to the woman, seemed to be completely up to the man. If he wanted her as a sex object, he could take her by force. If he did not want her, she could not entice him.

For eighteen of the couples in Carol Victor's survey, the violence was a turn-on for him, and a turn-off for her. The attitude of the wife toward the rape that followed was that her participation was self-deprecating, a bitter necessity to save her life. Sample comments: "Oh God, maybe he'll stop now." "Anything to get some peace." "I let him; I believe a wife should never refuse." "Violence turns him on. I bluntly refuse. He acts like an animal and forces me. So I can't refuse. He assaults; I must submit." "The worse he was, the more he wanted sex. I turned off, he turned on. He hit me because I 'incited' him."

The opposite was also true: "He hit me because he didn't want sex. Our marriage was never consummated." The husband's reason? "A woman like you makes a man mad."

The Middle-Class Taboo Against Getting Help

I have observed that battered wives from working-class families seemed to have much stronger resources than the middle-class wives I encountered. In general, the Gelles wives experienced less frequent, less severe, and less escalating violence, for example. These working-class women seemed to have less fear and more control over their own lives than the middle-class women with whom I spoke. These women, it seemed, felt too threatened to discuss their marriages freely, particularly if the wifebeater were at home.

In the psychological and sociological literature, which is remarkably remiss in not mentioning wife-beating, there is one highly respected volume that gives a few case histories. It is possibly the earliest mention in print. In Mirra Komarovsky's *Blue-Collar Marriage*,[12] involving couples interviewed in 1958–59, those wives who were physically abused seemed to have fairly strong resources, as did the Gelles women, and as the middle-class women do not.

Why are the middle-class battered wives so poorly protected? Their higher status leaves them more vulnerable. A devout Quaker who has worked with these women privately says succinctly: "The middle-class wife has more to lose, in status, possessions, and ego-loss." This woman is shattered by the shock of "lower-class-type" behavior appearing in her marriage. There is such a taboo in her world against taking a husband to court or calling the police because of him or even admitting the barbarisms that she has fewer options for relief. And she's aghast at the thought of going on welfare.

This is not to say that the lower-class wife does not have obstacles. She has a world of them. The very fact that she may be a candidate for welfare puts her in a position of disrespect with police, courts, etc. Her lower educational level makes her future unpromising. And her husband, unlike the middle-class man, has fewer restraints regarding visible violence and tracking her down when she flees or separates.

The middle-class battered wife does have a potential weapon not available to her sister, but she's seldom daring enough to use it.

If she felt comfortable with the concept of black-mail, she'd be protected. She could threaten to ruin her husband's career. But the kind of woman who marries a man comfortable with wifebeating is not the kind of woman who "enjoys a good fight."

On the other hand, Komarovsky's women seemed to maintain a certain fearlessness in the home, even occasional dominance or equality in the marriage, or a sufferance of the husband's need to swagger and pre-tend to be superior. Some happily married couples seemed to "relish a high-spirited contest of will in frequent arguments."

Some of the women seemed to know how to an-tagonize the husband and provoke him verbally. They did not seem to live in fear. Those who experienced physical abuse afterward were not reluctant to talk about the problem with relatives or clergy. They went to court without fear, and husbands appeared chastened by their wives' actions and did not retaliate.

One wife, a Mrs. M., told her abusive husband, "You run away from home, you run away from school, and you are running out here; you cannot face it." Because Mr. M. is not capable of defending himself with words "he turns in helpless fury to physical aggression."

There is a great difference in what happens next in *this* marriage and a typical middle-class violent mar-riage. Mr. M.'s violence, according to the sociologist, "not only fails to bring him victory, but creates a vicious circle of marital conflict in which he is ulti-mately the loser. The beatings get him into court. He sees the judge and the minister as his wife's and his mother-in-law's allies." Once, feeling some guilt, he "admitted that he had a violent temper and wishes he could control it better. His violent outbursts are used by his mother-in-law as an argument to remove him from control of money and to keep the savings in Mrs.

71

M.'s name." Although he hates the arrangement, he can do nothing but accept it.

I think many of the trapped middle-class wives mentioned in these pages would consider themselves fortunate to have Mrs. M.'s self-awareness and control of the situation.

Embarrassing Wounds

Of all the words to describe the battered wife's home life, one frequently noted is "embarrassing." The nightmare world carries an additional stigma. The middle-class wife is embarrassed at her choice of husband and her continuing commitment to him. She is embarrassed about her wounds, her scars. As chapter 2 has shown, some wifebeaters deliberately inflict injuries that will cause a long period of embarrassment. In medieval times, it was a common, cruel joke among peasants to injure a wife's nose in such a way that townsfolk would jeer at her whenever she was in public. Feelings of sympathy were not aroused, only mockery. Perhaps to a lesser degree, similar reactions still persist. In fact, one man—not a wifebeater—exhibited similar reactions to what he thought of as "funny" pain in "funny" parts of the anatomy. He heard of a wife being so injured in the buttocks by her husband's kicks that she could not sit, only stand or lie on her side. His comment was, "I can't help it. It's funny. If she was kicked someplace else, I could feel sorry for her, but that's just funny." He was incapable of thinking in terms of pain rather than scatological humor. And too embarrassed or threatened to face the reality of marital violence in his own social class.

The Process to Craziness

A typical wifebeater's taunt is, "You are crazy." And for many battered women, it becomes, to their perception, less of a taunt than an accurate description. After all, what's going on in her life is "driving her crazy": The rules of logic are not operating very well.

Expected responses do not follow customary actions. She feels persecuted, yet no one agrees. If she tried to explain, she might be accused of being paranoid. But the world really *is* a threatening place. She feels frantic or depressed or "at her wit's end" most of the time. People and institutions don't seem to understand her. It becomes easier to withdraw from them.

For the battered woman, the components of basic mental stability are awry. When she has become isolated from sources of possible help and from old friends and family, and from contacts with neighbors —a typical wifebeater's demand—then her world is peopled mainly by two individuals with the same viewpoint: her husband, who taunts her about her sanity, and herself, with ever increasing doubts about her sanity. With no fresh viewpoint from the outside world, she is stuck with the single input.

"A man may say, 'My wife is crazy,'" women's advocate Monica Erler points out, "if she doesn't enjoy traditional women's marital roles and chooses not to go along with them—roles such as sex on demand or nonshared housework and being a servant in the home. We have known of a few cases where a violent husband wanted to commit a wife like that [to a mental institution]. Or where the psychiatrist the battered woman consulted suggested that a brief stay in a good institution might be helpful in her adjustment to marriage, instead of offering therapy for the wifebeater."

And there was the case of the woman whose husband bit her as well as beat her. Esther never told anyone until she sought therapy and a divorce about twenty years later. Once, during her miserable marriage, her mother sent her some money to buy a small luxury for herself. (The mother knew that the well-to-do husband was very penurious in the living standard he allowed her daughter. But she never heard about the violence.)

Esther says that when she saw the check, "I suddenly thought, 'Now I am going to my mother. Everything will be all right then.' I began to shake convulsively. I could not stop trembling from head to foot. I didn't know what was wrong and went to a doctor my husband knew who told me I was having a nervous breakdown. He also informed my husband."

What was done? Nothing. Life went on as before. Some years later, a new neighbor called the police during the sounds of a beating. The police advised Esther to get an order of protection from family court. After ignoring two hearings, her husband appeared with a three-page statement for the presiding judge. He denied his violence. He said the biting was a figment of Esther's imagination. He detailed her "mental disturbance." He indicated she needed to be remanded to a mental institution.

Upon reading the statement, the judge asked Esther if she had an attorney and if she wanted to continue the action. "I was so confused and frightened," she recalled, "I didn't know what to do. I felt so alone. I stumbled around and mumbled 'no' to both questions. Later my husband grabbed the order of protection away from me and laughed at me. He said my performance in court proved I was crazy."

What Role Do Parents Play?

Many middle-class women I've talked to claimed a nonviolent background. A number of residents at one shelter I visited told me they'd come from warm, loving families and simply could not bear to burden their parents with their own problems, although the parents knew why their daughters were at the shelter. What childhood strengthening or weakening factors made one woman determine to end her captivity, despite the social and economic hardships, and another woman give up and "adjust" to her lot, with an increasingly battered personality? It may be that people are much more than the product of their early environment and heredity, developing inner strengths or weaknesses independent of childhood experience and logic.

Over two-thirds of the couples in the Growth & Life survey had not been physically abused as children themselves, and only 5 percent of their mothers had been beaten by their fathers.

The saddest statistic: There were marriages continuing for up to thirty-four years—women as old as fifty-nine. What wasted lives.

Among those who got themselves out of the nightmare were women who had made earlier attempts at remedying the situation by means of the police, family court, and some therapy—usually from psychiatric social workers or psychiatrists—with varying degrees of success. Most of the women left after five to nine years, convinced that there had to be more to their lives.

What kind of woman becomes a battered wife? Essentially, she is one who marries a wifebeater—and who is then psychologically and societally incapable of saving herself.

4

How Society Keeps Her There

The battered wife comes to believe she has no allies, no champions. And her conclusion is not paranoid, but starkly realistic. Although the world seems to reach out to others of society's neglected ones—earthquake victims, rare-disease victims, and even to violent criminals perceived as victimized by their backgrounds—the victim of conjugal crime seems to have very few who care at all about her. As social work professor Eleanor Kremen described it: "Procedures and recording systems of the police, the courts, hospital emergency rooms, traditional and even nontraditional social service agencies systematically ignore and obscure incidence."[1]

Guilty Until Proven Innocent

The battered wife lives in a Kafkaesque world. The constitutional right of being considered innocent until proven guilty doesn't seem to apply to her. The mere fact of her being so incredibly "punished" by her husband is interpreted too often by police, the courts, and the community as, "she must have done something terrible to provoke such a response."

The most common reaction by others to the plight of the battered wife has been contempt, criticism, or utter disbelief. Even the woman herself may deal with her nightmare with disbelief or torture herself trying to find a "reason." After all, it's an orderly world, isn't it?

From acquaintances who unexpectedly find out about the phenomenon, the reaction is often social embarrassment or bewilderment. Neighbors who cannot doubt its existence often find it more comfortable to put blinders on. Why? Partly because of the psychological need for strong denial when confronted with something too horrendous to make sense. It is not only the victim who needs to believe in an orderly world.

According to Dr. Martin Symonds, a psychiatrist affiliated with the Karen Horney Institute and specializing in the psychology of violence, a common attitude toward the victim of accidental violent crime is that the victim must have provoked it. The attitude is followed by a need to ostracize the victim because of fear of "contamination." The reason listeners feel uncomfortable is the "implicit demand" that they "do something." Yet there is nothing they can do. There is an "implied criticism that listeners failed to protect her from this tragic experience."[2]

Although she may think of escaping her brutal marriage, and actually attempt to do so, the average battered wife does not get out. She simply *cannot* because of the inherent psychodynamics and societal blocks and pressures. These include her unconscious psychological patterns and those of her husband, legal and economic reasons, children, health, threats, fear and danger, and overall, a vestige of hope that her assailant will change. All these factors combine to enforce her captivity. When she attempts to change her life, she finds no appropriate doors on which to knock. She puts up with it because she can do nothing else.

A CASE HISTORY

Betty was a battered wife who was determined to escape. She was twenty-six, attractive, and spirited, with a four-year-old daughter from a former marriage. A pattern of control developed with this second husband in which he began to insist on grocery shopping with her and in choosing her wardrobe.

"I am an independent person, but I was insecure at the time and I needed that. He was insecure, too, and having a wife in the traditional sense seemed to give him power," Betty said. When she sought to reestablish her own autonomy, he gave a drunken ultimatum: If things were not run his way, then she could just leave. Betty agreed to leave. That, however, was not the answer he expected. He hit her face so hard she had to tell her office she'd been in an automobile accident.

Twice she separated from him. Twice she succumbed to his promises that he would change. She tried to get him to stop his heavy drinking. He responded by carrying guns in his car.

One evening, after she'd come back from dinner with her parents, celebrating the return of her brother from overseas, her husband forced her into the apartment at gunpoint. "His eyes were wild with anger. He kept insisting that my brother was really my ex-husband." When the police came, she asked them to wait so she could pack and take herself and her child to safety. But they refused.

"He would not let me leave then. He made me take off my clothes. He got a .22 pistol, put one bullet in it, and said, 'We're going to play Russian roulette.' " Pointing it at her head, he pulled the trigger three times. Betty kept her sanity with a firm resolve: *I can't let him know I'm scared.*

Her firm resolve actually helped very little. She had to learn to hide her every feeling. "If he stayed out until 2:00 A.M. and I didn't say anything, then he thought I was seeing another man. If I complained, that was wrong." He raped her twice, snarling, "I'm going to see that you will never enjoy any man."

Why didn't she leave? "It is not as easy as many people think. I was a prisoner in my own home." Her husband deprived her of telephone, checkbook, her own car, money—and her job. She was afraid he would harm her little girl. He did beat the child, though not as severely or as frequently as her mother.

Betty got her chance to escape on very short notice. But she did not hesitate, because she knew she might not have another chance. One day her husband gave her a dollar to buy some groceries because he would not be home for lunch. Immediately she phoned her parents, asking them to rush into town to rescue her and the child. There wasn't time or extra hands to take many of her belongings. Again, the police refused her request for assistance.

Later, when Betty went back to get her things, she

found her husband had destroyed her stereo, television, records, and house plants, and had virtually torn the place apart.

"I called a lawyer," she said, "filed for divorce, and told him I wanted my car, half the money in the bank, and restitution for all he had destroyed. . . . My husband went to see the lawyer and told him how much he wanted to get back with me. . . . I got nothing."

The police discouraged her from getting a peace bond because "it was expensive and if they picked him up he could be released for twenty dollars and would probably be angrier.

"It is like he has sole control over you—your credit, your job, your coming and going. And if you try to get out from under that control, no one can help you. If I didn't have parents, where would I have gone?"[3]

Women like Betty have a terrible time getting another job once they leave their home address, even when they are trained and experienced. They hesitate to give references for fear the ex-husband, hot on their trail, will trace them and harass or harm them. Time and time again I have heard stories of how people cooperate, wittingly or unwittingly—and this includes secretaries, attorneys, clergymen, neighbors, former employers, "friends," social workers, family doctors—with the former husband-assailant. I have yet to hear of any cases where everyone worked to keep the information from him. In many cases, once the husband or former husband finds the intimidated woman, she sees no way out but to go back with him, as he demands.

Judges and Courts Against the Battered Wife

"A husband who has a little bit of knowledge . . . and is a little bit careful . . . can go on beating his wife systematically and there is nothing she can really do about it except to leave. . . ." This is the conclusion of one wife, disgusted with the legal system's failure to protect her from further assaults by her husband, while at the same time pressuring her to stay with him.

She was interviewed by Helene A. Pepe, of the Georgetown Law Center in Washington, D.C., in her study of the way the legal system operates in wife-abuse cases in the Washington, D.C., area.[4] Pepe says that wife abuse is essentially defined as noncriminal behavior, as recommended in the District of Columbia Court Reform and Criminal Procedure Act of 1970. This act established a new Family Division of the Superior Court and permitted dispositions of intra-family offenses through civil suits with a civil procedure, even though they are violations of the criminal law.

A battered wife may apply for a civil protection order, which is effective for a year. The order might require the wifebeater to participiate in psychiatric counseling or to avoid the presence of his victim. But as with most laws to protect the battered wife, as of this writing, it does not give much protection. In the District of Columbia, a hearing is often delayed five or more weeks, during which time, according to Pepe, the victim of the crime is *without* court protection. A striking example is the "irate husband who, two days before such a hearing, pulled his wife out of work and shot her to death. Ironically, the incident occurred at the D.C. Superior Court."

Another method of "protection" in the District of Columbia is to send a warning letter to the husband. Pepe cites one indication of the effectiveness of such a letter, wherein the wife said her husband "crumbled it up and tried to make me eat it. . . . He thought it was funny." The beatings continued.

Says Pepe: The vast majority of battered wives "are like sitting ducks with no more protection from physical abuse than before they filed the charges. . . ."

Sometimes it is the judge himself who gives the wife a sense of nonprotection from physical abuse. For instance, on October 7, 1975, in Kings County, New York, Family Court Judge M. Holt Meyer issued a temporary order of protection "not to assault, menace, harass or recklessly endanger." The next day, October 8, he amended it to "permit Petitioner (the wifebeater) to enter his premises in the company of a police officer." The day after that, October 9, he amended it "to permit the Petitioner to use force to enter his premises, by breaking locks if necessary."

A woman judge is not necessarily more sympathetic or helpful than a male judge. At the first New York State conference on the physically abused wife, the abused wives pleaded for ways to "assure themselves of firm police and judicial action against their husbands and . . . to sever ties with their husbands legally when they didn't have funds for a lawyer."

A mother of three, married for twenty-six years, who had "gotten three family court orders of protection in ten years" against her husband's violence, complained that both her husband *and the judge* told her the "piece of paper didn't mean a damn thing." To save herself and her children, she had moved out of her five-room apartment. Her husband, she said, "is sitting there with all my possessions. I'm afraid to go back."

The astounding response from a woman family court judge, Justice Yorka C. Linakis, was: "All the havoc that can be created by the absence of the father from the home can be tremendous, and Family Court judges are most reluctant to order spouses from the house. There is nothing more pathetic than to see a husband going to his home—usually in the company of a policeman—to collect his meager belongings."

Judge Linakis went on to say that she herself had seen many similar cases wherein wives misuse Family Court and orders of protection, which "they hang over the husband's head like a sword of Damocles."[5]

Undoubtedly the judge had seen such cases. But I submit that the women who were able to *use* the court, and their husbands, had never been severely beaten over long periods of time. As we have seen, the real battered woman finds Family Court and its procedures either too dangerous to her safety in its delays and "understanding" of the husband-assailant, or too counterproductive to her safety when it does issue an order of protection.

It is this very confusion of the vengeful, litigious wife, "enjoying a good fight," with the *real* battered woman who dares not make herself known, that contributes to the general indifference to her plight.

Sometimes, since she has no recourse to justice, she can't take it any longer and strikes back. Because she is physically weaker, she must choose a very powerful means of retaliating or protecting herself. Too often this is a lethal weapon. In the 1961 case of Patricia and George Stallworth in Michigan, the husband beat the wife three times in one day. The last time was his very last. She killed him.

George Stallworth assaulted his wife during the afternoon at her mother's house, again that evening at their country club—where a club officer intervened—and once again a few minutes later, beyond the protection of the officer, in the club parking lot.

"The couple left the club and as Patricia was about to get into a car George knocked her down, blacking her eye, and then he threw her on the ground and sat on her, beating her with his fists. Patricia got the knife out of her purse and opened it, whereupon George grabbed her wrist. Eventually a passerby took the knife away and gave it to George."[6]

Within a few hours, Stallworth was knifed in the lower abdomen; he died four days later. How did societal attitude contribute to what happened? The country club's officer did intervene, it's true, but only because the scene was making the other members of the club uncomfortable. Since George Stallworth was at it again within minutes, out of sight of his peers, it can be assumed that no one offered Patricia Stallworth rescue; it was simply suggested that the wifebeating be conducted elsewhere.

The action of the passerby in the Stallworth case is noteworthy. On seeing a woman thrown to the ground, eye blackened, and being beaten, whom did he assist? The husband. This pattern of passerby reaction was put to the test in an experiment that amazed psychologists at Michigan State University. They staged a series of physical fights in view of unsuspecting passersby. The researchers found that male passersby would come to the aid of men being assaulted either by women or by other men. They would rescue women apparently being hit by other women. But no passerby interfered when the assault was perpetrated by a man upon a woman.[7]

Sociologist Murray Straus suggests that the male witnesses refrained from aiding the female victim because wifebeating is some kind of norm, and these men inferred that the actor was the woman's husband. He refers to this as "the more general phenomenon of male hostility to women" in men who are *watching* a violent act against women, rather than committing it. This very "norm" of not interfering in what they thought was a marital dispute was, in fact, the reason given by several of the thirty-eight witnesses to the notorious murder of Kitty Genovese, all of whom "didn't want to get involved."

The Policy of Equal Blame

Social agencies have traditionally been counterproductive when treating the battered wife. More than one counseling agency has a policy of being so "fair" to the husband that its goal is to keep the victim under the assailant's roof and control. The goal of protection or a hiatus from violence is lost in the process. This philosophy is called "keeping families together." Other agencies have also been guilty of "seeing both sides" and distributing the blame equally, to the exclusion of seeing the heart of the problem.

One such agency is the Home Advisory Service Council of New York, funded by the Criminal Justice Coordinating Committee and offering this type of counseling free to certain couples referred by Family Court. Says the executive director: "These people know violence as a way of life and they beat each other up."[8]

I always find it incredible to hear terms of an evenly matched sparring applied to the one-sided war of the powerful against the weak, to hear "they" instead of "he."

Another partisan of the "equal blame, equal strength" theory is the supervisor of probation for this same family court. As overseer of the screening of the petitioners in family offense cases, she is another firm believer in examining the whole situation, "without prejudice to either party," and not breaking up families of wifebeaters.

Said she: "I don't want to see anyone hurt, but sometimes it's the woman's fault. Not all women are lovable, like not all men are lovable. But a man gets hassled at work, he gets hassled on the subway, he gets hassled at home, and then he punches out. It's not right, but . . ."[9]

The above attitudes were aptly summed up by Monica Erler, one of the administrators of St. Paul's Women's Advocates House for battered women and their children. She told me: "Society has always given a man a 'right' to violence if frustrated; a woman, never."

Wifebeaters are conditioned to this attitude. Battered wives are, also. And so many women try to ignore their own frustrations and to accept the hassling they get without reacting.

Social Agencies Against the Battered Wife

Social agencies have often been guilty of accepting both sides to the exclusion of keeping accurate documentation—and it shows up in the way they record marital violence. On the record, until recently, the battered wife and her problem did not exist.

Although the physically abused wife has frequently been encountered in a family social service agency, case workers have seldom recorded the violence as its own statistic. Wifebeating was—and in many cases still is, even as awareness is growing—hidden under more innocuous categories, such as *marital conflict* or *intra-family disturbance.*

The very first social work journal article on wife abuse appeared as late as January 1976, published by the Family Service Association of America, a federation of more than three hundred voluntary family-serving agencies located across North America. A Massachusetts caseworker, Beverly Nichols, noted that she "could find no articles in professional journals that dealt with abuse in marriage." Nichols observed that "caseworkers rarely pick abusiveness as the focus of intervention; rather they tend to ignore this symptom." Some social workers, when confronted with the problem, Nichols found, became "self-conscious and defensive, afraid of being judged as being too allied with feminism." There is often "embarrassment which appears as an avoidance of the issue. This reaction is due in part to the acceptance of a philosophy which tolerates the normalcy of male aggression in whatever form it takes."[10]

And the final result of all this is that the battered wife is once more trapped into staying in the violent marriage.

AND WHEN SHE "RECONCILES," WHAT THEN?

Women's Advocate Monica Erler says: "The problem of wifebeating is never going to be solved by counseling alone, because the traditional goal is reconciliation, seeing the woman as merely a part of a marriage instead of as a whole person in her own right." I asked her if there were ever any real reconciliations and newly happy relationships between former residents of Women's Advocates House and the husbands who begged them to return on promise of reform. "None that we know of," she said. "When we call them on the phone, they are guarded. They often cannot talk if they hear their husband coming. Recently I met a former resident in a supermarket with her husband. When she was alone, she came up to talk. Then her husband stopped her. So, reconciliations? I don't know."

The First Reforms Begin

The Family Service Association in St. Paul is one of the first agencies to confront the problem of wife abuse *directly,* without embarrassment, and reach out to help even those clients who have not admitted the problem yet. I talked with its executive director, Ronald G. Reed, about the agency's approach. Reed had designed an intake-interview form for all incoming clients, regardless of their stated reason for needing help. Its purpose was to gather the generally lacking statistics and "get a better picture of the number of clients we have where physical abuse of any family member was a problem." Many clients coming for other reasons—financial counseling, job problems, or even generalized marital unhappiness—might have violence in the marriage and never mention it. In the first month the new form was in effect, there were recorded zero assaults by wife against husband, and twenty-two assaults by husband against wife.

Reed pointed out that it is sometimes difficult for social workers "to confront the troubled family and just ask the simple question: 'Is abuse part of the problem?' "

It is partly a matter of not knowing what to do, he said. "And then there is the conditioning that 'some things should be kept in the family.' But if we give a *caring* message, let the client know we are concerned—and we are committed to that—it will let the family know that . . . if in the future they should have a situation like that, they may call on us. We are getting it out on the table and saying, 'We are willing to deal with this if you are.' "

Reed compared this to investigating child abuse, a project he was assigned to during his student days: "Although it was hard to go into homes and ask, 'Have you beaten your kids?' once I was comfortable enough with asking, the people *wanted* to talk about it. I think it will be so with spouse abuse."

Reed started one of the first couples therapy groups because he sees the problem as a family problem, not just the wife's problem. What seems obvious today was considered iconoclastic until recently. "Wifebeating is similar to incest in that the entire family covers up the 'private' matter, including the wife, who, by doing nothing, tacitly is complicit. The problem is covered up by many people involved in knowing about it. Ten years ago, for instance, doctors could not face alcohol as a health problem. They used other diagnoses because alcohol was such a stigma. I think the same thing is going on with wife abuse."

Researchers Micklow and Eisenberg[11] found that hospital and physician response to the problem could be summed up as a "failure to disclose." There was an absence of effective recording procedures. "Unlike child abuse, there is no specific code for wifebeating, even though doctors acknowledge a similar frequency of occurrence. This absence of records inhibits an ability to identify as well as aid the repeatedly assaulted wife. It further assures, through nondisclosures, that some assaults will never come to the attention of the legal system."

A Michigan physician interviewed by Micklow and Eisenberg expressed a common "nonjudgmental" approach to the problem of treating a battered wife. If a woman comes in with bruises, he asks about the cause. If she says, "I fell down the stairs," he accepts her explanation. "Upon examination, however," the doctor said, "I may feel that she didn't sustain these bruises by falling down the stairs. Somebody may have hit her. I accept the patient's story. . . . We don't have the time or the background for the reason of the assault. . . . It's a personal problem between a man and wife, and if she doesn't want to prefer charges, that's her privilege and her right and her business to do as she pleases. As far as I'm concerned personally, I don't care if she prefers charges or not."

A battered woman in another state spoke of the doctor she went to during her last pregnancy. The doctor was the choice of her well-to-do husband—as were most of the things and people that affected her life.

All during her pregnancy she was beaten. After each incident of assault, her husband stayed home to make sure she did not leave or make any phone calls. During her eighth month she asked the doctor for help for her latest injuries and her problem. The doctor told her coldly he was treating her for prenatal checkups and delivery only; he did not want to know about anything else. The husband was a friend of the doctor. The husband controlled the very sizable finances. Because she was so completely under the control of her husband, emotionally and financially, the woman felt powerless to seek a more compassionate physician. With very little confidence, she sought the moral support of her widowed mother, whom her husband provided with a small monthly allowance to enable her to continue living in her own home. The mother reminded her daughter of her "wifely duty." She spoke of how lucky her daughter was to have found someone who gave her a standard of living so superior to the one she'd known growing up. She said she should be ashamed that she upset her generous husband so much.

A major reason the older wife finds it so difficult to take action to leave the abuser is her deteriorating health. Jeanette H. Milgrom, a therapist with St. Paul's Walk-In Counseling Center, notes that, "Even women who must go to a hospital's emergency room repeatedly in order to get treatment for bruises and broken bones may not, at this time, receive comprehensive understanding or treatment from the medical profession. Sure, symptoms will be taken care of, but no one may ask how come a woman's ribs or nose were broken twice within the past six months. In addition, women who develop a lot of physical problems may be put on tranquilizers; this again treats the symptom and not the problem."[12]

Many of the residents of shelters arrive with various forms of medication—antidepressants and tranquilizers —prescribed by family physicians and psychiatrists. The medication has made it possible for them to *endure* their horror somewhat or to blank it out a little, rather than do something about it. It is the policy of a number of shelters that arriving residents check their medications in the office. They will be given them on request, but taking them will not be quite so automatic.

The Community Against the Battered Wife

Why do women go back to the men who battered them? Says Gary Schoener, also of the Walk-In Counseling Center, they do so "because there is no further support from the community. Their lives were tied up in the marriage relationship. They are not trained in how to pull out of a bad relationship. It is tragic. Even women who have been TV and radio panelists on battered wife programs, women who say they've found the strength to make a new life for themselves—even they go back."

The Police Against the Battered Wife

Dr. Morton Bard, a psychologist who developed family-violence response training programs for police trainees, stated:

"A request for . . . police intervention may be seen as public declaration that acceptable limits of aggression (perhaps a class-linked phenomenon) are being reached and that unacceptable violence is imminent. However, a declaration of this kind is made to a system which sees itself not as a helping resource but rather as one empowered to enforce compliance either physically, by legal sanctions, or by admonition; the disputants, on the other hand, may be seeking relief through immediate arbitration or mediation by a skilled authority.

"Limited by traditional role definition to perceive himself primarily as a law enforcer, the police officer may not be able to perceive this hidden agenda in the appeal for his intervention."[13]

Attorney Elizabeth Truninger of California has observed how the system can work against the battered wife, effectively forcing her to stay and put up with her husband's behavior.

Truninger conducted a survey [14] of private attorneys and legal services offices in the San Francisco area. She found that "less than one-fourth of the attorneys felt that the police were of help to their clients in dealing with violence, although it was generally accepted that 'calling the police' was often the only solution at the time." Police were reluctant to make arrests. ". . . The 'legal advice' given by the police was often incorrect and served to reinforce the assailant's belief that he had a right to behave violently."

Further, the attorneys surveyed said, "Police aggravated situations by a seeming insistence on defining the behavior as noncriminal. Police advise the wife

89

that she has a civil problem and recommend that she obtain a restraining order. Even after a restraining order is obtained, police sometimes tell the client-victim to call her lawyer, claiming an inability to enforce the order."

The fact is that police, nationally as well as internationally, are recommended to avoid arrest and seek mediation of domestic disturbance calls. This alternative, Truninger points out, minimizes the seriousness of the husband's actions and misstates the law. It also "effectively traps the wife with children in the home."

Truninger cited an example of police refusal to remove a violent husband from a client's home: "The woman had known her husband for some time before she married him. When he became violent then, she would call the police and have him put out of the apartment. But she had children by him and was pressured into marriage for the children's sake. Now when she calls the police, though it is still her apartment and she pays the rent, the most the police will do is escort *her* from her home."

Helene Pepe found that a similar attitude existed among police officials in Washington, D.C. She was told by a police spokesman: "A domestic dispute really isn't a crime. We really provide a counseling service more than anything else."[15]

The Law Against the Battered Wife

There are often technicalities in the law that play into the hands of the wifebeater. I've encountered story after story of a woman fleeing her home in terror and then initiating divorce or separation proceedings—only to find that her violent husband will get to keep everything and she will get nothing or very little by way of settlement, because *she* left *him*. The reason she left just did not count with the court.

For example, one woman, who was able to hold down a good job despite the horrors at home, finally took a big step by moving in with a former college roommate. But every weekend she'd return to cook a week's supply of food for her husband and college-age son, to clean the house, and mend the clothes. She tried to time her visits to hours when her husband would be out of the house. Whenever the two were there together, he would assault her on some pretext or other, often to "punish her for being a bad mother." His constant threat was to "ruin her so no man would ever look at her again." Every attorney she'd checked has said that in a divorce settlement she will lose almost everything she's built up over the years because, technically, she deserted the home and family. Her husband, a knowledgeable, high-salaried man, is well aware of his clout with the law, and taunts her with it as he drives his fist into her breast.

Marjory D. Fields, an attorney who helps indigent women in Brooklyn obtain divorces, always warns her clients, "Plan carefully. Once you leave, don't plan to come back. Ever." Freedom from violence has to be enough. It has to be worth the sacrifice of any amount of possessions. The wife's possessions too often become the husband's possessions, often for the purpose of destruction.

Fields adds: "The assaultive husband's due process rights prevent any form of effective protection for the wife."

Many attorneys advise a battered wife that she'll need stronger grounds than "mere" physical assault for divorce, separation, or bringing charges. Until 1977, two beatings in four years were not enough for a divorce in New York State. Further, many courts require complicated proof that the beatings occurred and that the husband was the instigator.

There have been repeated rumors—usually denied by police and the courts—that there must be a certain number of bruises or broken bones or stitches or occasions before it "counts"— kind of quota. Women coming to AWAIC Outreach meetings have referred to this quota as "the stitch rule."

The *Stanford Law Review*[16] reports, "A search of the few American cases and statutes available indicates they have been influenced by policy factors. For a husband to be guilty of the battery of his wife, something more than an unpermitted touching or even minor injury is required. One court has stated several times that either 'permanent injury' must have been inflicted or the husband's conduct must have been prompted by 'malicious and wrongful spirit.' Other courts have allowed the husband to defend on the ground that he was provoked by his wife, providing the husband has not seriously injured her."

Economics Against the Battered Wife

To add to her difficulties, a battered woman usually has little or no access to money for legal fees, which are considerable. In the District of Columbia, Pepe states, the awarding of counsel fees is discretionary with the court, and the wife "takes the chance that she may get stuck with the entire legal cost herself."[17]

Many battered wives feel that they must stay in the marriage for the sake of the children. It is true that children will have a lower standard of living if their mother leaves. Alimony is seldom granted and child support tends to be minimal and unreliable. Only 14.7 percent of the divorced women polled in a national survey were awarded any alimony at all. In the District of Columbia, an attorney found that "nearly one out of five persons granted alimony has to return to court, usually within one to three years, to ask for reinforcement."[18]

If the formerly battered wife has to take the children's father to court to collect child support, "this means more legal fees and expenses, with little chance of recovering back payments." So says Del Martin, of NOW's National Task Force on Battered Women/Household Violence.[19] "Courts consider the case closed when *one* payment is received. Of 29,489 cases of nonsupport handled by the Connecticut judicial system in fiscal year 1971–72, only 48 percent were 'closed.'" (That means that a shrewdly calculating wifebeater could submit to making one payment only, and then let his ex-wife begin the expensive child support collection process all over again.)

"Child support payments cannot be relied on to provide even a minimum standard of living, and employment prospects for the working mother are not attractive," according to attorney Elizabeth Truninger, writing in *The Hastings Law Journal*.[20] Internal Revenue does not recognize child care as an acceptable business expense. In a reliability study conducted by William J. Goode, professor of sociology at Columbia University, he found that 40 percent of divorced husbands in a major midwestern city rarely or never paid their child support payments, 35 percent always paid, 14 percent usually paid, and 11 percent paid once in a while.

With neither alimony nor child support to count on, the woman may become one of the 1.8 million female-headed families that in 1970 had income below the poverty level. The survey included those on welfare and those working. Sixty percent of all working women were found to earn less than $5,000, as compared to only 20 percent of all employed males.

The average battered wife who manages legally to get out of the violent marriage will have to go to work, probably at a relatively unskilled job, or go on welfare in order to live. Ironically, there are some reasons why going on welfare would be preferable. One is that good social workers have been known to move wives to other housing projects to help them escape the determined harrassment and retaliation of their violent ex-husbands. Another irony: For women with children, working will probably provide less money than the welfare stipend and its fringe benefits of various services like health care and day care and availability of job training and back-to-school programs.

It seems almost as if the professional world conspires against the battered wife and deliberately or unwittingly prevents her from leaving her tormenter while aiding him to continue his behavior. Where can the woman go when it seems as if nothing can stop her powerful husband, immune from all reasonably expected restraints and consequences?

Some wives hope they will find refuge in their parents and relatives, in their religious faith, or in psychotherapy.

The prevailing myth indicates that the family is the most logical resource in time of trouble. "Home is where they have to take you in when you've got no place else to go." Yet in counselor Carol Victor's survey of eighty of her battered-wife clients, more than half did not even attempt to seek help from family or friends. Those who did tried parents first and siblings next; then clergy, in-laws, and friends. "Families," commented therapist Victor, "tend not to want to know. They don't want the financial responsibility implied in helping. It might mean taking on the support of a grown daughter and her children for life. Many feel they should not interfere in a marriage. They see the situation as a social stigma and would prefer to avoid it. They have the attitude of 'you've made your bed, now lie on it.' And overall, they are *afraid*." And rightly so, for wifebeaters, all professionals in this field have found, do tend to retaliate against someone close who helps their victim.

There was a woman in Alabama who discovered that both family and church would regard the prospect of giving her safety as a social stigma, and therefore refused to do so. She was an active member of a popular fundamentalist church. Her entire family—parents, husband, children—were also regular churchgoers. The woman, college-educated, living in a very comfortable home, admitted after twelve years of marriage that her life was one assault after another. No one had even suspected, because she'd confided in no one, and her clothing hid the bruises. Finally, in desperation, she begged her parents to take her in with the children until she could think what to do next.

Her mother refused. "Marriage is made by God. Marriage is until death do you part. You took those vows. Now, live up to them, girl. Go back to your husband, where you belong, and see that you're a good wife from now on, hear?" was the motherly counsel.

Mary then asked her minister if he would talk to her husband. "Women can exaggerate so," the cleric responded. "God has given you a lovely home, beautiful children, and a good man. Why, I've known you both since you were babies. Your nice husband comes from a good Christian home, just like you. Now you go home and give God thanks for your blessings. And I'll pray for you."

Perhaps a psychotherapist would have a more worldly, more realistic view, would know that all God's children do not necessarily behave in a godly manner. A Boston physician's wife tells the story of how she tried to reason with her once-beloved husband after increasing incidents of sudden violence.

"I couldn't believe what was happening to me. I thought only poor, uneducated, alcoholic men beat their wives. I kept wondering who would believe me if I said my doctor-husband, that pillar of respectability in our community, beat me. . . .

"I got the name of a psychiatrist from a close friend after I told her a relative of mine needed help. On my first visit to his office, he asked if this had happened before. When I told him about the different incidents, he shook his head, saying he understood. Then he intimated that perhaps I had a masochistic need to be abused or had provoked Larry into hitting me for some unconscious reason."[21]

If the psychoanalyst had been more knowledgeable about the problem of husbandly violence, he could have helped the doctor's wife explore her alternatives and avenues of possible help—granted, they are seldom effective, but many women feel they must try—before she tried to end the marriage. He might have helped her come to her own conclusion that she had a right not to take what she'd been taking, and that her husband would not change without drastic measures imposed from the outside—no matter what she herself did or did not do.

It is disturbing to ponder these responses from professionals in social work, medicine, law, organized religion, and psychiatry—professionals whose deepest beliefs encourage the wifebeater by barring the way to relief for the battered wife.

In refreshing contrast, there is a young judge who

is unique in his grasp of the phenomenon. Jack F. Crawford is an innovative twenty-eight-year-old city court judge in Hammond, Indiana. In the spring of 1976, after becoming concerned over the number of repeat offenders among wifebeaters, Crawford began an experimental program. He appointed certain battered wives as probation officers for a period of six months to a year. Their probationers were their own wifebeating husbands. Although it is "too early to tell," the program seems to be working out well so far.

"We impress upon the husband that if he hits his wife again," says Judge Crawford, "he's not only hitting his wife, he's hitting his probation officer, and he's hitting somebody who works for this court—the idea behind that being that *the husband may not think twice about hitting his wife,* but maybe he'll think twice about hitting an officer of the court."[22]

"A Mere Playful, Loving Slap"

When I testified before the Public Safety Committee of the New York City Council on behalf of the passage of Councilwoman Miriam Friedlander's Resolution #491—to mandate the city's agencies to recognize the problems of battered women and develop programs to improve the situation—it happened that I was the first witness. So the material I was presenting (on the definition, scope, frequency, and multisocial levels of the problem, and the total lack of city facilities for ameliorating it) was very new to the councilman in charge of the hearings. At one point he questioned me. "Do we break up a marriage *merely* because a man beats his wife? Are we talking about a man who playfully slaps his wife? Who *lovingly* slaps his wife?" Later he wanted to know if a beating "*just once*" was really any reason for a woman to walk out of a long-time marriage.

No, the councilman was not a wifebeater, I was later assured by his co-workers—although his office was deluged for days by indignant women. I believe it was good to get that thinking out in the open. Clearly, he had no idea of the offense his words conveyed, nor of the tacit toleration they implied. He was no monster; he was Everyman. To my way of thinking, he became the unofficial spokesperson of the attitudes of society and of certain husbands, even those who are not violent themselves. The councilman's few innocent questions clearly show why the battered wife puts up with her horrendous situation, why she does not leave, why she does not report it, why she does not retaliate, why she is pressured into returning when she does manage to escape.

Actually, the councilman, before the end of the six-hour day of testimony, became a kind of hero. He had an open mind, despite the initial appearance, and he was very much moved by the testimony. When he heard from three battered wives who appeared with AWAIC's Maria Roy, he was convinced. He then became a champion of Councilwoman Friedlander's resolution and even suggested that additional specific mandates to city agencies be added.

The reason the battered wife does not leave is that she cannot. The psychodynamics of the people with the problem, and the pragmatic, unchangeable, solid reality of society's attitudes blocks her way to freedom from marital violence.

There is a danger of emphasizing the psychodynamics over the empirical societal conditions. As I see it, this perpetuates the "all rightness" of wifebeating and its inescapability. Instead of encouraging understanding and insight, overanalyzing the woman may put the focus in the wrong place. Consequently, it may seem like "substantiation" to those who see conjugal crime as only a private marital issue.

Enid Lloyd Keljik, a co-coordinator of the New York NOW's Task Force on the Battered Wife, emphasized at the hearings for the resolution that "intrafamily violence is first of all an expression of ingrained social evil and secondarily a personal, psychological illness of the victims; and that both battered and batterer are victims of social ills they did not make and surely cannot cure, at least not alone."

As to the question of psychodynamics, the mutual-dependence theory (discussed in chapter 2) could be one explanation why a battered wife might stay even if she were completely free to leave, aided and protected by societal conditions in her escape. But then, if society protected her leaving, her departure could hardly be called an "escape."

Until recently, those professions dedicated to the public good—legal, medical, psychiatric, and religious —have not mandated change in this social evil.

Where do society's "best people" get the notion of tolerance for wifebeating? How is it that decent, intelligent, law-abiding citizens act as though marital violence called for no outrage? The answer is deeply rooted in tradition.

How Does He Get Away with It?
Historical Precedents
for the Toleration of Wifebeating

> ... Scold her sharply, bully and terrify her. ....
> Readily beat her ... so that the beating will
> redound to your merit and her good.
> —*Rules of Marriage,*
>   Friar Cherubino of Siena

The tradition of wifebeating has been accepted by our most revered institutions and by highly respected nations. Wifebeating is a matter of historical record.

British Common Law "regulated" conjugal crime by permitting a husband to beat his wife only "with a rod not thicker than his thumb." This law, considered protective to the woman, was less harsh than Roman civil law, the law of continental Europe. Napoleon's civil code, which gave civil rights to many disenfranchised groups, such as Jews and homosexuals, took away all the status of women won during the French Revolution.

But these legal developments were relatively late in the sequence of institutionally condoned wife battery. Sadly, contempt for women has been interwoven with Western religious teachings, particularly those of Christian churches, almost from the beginning.

The concept of woman as subservient to man is quite clear in this Old Testament passage (Gen. 3:16) where God says:

> I will greatly multiply thy sorrow, and thy conception; in sorrow thou shalt bring forth children; and thy desire shall be to thy husband, and he shall rule over thee.

Although this was "modern" civilization's belief, women had not always been defined as base objects deserving to be beaten with impunity. On the contrary, early man approached the opposite sex with mixed feelings. He regarded her with awe, and even reverence. Most of the ancient world began by revering the female.

In fact, according to Robert Graves, ancient Europe had no gods, but a Great Goddess who was regarded as "immortal, changeless and omnipotent. . . . The concept of fatherhood had not been introduced into religious thought. She took lovers but for pleasure, not to provide her children with a father. Men feared, adored, and obeyed the matriarch; the hearth which she tended in a cave or hut being their earliest social centre, and motherhood their prime mystery."[1]

A typical Greek creation myth tells of Eurynome, Goddess of All Things, rising from Chaos and deciding to begin a work of creation. She catches hold of the North Wind, rubs it between her hands, and it becomes the great serpent Ophion. She dances wilder and wilder until the snake is "moved to couple with her." She lays the Universal Egg and bids the snake hatch it for her. "Out tumble all things that exist."

The snake-god in this case represents the father, not the Tempter. This father, however, is quite the opposite of the Old Testament patriarchal concept of father. While the couple is at home on Mount Olympus, Ophion vexes Eurynome so much by claiming to be the author of the Universe, that she bruises "his head with her heel" and banishes him to the dark caves below the earth.[2]

Biblical Interpretations

Many centuries later, the Hebrews, writing their own creation myth, would incorporate a snake story. Their God, the stern creator Jehovah, would also punish a snake, saying (Gen. 3:15): "And I will put enmity between thee and the woman, and between thy seed and her seed; it shall bruise thy head, and thou shalt bruise his heel."

Why did the Judeo-Christian approach develop as it did? If we look at the Bible as a literary work, we may get some understanding of this. Life was harsh for the desert patriarchs and tribes, and it produced a harsh outlook on life. Says one historian: "The male Jehovah is a stern Hebrew patriarch who leaves us in no doubt about the position of women. Far from being the mother of all the races of men, the natural order has been reversed, and woman is born out of a man, no more than a single rib."[3]

By the time the Book of Genesis was in its final draft, the patriarchs had accustomed themselves to putting women in their places—very lowly places. And their descendants, the designers of the early Christian church, who took over after Jesus himself had left the earth, were no different. Although Christ himself had egalitarian principles and honored many women as his beloved followers, the men of his times were not so advanced in attitudes.

"Since the Church fathers were male, and many of them became conscious of the physical desires of their bodies when in the presence of women, misogynism became engrained in Christianity," historian Vern L. Bullough notes. "These ideas . . . were carried over into the mainstream of Western thought. While the ordinary Christian man seldom achieved celibate life, he . . . tended . . . indirectly to blame his own inability to do so on women. Somewhat hesitantly Western man endorsed the idea of woman as temptress." It was St. Paul who stated it was "better to marry than to burn." (Cor. 7:9)[4]

Sociologists Suzanne K. Steinmetz and Murray A. Straus observed this unfortunate impact of the Adam and Eve story, stating, "The curse placed by God on all women when Eve sinned is only the earliest example in our culture of the sexually restrictive ethic, the placing of the 'blame' for sex on women, and the resulting negative definition of women—all of which tend to make women culturally legitimate objects of antagonism."[5]

The attitude that women are culturally legitimate

101

objects of antagonism is clear throughout the Old Testament. In the Book of Deuteronomy (25:11, 12), among the "divers laws and ordinances," there is one punishing a wife with mutilation if, in coming to the rescue of her husband in a fight with another man, she touches the opponent's genitals: "When men strive together one with another, and the wife of the one draweth near for to deliver her husband out of the hand of him that smiteth him, and putteth forth her hand, and taketh him by the secrets:

"Then thou shalt cut off her hand, thine eyes shall not pity her."

In another passage (22:13–21) there is a law regarding the disposal of a wife unable to prove her virginity: "Then they shall bring out the damsel to the door of her father's house, and the men of her city shall stone her with stones that she die . . . so shalt thou put evil away from among you."

The early Christian church, like all growing organizations, had many factions and splinter groups. In 325 A.D., a council was called (in what would be northwest Turkey today) to sort things out and to allow the strongest bishops of the Roman Empire to condemn as heresy those prevailing beliefs they did not approve. The surviving beliefs were then systematized into the Nicene Creed, which is still in use today. The council was presided over by Constantine I, "the Great," called by history the first Christian emperor of Rome because he was baptized on his deathbed. According to theologian Paul Tillich, "Constantine in Byzantium was the Christ for the whole Christian Church."[6] A fact of Constantine's life seldom mentioned in history, however, is that he had his wife, Fausta, killed.

It had been through marriage to Fausta, Maximian's infant daughter, whom Constantine had married in 298 by proxy, that Constantine had secured the empire. He executed her when she became an adult, of no further use to him.

By the Middle Ages, the status of women in the Roman Catholic church was so debased that, according to one writer, "men were exhorted from the pulpit to beat their wives and wives to kiss the rod that beat them. The deliberate teaching of domestic violence, combined with the doctrine that women and children by nature could have no human rights, had taken such hold by the late Middle Ages that men had come to treat their wives and children worse than their beasts."[7]

Further, the contempt of the Christian world toward women had reached such proportions that it was not uncommon to find two clergymen engaged in a heated argument about whether or not women even went to heaven.

Although omitted from most church historical accounts, the Christian Church, from Constantine on, has had a record of practicing and recommending physical abuse to women. The groundwork may have been laid officially in the first enduring systematization of church law, the *Decretum* (c. 1140), the work of Gratian, a jurist from Bologna: "Women should be subject to their men. . . . The image of God is in man and it is one. Women were drawn from man, who has God's jurisdiction as if he were God's vicar. . . . Therefore woman is not made in God's image. Woman's authority is nil. . . . Adam was beguiled by Eve, not she by him. It is right that he whom woman led into wrongdoing should have her under his direction so that he may not fail a second time through female levity. *(Corpus Iuris Canonici)*"[8]

The *Rules of Marriage* were compiled by Friar Cherubino of Siena sometime between 1450 and 1481. A section begins: "When you see your wife commit an offense, don't rush at her with insults and violent blows. . . ." But then it adds: ". . . Scold her sharply, bully and terrify her. And if this still doesn't work . . . take up a stick and beat her soundly, for it is better to punish the body and correct the soul than to damage the soul and spare the body. . . . Then readily beat her, not in rage but out of charity and concern for her soul, so that the beating will redound to your merit and her good. *(Regole della vita matrimoniale)*"[9]

Martin Luther (1483–1546), famed for the reformation of the established church, might also be famed for his remarkably anti-establishment views of women. According to the Family Life Committee of the Lutheran Church, he viewed women as a kind of "friendly rival." Lacking "the fear of some of his clerical predecessors," he dared oppose the common practice of ridiculing women in public. His counsel to men was that "no matter how antagonized they might be by the female, [men] should always keep in mind that women are also God's creatures." He considered it only right that he "upbraid the Archbishop of Mainz, who had been quoted as condemning the 'stinking, putrid, private parts of women.'"

Nevertheless, Luther was not beyond a casual reference to his practice of, and acceptance of, a non-severe form of physical abuse to his wife, the former nun Katherine. It was no guilty confession. Instead, the reference was in the context of thankfulness for his happy marriage: "I am rich, God has given me my nun and three children; what care I if I am in debt, Katie pays the bills. . . . George Kark has taken a rich wife and sold his freedom. I am luckier, for when Katie gets saucy, she gets nothing but a box on the ear."[10]

Man, the Manipulator

Throughout history there has been an almost desperate need on the part of men to try to manipulate conditions so that they themselves might feel superior to women and ease that awful gnawing suspicion that they were in fact not superior at all.

Scholar Joseph Campbell has observed: "in the very earliest ages of human history the magical force and wonder of the female was no less a marvel than the universe itself and this gave to woman a prodigious power, which it has been one of the chief concerns of the masculine part of the population to break, control, and employ to its own ends. It is in fact more remarkable how many primitive hunting races have the legend of a still more primitive age than their own, in which the women were the sole possessors of the magical art."[11]

Part of the magical force attributed to the female was the belief that somehow ancestral spirits in the form of living germs found their way into the maternal body. Eventually it dawned on man what his sexual contribution meant, and he marked the discovery by doing something about that old concern of his. He looked for effective ways to break and control the woman, employing her to his own ends. He became the patriarch. Society did an about-face.

Many ages later, one patriarchal figure, Sigmund Freud, added to the sexual repression of modern woman with his notions about masochism or orgasm. While his disciple Jung conceptualized the archetype "Great Mother," Freud saw woman as suffering from penis envy. From the few Victorian women patients he psychoanalyzed, several of them prime examples of hysteria, he became convinced that they felt inferior (or were indeed inferior) because of the lack of a penis. And the male, "conscious of his possession, feared women wanted to castrate him. In brief, the narcissistic rejection of the female by male is liberally mingled with fear and disdain."[12]

Freud's noted woman disciple, Karen Horney, observed a very different dynamic. After treating many American men and women, she came to see that instead of women suffering from penis envy, the fact was that men suffered from womb envy. She held that the Freudian theory was an attempt to deny the existence of the intrinsically "sinister" female genitalia, which represents a fear of maternal envelopment. In other cultures men had expressed their fears that the woman, sexually inexhaustible, would suck him dry of his strength or that she might possess a vagina *dentata* ("with teeth") and castrate him with it.

Horney reasoned that men had developed two techniques to deal with their fear of women: disparagement and idealization. By using disparagement, the male could reassure himself that there was nothing to fear from so poor and inadequate a creature. By using idealization, he felt reassured that there was nothing to fear from so saintly a being.[13]

With that theory, in a sense Horney summed up Western man's rationale for marital violence. If his wife did not accept her disparagement sufficiently, or if she did not live up to his idealization, he could call up the Adam and Eve story and justify himself for whatever he did to her. And society would let him get away with his wifebeating. Not only could he get

105

away with it—he could have it sanctioned by the courts.

Common law reflects the customs of the people of a nation. The early British judges based their decisions on what the community seemed to feel was correct. Women had no voice in these matters. After a number of courts had made similar rulings, the first decision then would become the precedent, and what was once custom now became law.

Sir William Blackstone wrote the *Commentaries on the Laws of England* (1765–1769), which "had great influence in the American colonies, where it provided the colonists with their chief source of information about English law."

Blackstone saw nothing unreasonable about the wife-beating law. In fact, he believed it to be quite moderate. He wrote, "For, as [the husband] is to answer for her misbehavior, the law thought it reasonable to intrust him with this power of chastisement, in the same moderation that a man is allowed to correct his apprentices or children."[14]

With Blackstone as a guide, America's first states formed their wifebeating laws. In 1824, Mississippi held that some "moderate chastisement . . . would be allowed in order to enforce the salutary restraint of domestic discipline." The court further sought to protect the husband from his wife's attempts for justice: "Perhaps the husband should still be permitted to exercise the right to moderate chastisement, in cases of great emergency and to use salutary restraint in every case of misbehavior, without subjecting himself to vexatious prosecutions, resulting in the discredit and shame of all parties."[15]

And who would determine what constituted "misbehavior" or how injurious the "salutary restraints" might be? In this decision the husband was the only one in a marriage who had civil rights. In other words, it was all right for a husband to beat his wife as far as the early American power structure was concerned, and it was *not* all right for him to be stopped or dealt with in any way by the law. It was all right for a wife to be injured by her husband, but *not* all right for her to "vex or discredit or shame" herself or her husband by seeking prevention or relief.

In 1871, Alabama and Massachusetts repudiated the tradition of legal wifebeating. In spelling out what actions by husbands were no longer allowed, the legal language exposed, rawly and vividly, what had been the legal fate of wives under American and British law:

". . . And the privilege, ancient though it be, to beat her with a stick, to pull her hair, choke her, spit in her face, or kick her about the floor, or to inflict upon her other like indignities, is not now acknowledged by our law."

In 1874, the North Carolina court seemed to have recognized the wife as a human being with rights the same as a husband. The court wrote: "We may assume that the old doctrine that a husband had a right to whip his wife, provided he used a switch no bigger than his thumb, is not the law in North Carolina. Indeed, the courts have advanced from that barbarism until they have reached the position that the husband has no right to chastise his wife under any circumstances."

Enlightenment at last?

Well, yes and no. There is a Catch-22. That old inherent right about the sanctity of a man's castle and the nonsanctity of a woman's castle caused the court to add a qualification that it wasn't going to hear any trivial complaints:

"If no permanent injury has been inflicted, nor malice nor dangerous violence shown by the husband, it is better to draw the curtain, shut out the public gaze, and leave the parties to forget and forgive."

The double standard implied here was that the wife was legally expected to forget and forgive being beaten. But the husband, instead of forgetting or forgiving any annoying little act of hers, could get away with the aforementioned "barbarism."

In 1886, a Pennsylvania citizen tried to have wifebeating made illegal. A state legislator named C. Adams received a bill from a constituent to be placed in the statute bill. The bill was to criminalize wifebeating, and make it punishable by thirty lashes. Its rationale was that by beating the wifebeater, the community would be saved the taxes needed for prison upkeep and the charity support of the wife and children. The corporal punishment was considered more humane than imprisoning, in that the family would be kept intact and continue to be supported by the non-incarcerated husband.

The bill read, in part: "Be it enacted by the Senate and house of Pennsylvania . . . that whenever hereafter any male person shall willfully beat, bruise or mutilate his wife, the court . . . shall direct the infliction of corporal punishment upon such offender, to be laid upon his bare back to the number of lashes not exceeding thirty, by means of a whip or lash of suitable proportions and strength for the purpose of this act."

Justice at last!

Wifebeating in Nineteenth-century Europe

The proposed bill, however, did not pass.

Although history has hidden many of the details of legal, religious, and societal cooperation with conjugal crime, history does document the fact that men (fathers or husbands) considered themselves *owners* of women.

Napoleon Bonaparte, one of the world's most influential lawmakers, was dedicated to the ownership theory. He legislated women into a position where they were victims of whatever abuse their husbands meted out, and wrote no law to protect them.

Napoleon's civil code (1800–1804) still has influence. It is still the law of France (with certain modifications, including recent ones on behalf of women's rights). "It is still the law of Belgium and Luxembourg," according to one historian. It influenced the civil laws of Holland, Switzerland, Italy, and Germany. It has left its "imprints of political equality *and a strong family* on countries as diverse as Bolivia and Japan."[16]

The code changed the laws of privilege operating under the aristocracy before the French Revolution (1789–99). But it also changed the laws of equality of men and women that had been enjoyed through the Revolution. It is that legalized ownership and dominance of men over women which the innocuous-sounding phrase, "a strong family" implies but seldom acknowledges when it appears in print.

Married women had enjoyed wide freedom and separate property rights under the old regime. The revolution itself had broadened their rights. But Napoleon's view was that women must be treated as lifelong irresponsible minors.

According to historian Christopher Herold, Napoleon told the council of state: "The husband must possess the absolute power and right to say to his wife: 'Madam, you shall not go out, you shall not go to the theatre, you shall not receive such and such a person; for the children you bear shall be mine.'

"A French husband under the old regime would not have got very far with such a speech. Napoleon . . . was determined to reform family life on Roman, or perhaps Corsican, principles. . . . Just as Napoleon was the sole authority in the state, so the husband and father was to exercise authority over his family."[17]

So biased was Napoleon that he blamed only the woman in any two-spouse action such as adultery or divorce. Furthermore, he wanted women to suffer equally—the only time they were deemed equals—when their husbands were punished under the penal code.

Napoleon said that adultery was common, could "happen on any convenient sofa." Though he said nothing of their partners, he wanted restraints imposed "upon those women who commit adultery for trinkets or verses."[18]

Again, though he said nothing of the partner, he wanted to make divorce difficult, because "a young woman will be ready to marry a quite unsuitable man, for fashion, convenience, simply to get a roof over her head. The law must warn her against this . . . in truth there are only three valid grounds for a divorce: attempted murder, adultery, and impotence."[19]

And so then what happens to wifebeating as a cause for divorce? Unless it were proved attempted murder, or unless the husband also wanted the divorce, the wife would have to continue living with the wifebeater.

According to biographer Emil Ludwig, Napoleon's strong family feeling leads him to add that maltreatment, perversion, and adultery should be concealed beneath "the formula of mutual desire."[20]

The Napoleonic penal code was severe and barbarous, given to branding and cutting off the hand as punishments. It also favored punishing wives of criminals, as somehow being natural accomplices, or even masterminds of the crime.

Napoleon declared that in order to humiliate the bankrupt, "prison would do it, even if it were but for an hour. It was also desirable that in every case the woman should share the misfortune of her husband."[21]

Napoleon's sardonic reasoning as to why a wife should follow her husband to his place of punishment covers his contempt for womankind with sugarcoating: ". . . For how can we forbid a woman to do so when she is convinced of her husband's innocence? . . . Many men have become criminals owing to their wives. Are we to forbid those who have been the cause of the misfortune from sharing that misfortune?"[22]

What gave this lawmaker his notions of right and wrong in marriage? Genesis again. When one of his councilors of state questioned him about the severity, he brushed it aside, saying, "Do you not know that the angel told Eve to obey her husband?"[23]

At Last, a Champion

After the French Revolution an equally keen advocate of *ending* the subjection of women was born across the English Channel. The British philosopher John Stuart Mill (1806–1873) wrote critical essays and petitioned Parliament on behalf of women's rights. As strong as Napoleon's belief that his male superiority theories were proved correct via history and the Book of Genesis, Mill's beliefs that historic trends proved just the opposite were argued even stronger and more eloquently.

Mill, one of the Enlightenment's most distinguished literary figures, was known for his philosophic investigation and analysis of human nature. The results of his investigation showed that the subjection of women to men was based on theory, not experience, "because no other system had ever been tried." (Not in the presently established nations, that is. Matriarchy and equality had worked out well in pre-Christian times and in some early tribes.)

"From the very earliest twilight of human society," he wrote in *The Subjection of Women*, "every woman . . . was found in a state of bondage to some man." The bondage of his enlightened day was the "single relic of an old world of thought and practice. . . ." He pointed out that the trend of his times was toward freedom and away from old bondage. "Human beings are no longer . . . chained down by an inexorable bond to the place they are born to, but are free to employ their faculties, and such favorable chances as offer, to achieve the lot which may appear to them most desirable." Therefore, the present lack of rights for women, especially married women, "stands out an isolated fact in modern social institutions."[24]

Mill wrote passionately of the plight of the battered wife in 1869. Ironically, he could be writing about conditions today.

"When we consider how vast is the number of men, in any great country, who are little higher than brutes, and that this never prevents them from being able, through the law of marriage, to obtain a victim, the breadth and depth of human misery caused in this shape alone by the abuse of the institution swells to something appalling. . . . Yet these are only the extreme cases. . . ."[25]

Battered wives of today are handicapped in getting help because unthinking society too often refuses to take them seriously. Individual cases are labeled extremely rare; the evils of wifebeating, exceptional. Mill also encountered a fascination with the few specific cases publicized, and at the same time a general blindness to the existence of the widespread problem.

"The sufferings, immoralities, evils of all sorts, produced in innumerable cases by the subjection of individual women to individual men, are far too terrible to be overlooked. Unthinking or uncandid persons, counting those cases alone which are extreme or which attain publicity, may say that the evils are exceptional;

111

but no one can be blind to their existence, nor, in many cases, to their intensity. . . ."[26]

In the 1860s, as well as the 1970s, husbands had the power of the law on their side and the power of too little public outcry on behalf of battered wives. Yet now and then there was a demonstration of opinion. In some villages in the British countryside, for instance, there was the communal custom of "rough music," when the villagers would turn out and serenade a violent man with a clattering of pots and pans to shame him. But this was not the custom in London, or in the circle of Mill's readership:

"And it is perfectly obvious that the abuse of the power cannot be very much checked while the power remains. It is a power given, offered, not to good men, or to decently respected men, but to all men: the most brutal, and the most criminal. There is no check but that of opinion, and such men are, in general, within the reach of no opinion but that of men like themselves. . . ."[27]

Throughout modern history, some reformers have thought it wise if tougher requirements for marriage were enacted, and at the same time, easier requirements for ending a marriage. The thought seems to have occurred to Mill as well.

". . . Men are not required as a preliminary to marriage to prove that they are fit to be trusted with absolute power over another human being. . . . The vilest malefactor has some wretched woman tied to him, against whom he can commit any atrocity except killing her—and even that he can do without too much danger of legal penalty.

"And how many thousands are there in every country, who, without being in a legal sense malefactors in any other respect, because in every other quarter their aggressions meet with resistance, indulge in the utmost habitual excesses of bodily violence towards the unhappy wife, who alone, at least of grown persons can neither repel or escape from their brutality; and towards whom the excess of dependence inspires their mean and savage natures, not with a generous forbearance, and a point of honor to behave well to one whose lot in life is trusted entirely to their kindness, but on

112

the contrary with a notion that the law has delivered her to them as their thing, to be used at their pleasure, and that they are not expected to practice the consideration towards her which is required from them towards everybody else."[28]

Some of Mill's accusations may seem extreme, but they were less extreme than the conditions of the real life of the nineteenth century. As Wendell Robert Carr pointed out in his introduction to *The Subjection of Women*, "Under the present laws of marriage, Mill declared, wives could potentially be forced to endure not merely the traditional forms of slavery, but the 'worst description' of bondage known to history. Unlike other slaves, a wife could be made subject to duty 'at all hours and all minutes.' She could be denied even Uncle Tom's privilege of having 'his own life in his cabin.' She had no legal means, as existed in some slave codes, to compel the master to sell her. And worst of all, she could not refuse her master even 'the last familiarity' but must submit to 'the lowest degradation of a human being, that of being made the instrument of an animal function contrary to her inclinations.' "[29]

John Stuart Mill's essay has become a kind of Bible among today's groups working on behalf of the battered wife, establishing shelters and hotlines; developing reeducational programs for institutions encountering the problem; proposing changes in state laws. It is quoted and reprinted everywhere.

Mill was one of the few men of history with power enough to influence society who spoke out against wifebeating. He is a hero who made the unspeakable *speakable*. The way his eloquent words were received in his own time, however, is quite another matter. He was denounced as a traitor to his society and his sex.

"Of anything Mill ever wrote, *The Subjection of Women* aroused the most antagonism . . . not only his enemies but his friends were horrified," so says his biographer, Michael St. John Packe.

Mill kept the manuscript of *The Subjection of Women* "lying by him for eight years, awaiting the decisive kindling moment" for publication and for stimulating discussion.[30]

In 1874 there was enough evidence to bring statistics of suffering women and children to the attention of Parliament. The prime minister, Benjamin Disraeli, promised to do something about it, but did not act on his words. Life continued as before for the battered wife.

A Feminist Takes Up the Cause

In 1878 a well-known feminist of the day, a woman "of the ranks, constitutionally qualified by the possession of property . . . and naturally qualified by education and intelligence," decided to do something about the lapse. A learned journal of the time, *The Contemporary Review,* published her paper proposing a bill giving some measure of protection to battered wives. Frances Power Cobbe felt it was her duty and responsibility to work for her more unfortunate sisters because she herself "had never received . . . from the men . . . anything but kindness and consideration." She entreated other women like herself, "who are prone to think that the lot of others is as smooth and happy as our own," and the "gentlemen of England—the bravest, humanest, and most generous in the world—" to realize the hopeless condition of the battered wife and to support remedial action.[31]

Mrs. Cobbe summed up the situation aptly—for her own times, and, alas, for our own, a century later. She made the astute observation that "the abstract idea of a strong man hitting or kicking a weak woman—*per se,* so revolting—has somehow got softened into a jovial kind of domestic lynching, the grosser features of the case being swept out of sight, just as people make endless jests on tipsiness, forgetting how loathsome a thing is a drunkard. A 'jolly companion' chorus seems to accompany both kinds of exploits. This, and the prevalent idea . . . that the woman has generally deserved the blows she receives, keep up, I believe, the indifference of the public on this subject."[32]

She expressed her shock at clerical idolization of wifebeating as somehow beautiful and Christian, as exemplified by a Rev. F. W. Harper, writing in the *Spectator.* "I make bold to believe that if I ever should turn into a wife I shall choose to be beaten by my husband to any extent (short of being slain outright) rather than it should be said a stranger came between us." Then he bids his readers remember that the true idea of marriage is "the relation of Christ and his Church." Mrs. Cobbe exclaimed: "Heaven help the poor women of Durham and Lancashire if their clergy lead them to picture a Christ resembling their husbands!"[33]

The nineteenth-century author noted that "wifebeating exists in the upper and middle classes rather more, I fear, than is generally recognized. . . ." But she expressed special alarm at certain districts notorious for their brutal assaults on women, such as the "kicking district" (kicking the wife's face with hobnailed boots) of Liverpool. There, "Legree himself might find a dozen prototypes. . . .

"There are also various degrees of wifebeating in the different localities," Cobbe wrote. In London it seldom "goes beyond a severe 'thrashing' with the fists —a sufficiently dreadful punishment, it is true, when inflicted by a strong man on a woman; but mild in comparison of the kickings and tramplings and 'purrings' with hobnailed shoes and clogs. . . . Nowhere is the ill-usage of woman so systematic as in Liverpool and so little hindered by the strong arm of the law; making the lot of a married woman whose locality is the 'kicking district' of Liverpool simply a duration of suffering and subjection to injury and savage treatment, far worse than that to which the wives of mere savages are used. . . . The condition of the women [might] be most accurately matched by that of the negroes on a Southern plantation before the war struck off their fetters."[34]

For many women living in the "kicking district," to be *treated like a dog* would only be welcome relief. "Human beings no longer live like animals in a condition wherein the natural sentiments between the sexes suffice it to guard the weak, where the male brute is kind and forbearing to the female, and where no Court of Chancery interferes with the mother's most dear and sacred charge of her little ones. Man alone claimed to hold his mate in subjection, and to have

115

the right while he lives, and after he dies, to rob a mother of her child. . . . Man needs to be provided with laws . . . to form a substitute for chivalry."[35]

The bill she proposed would "afford the poor women by means easily within their reach, the same redress which women of richer classes obtain through the divorce court." A judicial separation (not divorce) would oblige the husband to pay a weekly sum for maintenance, "paid through and recoverable by the relieving officer of the parish," so as to afford the victim greater security and "obviate the chance of collision with the husband."[36]

Mrs. Cobbe recognized that a full divorce "ought to be given to the wife in cases of brutal assault," but it seemed "too dangerous an incentive to commit or to provoke assault." She recognized too that either husband or wife may "fall into vicious courses since marriage is closed to them," but on weighing the benefits, she noted that the wifebeater is always a man of "loose and disorderly life," while the battered wife is generally a law-abiding, humble citizen. "The decent respectable wife, such as I hope I have shown a large class of beaten wives to be, would of course live like a well-conducted widow."[37]

Although this proposed bill didn't make it into law, there began to be enough pressure from sympathizers to produce a number of reforms. The reforms, however, mostly dealt with the legal status and property rights of married women. Today, as Erin Pizzey can attest, and as the 1975 House of Commons Select Committee on Violence in Marriage has documented, wifebeating in the extreme is still an everyday occurrence in England.

The Past Is Present

The bizarre history of tolerated conjugal crime continued well into this century. However, as more facts are uncovered and brought to light, the existence of violence in marriage can be acknowledged and better dealt with. The laws giving protection to battered children and the reformed laws on rape prosecution came about in much the same way.

In contemporary Britain, Erin Pizzey, almost single-handed and without funding, started the first emergency shelter for battered wives and their children. By exposing wifebeating wherever she found it, she was able to get funding and to see the establishment of almost a hundred more shelters. The shocking element in the success story is that they are all used and even more are needed. But her work did lead to the Parliamentary committee and it will lead to the necessary laws.

Today's men and women have been reexamining their values, their sense of the dignity of the individual, their expectations of life and of marriage. It's time to reexamine the conscious and unconscious beliefs that led to the toleration of violence by husbands. Disputes between men and women must be settled on some other basis than physical abuse.

It will take a raised societal consciousness. It will take reeducation. It will take new laws. In the meantime, the movement against conjugal crime is growing. The topic has already become a new favorite for masters' theses in police work and counseling, and doctoral dissertations in social work, sociology, theology, medicine, law, and psychology. Two law students at the University of Michigan, Sue Eisenberg and Pat Micklow, did a groundbreaking study of the ineffectiveness of the legal and health care delivery systems to help the battered wife.[38] And the first professional guide for lawyers, police, therapists, social workers, physicians, and others who encounter the battered-wife syndrome in their work—written by these professionals for their colleagues—was published in 1977.[39]

Each time the media covers the topic, hotlines around the country record an increase in revelations from middle-class wives that they too have decided to end their long silence. Well-known men who believe(d) in violence to women openly admit it—although not always with any indication of guilty conscience.

A famous British actor, for instance, boasted for publication in 1976: "Women probably think I'm sadistic . . . but basically the only way to make a woman feel secure is to give her enough of the old oats. . . . Yes

I've smacked a couple of women in the past. . . . You put her across your knee and give her one. . . . When I'm really angry . . . I kick them out of the door. Yes, physically."[40]

Aristotle Onassis is said to have beaten a woman he lived with for twelve years "until he quit from exhaustion." The next day instead of apologizing he said, " 'All Greek men, without exception, beat their wives. It's good for them.' "[41]

The Sicilian-American film director Martin Scorsese *(Taxi Driver)* did a vivid wifebeating scene in *Alice Doesn't Live Here Anymore*. He has said: "I had to come to terms with what I can only call my own hatred of women. Growing up, I got this Sicilian thing of treating women like rags or furniture. *Mean Streets* shows the violence I was brought up to feel toward women."[42]

Will the next generation also be brought up to feel violence toward women? And the present generation —those victimized children who are being brought up witnessing the violence of father to mother—what will become of them? Are they doomed to repeat the cycle of the battered and the batterers? The next chapter will take a look at the effect of wifebeating on the witnessing children of today.

How It Affects the Children

"I have to keep a home going for the children. What sort of home could I manage on my own?"

"Children need a father."

"He loves the children; I can't separate them."[1]

These are typical "reasons" given by middle-class battered wives for why they haven't left their husbands, or why it took them so long to leave. Do their children agree with their reasoning? Here is what some children had to say about the world their parents created for them:

"I beg my mother to leave him and take me with her, and she keeps telling me it's not good to grow up without a father. But I don't need *that* father."

"I'm going to kill my father one of these days if he doesn't cut it out."

"I don't want to talk about it. I don't want to know about it. I used to throw up when he'd start that, I'd be so scared. Now I sneak out of the house."

"I'm not going to help her anymore. She doesn't do anything to help herself, and I don't know why. Do you think she maybe likes it? I've heard of people like that."[2]

The child of the wifebeater has more hope than his or her mother, knowing that in a certain number of years, he or she will be grown up and able to escape, whereas the mother will only be more deeply entrapped. In the meantime, the child has an outside world. The father may keep the mother isolated, but the child has to go to school, and so has some chance of developing other, nonviolent, nonvictim role models.

Some of the problems peculiar to growing up with a wifebeater come from the very fact that others cannot believe the life the child must lead. Such children discover they are very different. Many things taken for granted by everyone else simply do not exist in their own lives. Many feel they don't dare bring a friend home, could never have a party, cannot explain why a holiday with daddy is not an event to look forward to. They are ashamed and humiliated at what goes on in their home, afraid someone will walk in on it, and yet also wishing a strong rescuer would come along.

The Dick-and-Jane life in schoolbooks, as well as the reports they hear from their peers, do not have any relationship to the life they know as real. A constant conflict is between fear of telling and longing to tell someone who would make it all better. The rationale is that if they do confide their plight, the odds are they won't be believed, and not being believed, their very being is negated.

Other people keep saying things—just normal, everyday things—that are painful testimony to the fact that the wifebeater's family is different from everyone else's. The child hears some other father saying, "Well, you know how fathers are . . . I could never refuse my kid anything," or, "I'd never let anyone harm my child," or, "My family comes first with me." Yes, this child knows how fathers are, and it's nothing like that.

Someone else's father might say, "If my wife doesn't stop that, I'm going to kill her,"—but it's a *joke,* unlike the threat of their own father, who really tries to kill. Or they may hear someone else's mother saying, "Oh, if I do this, my husband will be so furious, he'll beat the life out of me,"—but again, it's a *joke.* She's not truly afraid of her husband, nor will her husband try to kill her. Other people's lives are very different.

Life as Viewed by the Witnessing Child

The witnessing children are the most pathetic victims of conjugal crime because their childhood conditioning will color their entire lives. All other input will be processed through the mire of the first marriage they ever saw and their earliest role models of husband and wife, father and mother. Daddy is cruel to mommy, who can't do anything to change it. No one seems to care, neither in the house nor out in society. The nightmare apparently is to be regarded as natural—or nonexistent—since it is neither acknowledged nor alleviated. To the child growing up in this environment, it seems as if all power is on the side of the wrongdoer. Nice people finish last. Perhaps wrong is right, after all.

Growing Up in the Wifebeater's Home

VIOLENCE DURING PREGNANCY

The children's problems begin early—for some, even *before* they are born, when the father directs his attack to the mother's belly. Frequently, this violence begins with the first pregnancy. In other cases, Dr. Richard J. Gelles found, marriages that were already violent became worse during pregnancy, a time of crisis, of conflicting emotions. Gelles pointed out several factors that may contribute to the crisis and to prenatal child abuse:[3]

1. *Sexual frustration.* The factor of sexual frustration is obvious, ranging from the wife's discomfort and her perception of herself as growing unattractive, to her husband's similar view, or the superstition that abstinence should be the rule.

2. *Family transition, stress and strain.* The transition from carefree courtship or honeymoon to the responsibilities and maturity required by pregnancy and parenthood is not always welcome. Even when it is, it brings its own stresses. If the wife is already pregnant when the couple marry, or if the baby is conceived too soon after marriage, the transition may prove too rapid for the potential wifebeater to handle.

"I think because neither of us was ready to have any children—and I got pregnant three months after we married," was the guess of one pregnancy-battered wife. "We had a place we could go to on weekends, and he didn't want to stop doing anything. If I couldn't go, he would just go without me."

3. *The biochemical changes in the wife.* Certain changes of pregnancy, causing irritability, depression, an overly critical nature in the woman, were unex-

121

pected by the wifebeater, who was not prepared to be tender or understanding and didn't care to try.

4. *A desire to end the pregnancy.* For three wives in Gelles's survey, the beating was followed by a miscarriage, while a fourth gave birth to a handicapped child. Gelles suggests that "for many families, violence which brings about a miscarriage is a more acceptable way of terminating an unwanted pregnancy than is abortion." In couples whose views against abortion or birth control are unalterably rigid, it may be more acceptable "socially, morally, and even legally. . . ."

5. *Defenselessness of the wife.* Studies have shown that "aggression is more likely if the other person [the victim] is perceived as unwilling or unable to retaliate." The pregnant wife is especially vulnerable.

Other reasons may lie buried in the wifebeater's unconscious. Freud saw the woman as a mystic threat that men must struggle not to identify with. Pregnancy, of course, emphasizes her femaleness and makes her more threatening still. Some men suffer from unconscious womb envy, as discussed in chapter 5. Or, the man may be retaliating for the wrongs—imagined or otherwise—he felt he suffered as a boy at the hands of his mother.

But no matter what the cause, violence during pregnancy affects the unborn child and presages the direction its life will take.

INFANCY AND EARLY CHILDHOOD

The infant in a violent home often reflects his upset in poor health, poor sleeping habits, and excessive screaming (all of which may, in turn, ignite the father to abuse the mother more). "Under three or four years of age, they show their terror by yelling, hiding, shaking, and stuttering," says therapist Carol Victor. One expert who has worked with abused children suggests that infants who are not abused themselves but who witness abuse may develop in a similar way. Dr. Carolyn Levitt, head of the Children's Hospital Clinic and member of the Ramsay County (Minnesota) Child Abuse Team, says: "The battered infant is chaotic, frightened, cowering; afraid of us doctors, too . . .

frightened of anyone he is unsure of. At least he *knows* the battering parent; he gets psychic clues as to what's going to happen next. But he has no experience that it's safe with *us*. He clings strongly to the parent, including the battering parent. He is afraid of all men, or all women." This panic over encountering any man has also been observed in several children staying at shelters.

Noor van Crevel, a Dutch counselor in the field of conjugal crime, has encountered fierce aggression in the boys, even at two years old. Sometimes it was merely a cover-up for his fears and sensitivity; sometimes it was a deep-rooted hostility. She states that "Small boys often picked up from their dads the notion that a 'real' boy is a good fighter and has a loud mouth, and are confused about what they really feel. Underneath they may feel constant fear of being found out for the weaklings they are convinced to be, or have a constant hunger for affection."[4]

The hostility type of aggression, seen in those in van Crevel's shelter, usually requires motivation and therapeutic help, and neither parent nor child may be so motivated. For the cover-up façades, however, the shelter provides alternate outlets for aggression, such as carpentry, as well as protection and affection, in hopes of breaking through.

After the age of four, little boys are often "badly in need of a new orientation toward their own maleness," says Noor van Crevel.[5] The conversations among the shelter residents comparing experiences do nothing to improve their negative image of men, and unfortunately, some mothers tell their son he reminds her of his father. Once relaxed in the freedom of the shelter, some boys grab at any chance to identify with a good man—the handyman, the playworker. If the mother can be aware of the problem and let the son "develop along his own lines," some new orientation can occur.

AFTER FIVE OR SIX

As the child gets older, he may try ineffectively to push the father away, or beg him to stop (which in turn may endanger the child). Or the child may catch on to the fact that he is not supposed to do anything, and respond with immobilized shocked staring, with running away and hiding, or bedwetting and nightmares.

Carol Victor feels that "after five or six, there are often strong indications of losing respect for the mother. Some identify with the aggressor instead of the mother. The dynamics can get very confused. One daughter refused to testify against her father, saying very proud, 'My father can beat anyone.' "

Other children continue to try to halt the violence in their own ways. Noor van Crevel describes an eight-year-old girl who "developed a frantic set of tactics to divert her father's attention from her mother, even to the point of taking her mother's place in the marital bed." A six-year-old boy wanted a walkie-talkie for his birthday, "so he could install a hotline to the nearest police office"; and a ten-year-old was devoting himself to athletic training so he could outrun his dad."[6]

TEENS

Living in a household controlled by a wifebeater can turn some children not into frightened wrecks, but into calculating little mimickers of the ruling power. I have seen nothing on it in the literature. Only those who actually work in the field regularly know this "bad seed" aspect. Their mothers may think they are staying in the marriage "for the sake of the children," but the bitter truth is that their children will not allow them to leave. The wifebeater does not harm the kids. The kids, getting older and harder, have all the material advantages of a middle-class or upper-middle-class home, advantages that will end if the home is broken up. They no longer care about the mother's suffering; it's just part of the daily routine. They depersonalize her and block her from their consciousness and conscience. She couldn't be worth much if she got herself into such a fix, now, could she?

In their teens, both girls and boys may finally pick up the expected pattern and actually join in beating the mother. Some toddlers hit their mother or kick her to gain her attention. A counselor reported one boy saying coolly, "My old man can do anything he wants, as far as I'm concerned. All women are a pain to all men, just like he says. Sure, I hit her sometimes. Why not? He does."

I met one very quiet woman at a shelter who was there for the second time. Her children hated her for daring to leave them and the husband, because it meant losing their personal slave. They phoned the shelter frequently with threats and cajoling, to get her back.

One night her teen-age daughter enticed her to come with her in the car "to the movies." She did not return that night. A few days later the woman stopped by the shelter for a moment to return something. She was walking with difficulty and in obvious pain from a beating. She confided in the residents that not only her husband but her children had attacked her.

"I'm one of the dumb ones," she said hopelessly, as her children awaited her outside in the car. "I have to go home to my family."

Joining in the attack with the wifebeater offers some children the safety of siding with the winner. It is the easiest, most expedient way.

What Kind of Mothering Do Witnessing Children Get?

Women living with the terror become dominated by the problem and the pain. It's on their minds most of the time and they can't think past it. They are sometimes too enmeshed to think clearly about their children's welfare. They become so worn down, so needy themselves, they have less and less to give to their children.

Thus, children grow up with the confused feeling that the mother is not quite a grown-up because she cannot save them from harm, any more than she can save herself. They often try to make up for it by mothering *her,* growing up fast so they can protect her. At the Women's Advocates House in St. Paul, a child told the staff that her mother used to have a violent boyfriend. The child, at about eleven years old, would open the front door, hold out the man's car keys, and tell him to leave. And he would! What did the mother do? "She told me not to interfere, that she could take care of herself." And could she? "No."

Noor van Crevel also found problems with a girl in the Dutch shelter who had taken on the responsibilities, far beyond her years, of mothering her mother. She listened supportively to all her mother's complaints. In the shelter she didn't know where she fit in. She felt too old to play with the other kids, or for school, yet the women residents didn't recognize and welcome her as a peer the way her mother had.

In fleeing to the nonviolent atmosphere of the shelter, mother and daughter actually may resume a more normal relationship. The mother may, for the first time in her life, develop friendships with other adult women—leaving the daughter bewildered and protesting at being cast as "just another child. Or the daughter may make a positive use of the shelter by relaxing her grown-up attitudes and regressing rapidly to the fearful, whimpering, dependent child that lives deep inside her and never got a chance to show itself. In that case, the mother protests: she is disappointed and unwilling to make the necessary adjustments by growing up herself."[7] At the Dutch shelter, these spontaneous breakthroughs were looked for and encouraged, while simultaneously giving emotional support to the one who felt left out.

Generally, a new sense of respect and self-respect developed in the shelter, as both mother and child saw each other in a new light. It was very good for both when the child, who had known the mother only as a person who was treated with contempt, saw her standing up for her own rights and actually *liked* by other adults.

Carol Victor describes another syndrome typified by a mother who has bent "over backward to validate her need to feel, 'I'm a good mother.' She stays, 'for the kids' sakes.' During this time, the husband successfully convinces all of them—mother and the children —that she's not a good wife. The irony is, in the end, the kids have little or no feeling for her. Only terrible anger at the mother. No respect."

Some children may wonder if they themselves are the cause of their mother's predicament. It is not unusual for a mother to hint that this is the case, or that the pregnancy and subsequent issue made it impossible for her to escape.

The existence of a child does serve to entrap the battered woman. But it also may be the spur for daring to escape—to a lower standard of living, true, but to safety. Noor van Crevel noticed a certain ambivalence in the mothers: "On the one hand, overconcern . . . and on the other hand, hidden or open resentment."[8]

Children Who Try to Help—and Those Who Don't

At one shelter I visited, there was a young teen-age boy, big and strong for his age, who was kind, obedient, and helpful to his mother, and quiet and passive around the house. He told me he regretted that he wasn't "strong enough yet" to do anything about his father. When he got to be a little older and stronger, he said, he thought he'd pay him back, although perhaps he'd really prefer to "just go away and forget it all."

"Some sons try to protect the mother," says Carol Victor, and some keep out of it. And after they are older, some beat the mother, too. They are angry at her for taking it. They love her, so they are doubly angry. She must be unworthy, they decide, because she allows it.

There may be very different reactions within the same family. In Carol Victor's survey of eighty clients, she found that in a family of two brothers, the seven-year-old was confused and frightened; the ten-year-old became angry and tried to intervene.

A mother of three, with two daughters under ten, said: "They stay and hold on to me, try to get in between. Their six-year-old brother says, 'I'm going to do something to him.' "

In another family, the mother related that "The boys would grab my husband and hold him down; the younger ones would hide. They'd see it coming and beg me, 'Don't say anything at all; maybe he won't hit you.' "

And in a third family, the fifteen-year-old boy laughed at his battered mother, the thirteen-year-old girl tried to protect her, the little one just watched.

Why are some kids moved to try to help, while others look out for their own survival only, even when it includes joining with the father?

Nancy Smith, the child advocate at Women's Advocates House in St. Paul, says: "Different kids make different choices. It's a preconscious decision, based on what they see and hear, based on their survival, using all their capabilities at the time. One may try to make everything okay, while another may decide, 'People who rescue are incapable of being rescued themselves'—and that's smart . . . *then*. But the boy may keep that mentality even after it's outgrown. It's inappropriate for the adult son.

"The children who don't intervene are used to seeing it, and nothing much moves them. They chose from a selection of messages also—'you are a bad kid, dumb, good, no-good, special, smart, daddy's boy'— and live out their life that way."

The Hazards of Helping Mother

The witnessing children who try to make the situation better face danger and discouragement. There is, of course, the exceptional situation of a son who had grown stronger than his father, but otherwise, efforts usually prove futile. When children seek help from other grown-ups, they tend to meet with disbelief, even disapproval—although I believe that from now on at least that particular problem will diminish. Margaret Ball, area director of the Family Service of Detroit and Wayne County, Emergency Counseling Central District, addressed herself to this problem:

"Adolescents ask for help sometimes. They and also younger children go to school (may be sent by the abused parent) to exhibit injuries as a plea for help— consciously or unconsciously. They are similar to the abused wife in that they are:

1. conflicted in loyalties as to complaining against a person they also love;

2. not sure they have rights against parent or in conflict with parental rights;
3. experiencing shame (they are 'bad') in belonging to such a family and even 'deserving' abuse.

Some adolescents are more aggressive, even vindictive, and tend to be viewed as suspect by the authorities and discounted as reliable."

Not until public consciousness is raised, and old laws are modified and new ones passed, will a teenager's cry for help for his family be seriously heeded and seriously met.

The Survivors

For many of these children, the future is bleak. "They may grow up into a loser cycle, without making any effort to change," says Nancy Smith, child advocate at Women's Advocates House. Yet what is particularly interesting to me is that many shelters report that some of the children coming there are not at all difficult but are surprisingly friendly and outgoing, showing few problems.

What chance have they to become "normal" persons, not too psychologically scarred? "Trust is the key," says Smith. "The key to anyone is how they relate to other people and to whom. These children may not even trust themselves. Many of these mothers have trouble trusting, but if the mother can convey enough love and trust and security, the child may have a chance not to become the next generation of battered and batterers. And even the other children, if they can get help, can get an idea for change."

The simple fact of being sheltered from danger can reduce the "close, anxiety-ridden tie" with the mother, as Noor van Crevel has found. Once the child sees the mother is safe, he can relax the vigil and become more of a child.

Some children recognize their own precarious situation and determine to be "normal" by trying to reject the values of the violent home. Instead, they start trying to make up for the absence of love and decency. Being so conditioned to constant fear, however, it takes hard work to begin to see life with other reactions.

There may be a problem with authority figures. There may be a problem of needing nurturing, endlessly seeking it, always needing it. Conversely, there may be fears of one's own dependency needs, leading to Don Juanism, the fear of commitment to one relationship. Whether the witnessing children try to help or go the other way, they may feel that they can never make life right, never produce anything good, that they will always be doomed to failure in any undertaking.

None of these eventualities need be considered *fixed* or inevitable. But a person who really cares about such a child—or the child himself, if there's no one around who does care—should be aware of what may lie ahead and attempt to initiate various forms of help and self-help as early as possible. (See chapter 9, a handbook of guidelines.)

Sex and Relationships

We have seen that workers in this field will attempt to help little boys form a better male role than the one they have known. For the girls, however, the open distrust of men is sometimes seen as protective armor until they are old enough to validate other, better experiences. "Open distrust of men is perhaps not the most inadequate means to come to terms with one's experience. Growing girls are sometimes telling their mothers that *they* won't fall into the trap of marriage," notes Noor van Crevel. Unfortunately, the mothers "rarely react in such a way that the girl can make sense of it." Mothers counter with remarks like, "You'll change, wait till you're eighteen," or, "Poor girl, what a shame, at her age," or, "Shut up, what do you know about life?"—all very confusing messages. "Girls who are critical of their mother's attitude and speak their own minds are watched with a blend of (secret) admiration and (open) disapproval, and never unambiguously supported in their quest for independence. The whole subject is still weighed down by traditional notions about femininity, even among the victims of traditional maleness, or perhaps precisely among those."[9]

Among the many problems of growing up in the wifebeater's house are the unhealthy, untrue notions about sex and love foisted on innocent children. As awareness of sex grows, the violent home teaches that relating in a sexual manner is akin to rape. It is often an expression of power or anger, not of love, not tenderness or communication of healthy sensuality. Wifebeaters tend not to keep these matters private. The environment may lead a child to homosexuality or an inability to maintain permanent intimacy with either sex, an exploitiveness with either sex, or a deep dependence on anyone who seems both strong and caring.

Incest—and Cover-up

Incest, whether in the form of insinuation, or covered-up hints or overt acting out, is not unknown in these families. Erin Pizzey has found the problem among many children at her Chiswick Women's Aid in London. Carol Victor has found it among her clients coming for therapy at Growth & Life Center. Sgt. Carolen Bailey, of the St. Paul, Minneapolis, Police Department, says:

". . . We've found enough of it [incest] to be significant. But as in wifebeating, the entire family keeps silent about it. The mother may try to protect the child, but she's handicapped by her dependency. She takes the guilt on herself, but doesn't know what to do."

Yet when she learns there *is* something she can do —seek counseling, escape to a shelter—she will use it. That has been the experience of Ronald Reed, head of the Family Service Association in St. Paul, in dealing with the incest problem. "One who has been degraded all her life simply perpetuates the problem," says he. "But when the family knows there is help available, they are often willing to take advantage of it."

But when they don't know, or won't take advantage of it even when they do, what then? There was a woman at a shelter who finally left her wifebeating husband

131

when she found out by accident that he had also been sexually abusing his two preteen-agers from a former marriage, eight and twelve years old, and living with their mother. They had been too humiliated and terrified at first to tell. The father denied it, refusing to consider counseling or leave his house. The woman hadn't wanted to deprive her own kids of a "good home" and what had seemed to be a good father ("he never laid a hand on them in anger"). However, when she found out about the incest, she removed herself and them from the home.

Carol Victor found that in many cases, "the fathers physically abused the daughters, or one of the daughters in particular, as well as the mother. The abusing has often sexual overtones. If the father is a woman-hater, then he may abuse the daughters only, not the sons."

Do Wifebeaters Harm Their Babies?

Dr. Peter Scott, the psychiatrist who did a study on battered wives,[10] looked for a possible relationship between wife battering and baby battering, and wife killing and child killing. In small sample studies (125 men and 89 women in a prison population) of mothers and fathers who had battered their offspring, 25 percent of the men had also battered their wives. In another study of 50 men charged with killing their child, one-fourth were also wifebeaters; and one-fourth also battered other women in the family. In still another study, this one of 40 wife murderers in England's Brixton Prison, there were 5 cases of child battering.

Dr. Scott observes that "I would be unwise to draw firm conclusions from retrospective study of such a small sample in such a sensitive area, but at least it is clear that the two sorts of violence [to wife and to children] certainly overlap to some extent."

Toward Some Solutions

There are two problems, as I see it. One is the spillover of violence by husbands onto the witnessing children. Society has begun to take corrective steps in this area, with the mandated child-beating reporting laws. It is possible, however, that in many cases, the mother may be either too terrified to reveal the problem or else forcibly prevented from taking the battered child for medical care. And middle-class parents may fear the social stigma of such an act.

The other problem is one society must begin to counterbalance now: the emotional damage to the young witnesses of wifebeating. They will grow up with psychic scars, at least, making their lives unnecessarily burdensome. When no one believes them, or actually thwarts their efforts to bring some sanity to their family, the children are further burdened.

I propose one inexpensive solution, which any group considering itself a friend of children—I'm thinking especially of churches—could put into effect: establish a well-publicized hotline for children so that they can call, anonymously, a nurturing, trustworthy adult and unburden themselves. The mother might not be able to do anything to help herself, but a child can be helped, at least by listening and believing.

Whatever the church's beliefs on the duty of a battered woman to stay in her marriage, it cannot deny that helping the child is a priority. I would point out, however, that Margaret Ball of Detroit's Family Service, says: "If a wife chooses to remain in an abusing situation, it is her choice. However, she must face the fact that her children, seeing their mother accept abuse, are being prepared to become abused and/or abusing adults."

Toward a Responsible Parenthood

Researcher Richard Gelles suggests a reeducation toward more responsible conception and parenthood. "It is a known fact," writes Gelles, "that unwanted children are the most frequently abused children. . . . We have also seen that many wives are battered during their pregnancy because they are carrying unwanted or unplanned for children. Therefore, one of the initial steps in formulating a strategy of intervention in cases of violence toward pregnant women is to provide an avenue to prevent or ease the stress of an unwanted pregnancy. Effective planned parenthood programs, dissemination of birth control devices, and the removal of legal and social stigma of abortion are all steps in the direction of reducing the likelihood of stressed pregnancies ending in attacks on the pregnant wife by her husband."[11]

I heartily agree with Gelles's suggestions, though I fear that the very men who need to be touched by them are the ones who will refuse; and I am seriously concerned by the elements of society that will deny poor, uneducated women, or frightened, nonassertive women access to the knowledge they need. A very vocal minority believes that all conceptions (some include rape and incest) must result in a living child, regardless of how horrendous that existence will be, and regardless of how thoroughly unwanted the child is. It also believes that all sexual intercourse, even that expressly unwanted by the woman, ought to result in conception.

So far, the militant antiabortion lobbyists have done nothing to take responsibility for protecting the endangered *children* they demand be born, only the fetuses. I would like to see them help these children by using their effective organizational skills to raise money for shelters for battered wives and their victimized children, and to begin adopting the unwanted children who are abandoned.

In 1975, 770,000 women were turned down for legal abortions—mostly the young, poor, and rural, "and almost half a million of the women who did undergo them had to travel to another county or state to do so." (A battered wife could not make such a trip if her wifebeating husband chose to forbid it.) The reason for the nonavailability for these *legal* abortions (legal since the January 1973 United States Supreme Court decision for the *right* to abortion) is, as studies by Planned Parenthood show, that "most hospitals still prefer to avoid the operation. Their medical boards fear pressure from antiabortion groups, and many physicians in private practice find abortion a distasteful and boring surgical procedure."[12]

Yet legal abortion has staved off battering and saved lives. Says Planned Parenthood: "Because abortion is more readily available, fewer women at all social levels are dying from self-induced or other unskilled abortions. Before the Supreme Court decision there were 30 deaths for every 100,000 illegal operations. Today . . . abortion is safer than tonsillectomy or even childbirth. There are 3.1 deaths per 100,000 legal abortions compared with 14 for every 100,000 live births.

"In addition to reducing deaths, abortion saves taxpayers $550 million in welfare costs that, the Department of Health, Education, and Welfare estimates, would have gone to support unwanted babies to low-income women."

Although it costs Medicaid only $50 million as against the $550 million in welfare costs, "the persistence of the antiabortion lobbyists, a force whose influence has increased markedly," pressured Congress to approve banning Medicaid funds for most abortions. "One clear effect of the legislation will be to make it much more difficult for poor women to gain abortions."[13] More unwanted, mistreated children, more future sociopaths, more violent crime among younger and younger children, more welfare rolls, more battering . . . where is the sense in forcing their notions on the public?

7

My Own Story:
The Skeleton in the Parsonage

I would prefer to forget the terrors of my childhood
—my life is now far removed from them. But the terrorist was my violent father, a Christian minister. His
first target was my mother. And as I grew and tried to
be the peacemaker, he turned on me.

Conjugal Crime has shown that some wifebeating
husbands can be helped with therapy when their motivations to change are strong. But this wifebeater, my
father, would have never gone for counseling. After
all, as a clergyman, he *gave* counseling. He had no
intention of reforming. His brutality stopped only because the participant in this unhappy drama died.

Everyone has her or his individual way of surviving.
(You will see that my mother's and brother's ways
were quite different from mine.) Although I was physically helpless against him, I was determined not to let
my father touch my spirit. Why he refused to recognize
right from wrong, why he was so evil to my mother—
that was beyond my comprehension. I could see, however, that he didn't know how to love. I was a very
pragmatic and objective child and managed to escape
the gnawing worry many unloved children have that it
must be their fault. My survival depended on my steel-
ing myself against my father's influence, on keeping an
emotional distance from him and all he stood for, and
dedicating myself to seeking the good and healthy
things of life elsewhere.

A hypocritical environment prevailed in our household. In his job, my father played the role of the man
of God, and we dared not do anything to spoil that
image. Yet he also believed that he was right to torture
my mother, and that if I were a good daughter, I
would agree with him. I never saw any evidence of

136

compassion from him, or sorrow, or guilt, or a sense of responsibility for the horror he was inflicting on his family.

My father's particular brand of violence followed a pattern I have not encountered elsewhere in any research. Every so often he'd announce, "You're asking for it. . . . Don't tell me I didn't warn you. . . . You're going to get it." The war cry was directed at my mother; the children were also on notice. But what had the woman done? We didn't dare ask as the question would undoubtedly bring on a beating. There was no mystique to it. It was his nature, predictable, with no cause and effect.

Tension would build up over the hours, days, weeks, as he prepared to explode. Smugly he'd repeat his warning, but we were helpless to do any better than try our best. We were three hapless, cautious hostages.

He found his excuse mostly at dinner. The violence could be triggered by not passing the salt fast enough after he'd been deliberately unclear that's what he wanted. Or by guessing wrong what to do about our usual custom of saying grace before meals.

Usually he preferred to say the prayer himself, adding some warnings about behavior and respecting him to the thanks for the food. But sometimes he'd set off on a tirade at the beginning of dinner and start eating without grace. The three of us would then begin eating too. Sometimes, unfortunately, he could sense which of us was the most frazzled, the one closest to breaking down in forbidden tears, if forced to speak.

"You!" he'd thunder. "You say grace."

The inevitable choking and stumbling would become his trigger.

No one in the church or community reached out to him, no one ever gave any indication of suspecting or caring about his pathological behavior. Although I looked for them, there were no "rescuers"; traditionally, an integral part of Christian faith. My father, for instance, in his capacity as clergyman, and known to be a tough, strong man, was often called to the hospital to handle a patient who went berserk. And there was one congregant who periodically held his wife and children at bay with a knife. Their neighbors would call the police. The police would call my father, and *he* would go to the rescue, unarmed, successfully talking the man out of his violent state because he had no fear himself and was very good at that sort of thing. I grew up hearing his stories of how he had rescued others, so it seemed perfectly logical that someone would rescue *us*.

As to why this man chose the ministry as a career, today I can see that all his delusions of grandeur probably stemmed from an underlying lack of self-esteem that he repressed by indulging in a great sense of omnipotence. Running a church, making executive decisions, with people looking up to you and coming to you for counsel, presiding at the ceremonies of life and death—a job like this would provide a suitable power trip. I suspect that his success at getting away with his crimes inflated his sense of omnipotence and guiltlessness to the point where he may have become psychotic.

There, I've revealed a lot. Very personal facts. This detached analysis hasn't been too painful, but now the conflict begins. Reliving the details is the hard part, and when I get to the most painful memories my mind balks and goes blank. Originally I'd intended to present this as an in-depth anonymous case history of an intractable wifebeater and his effect on his world. Then I began to sense that my moral responsibility lay in being a straightforward witness to what I had experienced, making some good come at last out of my parents' tragic marriage.

I believe that revealing this shocking story of a well-respected professional man who also happened to be a confirmed wifebeater may be a powerful consciousness raiser. It may do more to move people to take legislative and compassionate action than any research or interview material I can present in this book. There's no better evidence of what can happen to both the wifebeater and the battered wife—as well as to their witnessing children—when conjugal crime is allowed to continue for a lifetime, unacknowledged and undeterred. There's no better evidence to show how a middle-class, gentle woman can be so trapped by her own values, and how good people can refuse to accept any responsibility for the living nightmare they see before them.

The roles in our household were clearly defined. My father thought of himself, it seemed to me, as almost-God. The children were to revere him, honor and respect him. ("I don't care about love," he'd sometimes say when I'd try to calm his violence, "I want respect.") We were to obey immediately, and never question anything he did. Any sign of fear or anxiety regarding him would be punished; instead, we were to behave as though we wanted and enjoyed his company. He was to be considered the beneficent captain of the ship, wise, sought after, charming, and very good to us.

We were to watch calmly, without reacting, without visibly flinching, whenever this self-righteous man punched my mother, pummeled her, kicked her, taunted and mocked her. We were not to intervene. He expected us to approve and learn from it. When he knocked her abjectly to the floor, kicking her body where it wouldn't show, he would proclaim, snarling, "You asked for it!" If he noticed her moans of pain, he'd only hurt her more, threatening, "You're trying to attract the neighbors: now you'll really get it."

At these times I was not allowed to leave the room, or hide, or even cover my face. If I cried out, he'd turn his fury on me. So I'd stuff my hand into my mouth and somehow stop time and feelings until he was finished. Then he'd rush out of the house, go off in his car, and not come back until the household was asleep. And I would run sobbing to my mother, "Please, let's leave him, I hate him, I'm going to *tell*." But who could I tell? Who was stronger than he was? I wasn't allowed to speak of it, anyway.

I think I'm fortunate that the scars of these experiences haven't crippled my adult self. Today I don't have a strong memory of past time in any way that is measurable. Rather, I find I remember events as happening a long or short while ago, lasting a long or short time in *emotional* experience, not by calendar date or clock time. Perhaps memories take an easier

139

perspective that way: the good things of life can come to the fore.

At that time, however, my father's special goal was to get me to show an obvious preference for him over her. I could not. This denoted "lack of respect" in his eyes, and so he began to consider me his enemy. Mine was not a good position to be in.

Mother's role was to act as his assistant in the business of running the church, as long as she didn't become favored over him among the parishioners. She was to go along with his rules for the children, including those regarding her own self-image. (And this was a woman with several graduate degrees!) Her way of coping was to try never to offend him, and to lose herself and her pain in her devotion to her religious calling.

She had inherited a comfortable sum from her mother, and then a larger sum from her father. The day we heard about the settling of my grandfather's estate, my father decreed: "I've supported this family long enough. Now it's *your* turn." He never again contributed to the household expenses or children's education.

He concentrated so much on his inexplicable vendetta against his wife—darting hateful glances at her, mimicking her, tricking her into daring to argue with him so he could beat her and claim he'd been provoked —I used to wonder when he had time or energy for his work. Yet he appeared to accept her as a full and useful partner in the church—which she certainly was.

At times he'd brood behind his unread newspaper, without answering anyone who spoke to him. That's because he was "Goddamning" his disrespectful family. My brother Buddy and I were astonished at how this minister took the Lord's name in vain, saying "God damn you" to us sometimes, and "God damn your soul" often to mother. So after a while, we used the initials as a nickname behind his back, "Old GD." That was our one daring little bit of defiance.

I ran scared most of the time, but a strong sense of outrage kept my fears from overwhelming me—and probably kept me sane. It was apparent to me that the responsibility for my life was entirely on my own shoulders. The only person I had to count on, ultimately, was myself, no matter how inadequate, and so I'd better get going. The present horrors would not be all my life was about. From the earliest years I had a cause, a crusade: to rescue mother and Buddy, and to try to make my own life as different from my conditioning as possible.

I had strong positive feelings toward my mother in those years. I pitied her, tried to rescue her, to be a big sister to her. I lived for the day I could get out safely. Mother knew this, and approved, thank God. But she warned me never to discuss our problems with outsiders. She said no one would believe me if I ever sought help or guidance or even shared my anxieties; and my father might kill me if he found out. I felt frustrated at her restraining me then. Now I think she may have been right. There were no havens for runaway teenage girls in those days.

She met my need to speak of rescue schemes, escape plans. I met her need to complain to someone. However, as soon as she'd aired the feelings of the moment, the problems were dissipated enough for her to deny that much violence had occurred. She would admonish me, gently, as if to soothe me, "There, there, it's all right. How can you talk about your father that way? He loves you." It was as though, once having got her feelings out and onto me, she didn't have to own them anymore.

When he'd plunge out of his chair to go over and hurt her, I'd hurry between them, begging, "Please, daddy, please don't. . . ." In the emergency of the moment, I'd forget that I'd only be hurt myself. I just couldn't remain the nonreacting observer my father required. My little brother, on the other hand, was very good at watching without comment. When I tried to draw him into my plans for escape or rescue, I met with little enthusiasm. It puzzled me then. Now I realize he might have been petrified. I didn't know then about the Freudian concept of "identifying with the aggressor" as a form of self-preservation. Or of little boys' unconscious fear of their fathers. It must have been excruciating and confusing for Buddy to see his sister trying to protect his mother while he did nothing. It took me a long time, I'm sorry to say now, to understand that my brother was also a victim, seeming heartless but actually suffering.

My belief, from childhood on, was that our confidence and morale would be strengthened if we were good friends, giving each other mutual support in life, and especially banding against the aggressor. Since this was not his belief, I'm afraid that difference added to his eventual alienation from me. And it may have made it easier for him to accept our father's later manipulative offer: If Buddy agreed to discontinue his relationship with me, and prefer father over mother, the boy could then become the sole inheritor.

Part of our father's pathology was his attempt to pit us against each other, while at the same time ruling that we act like friends in public. If we were chatting and laughing at dinner, for instance, he might silence us with a blow for "monopolizing the conversation." If we learned that lesson thoroughly, he might on another occasion berate us for not acting like loving, companionable brother and sister. When he wanted to spank one of us with his leather slipper, he would send the other child to fetch it. When I was the one who had to get the shoe for him I would hide it and call downstairs that I couldn't find it, hoping he'd leave Buddy alone. While I don't understand completely what forces made me the only one to react so strongly against what was going on, I know my gut feeling was that I would have died before I approved of the violence. And in many subtle ways, I did die.

As our life continued without any relief, I decided there had to be some mistake. My mother, my little brother, and I formed one family unit, in my concept of things, and that man—how did he get there? He wasn't even like the rest of his family—his brothers and sisters, mother and father, behaved like normal, peaceful people.

My wishful thinking led me to hope that my mother had amnesia and was with him only by accident; soon our rightful father would come and save us. Or that we were adopted (somehow this fantasy also included mother).

My mother's two brothers were exceptionally successful men. And I was awed at the fact that they were exceptionally devoted, loving husbands. Neither had children. They lived rather elegant lives in exquisite, small mansions on acres of grounds. Now *there's* where we come from, I'd think, and that's my background. "Why don't you tell your brothers, mother? They'll rescue us," I'd urge her. "No, I can't," she'd say. "I just can't let them know how my life turned out. They never did approve of my marrying your father." I wished I could get to know them better, but my father discouraged it.

Was it ever otherwise? Were we ever a normal, loving, nonviolent family? It seems, looking back, that we were always in the midst of the reign of terror. And yet in my earliest days I did not hate him. I did not fear him. He loved to show me off, the fragile toddler, with the perfect little manners, dressed at the best shops, taken along on his rounds to parishioners' homes and offices, banks and restaurants and factories and hotels, and to meetings where he was the speaker, and sometimes I'd have to be the little speaker after him. These "memories" are less my own than what I remember mother telling me. At the point where my own memory begins, I remember feeling exploited, a foil for his own loud showing off. Why was I so negative toward him? Were the beatings just beginning then? Did they start without the requirement that I watch? My mother said they began when she was pregnant with a baby who died.

Buddy was born when I was in the first years of grade school. When I visited my mother and my new baby brother in the hospital, my parents seemed glowingly happy. They both embraced me and each other —a rare occurrence—and my father actually seemed loving and tender toward my mother. Like a real father, a real husband. And the homecoming was a sweet memory too. I was allowed to hold the baby, and to help my mother take care of him. Later, Buddy took his very first steps into my arms—he wouldn't go to either of them. They told everyone how proud they were of me for having "taught" the baby how to walk.

143

Mother said I was "a good little mother." Seems like a happy, normal family, doesn't it? But were we?

How old was I when brutality to mother became an established way of life in our house? I guess it must have been when I was in the third or fourth grade. My recollection starts in the middle of the incident, after my father had threatened either me or my mother or both of us. I remember standing in the living room under the chandelier. I could tell he was about to harm us. I just couldn't, wouldn't take this any longer. Grabbing my mother's hand, I started rushing her up the curving staircase into the upstairs bathroom. Heart pounding, I turned the key. Safe!

But no. He came racing after, banging on the door. "Open that door, damn you. Open it, I said!" Urgently, mother whispered to me, "We've got to open the door, he wants us to open it." Was she crazy? Let him in to kill us, or God knows what? Do some permanent harm to us? Not I.

"I'll break down this door, damn you!" he shouted, shaking it. Yes, he could easily do that. I opened the window and calculated what a jump of one story would do. Would it mean a broken arm or leg? Then I'd really be his prisoner. Could I leap over the gravel driveway onto the softer grass? My mother would probably know these things, but she was totally out of it, as far as I was concerned. She could not take care of herself. She could not take care of me.

It ended, somehow. He did not break down the door. Instead, he rushed out of the house, into his car, and drove off, and didn't return until late that night when we were all asleep. The next day was just like any post-beating day, no one said anything, everyone tiptoed around trying to be invisible, giving no indication that anything had happened—or in this case, had not happened. I thought about it a long time . . . if I could only pull that off again . . . would it be possible to skip some of the actual violence? Possibly he might be satisfied just going through the previolence stages and then would slink away? But there was never a similar opportunity.

Life limped along as usual. Out of the house, at least,

144

there were friends and school. I wouldn't have dreamed of bringing anyone home with me, but I was thankful I was allowed to sleep over at girlfriends' houses. There, at last, I saw what I'd always suspected: that Old GD was the only monster in the civilized world: He didn't represent all men. Future boyfriends or husbands were not going to be like him. In my limited experience, most men, and even some clergymen, were all right. Other women did not seem to be afraid of their husbands.

But we were afraid of him. And he got worse: The violence escalated year by year. I wasn't keeping records but I'd say it increased to perhaps once every three or four days, with the worst times—the ones he called "You asked for it"—happening once every three or four weeks. Life was not worth living; not there. I was only in grade school but all my energies were concentrated on preparing to get out some day. I saved my Christmas checks and nickels and dimes from my allowance. In case he kicked me out, or I had to flee for my life, I wanted to have something to count on.

And then one day, I think at the beginning of my teens, I saw a rescue for us all. Old GD had become interested in a missionary-type job overseas. It was just right for him—a lot of glory, because it could be dangerous, and a lot of power, bossing around people who had to obey him. He started indoctrinating Buddy with the belief that it was all right to ignore anything mother said to him. Generally, I did not believe in longing for something that was impossible, but his behavior indicated that he really intended to leave us, and at the same time leave mother with an unexpected discipline problem on her hands.

Then he seemed to change his mind. There was no more talk of leaving. One afternoon, his violence to my mother was more brutal than I had ever remembered, some of it spilling over onto me. He sent me up to my room, threatening that if I didn't stop crying, he'd "really give me something to cry about."

Soon I heard him on the stairs. But he didn't come after me; he went straight into the library, next to my room. Silence. What was going on?

Then, "Come in here, young lady." Forgetting to take Kleenex, I obeyed. Instead of the usual thundering "Sit down!" *Pow! Crack!,* he began in a soft, self-pitying tone:

"Well, I guess no one in this family loves me."

Silence. I needed all my wits about me. The correct answer, of course, was "No, no, daddy, we love you." But in that moment, something gave me more courage than I'd ever had: The safety of my family and my own sanity hung on how I would respond.

"I'm sorry," I began, thoughtfully, respectfully, "but sometimes it's hard when we're so afraid of you."

"All right!" he shouted triumphantly. Triumphantly? It was the right answer? And he didn't hit me! "You did it! Remember, *you* sent me off into those jungles. If I don't come back, remember, *you* killed me. If I get sick or injured, remember, it was you who made me go. The responsibility lies on your head, young lady!"

It was too good to be true. He was really going to leave us. What a coward he was, dumping it all on me, but I'd take the responsibility gladly. Now all I had to do was hide my relief and elation for the next several months, while he carried out his plans. . . .

Although he never sent any money the entire time he was gone, those next few years were the best of my homelife. At first, to celebrate his absence, I'd dance through the exorcised rooms, singing my own psalms of thanksgiving and joy. Soon I was able to begin normal teenage dating. It was an untroubled time, and lots of fun. With the wifebeater out of the house my mother and I were able to share the same values. We were in agreement on most things, and talked them out. We both believed, as it happened, in the ideal of the virgin bride.

From across an entire ocean, however, my father's damning letters accused me of being a "bad girl." He had certain informants, he wrote, in fact he had friends all over the world, who were reporting on everything I did, so I'd better watch my step. I never could discover who my enemy was. Or why he/she/they were lying about me. It wasn't until years later that it occurred to me he could have made it all up.

146

When Old GD returned, I was safe in college far away from home. Around this time, my mother became bedridden with some mysterious malady she refused to tell me about. She had a nurse, but I couldn't get any information out of her either. I spent my allowance on long-distance phone calls to the family doctor and then to my best boyfriend. All I got were evasions.

Had Old GD gone too far? Was she dying? I was frantic and had no one to turn to.

Then I heard about a professor of psychology on campus. I wasn't sure what psychology was (we had led a very isolated, provincial life), but I looked her up. And she believed me. She understood everything I was saying. I explained my theories about my parents, about how my father "needed" to smash my mother and sometimes me, that there was no cause and effect, about my pity and anger over mother's helplessness. I told her my own plans for a better life for myself, removed from all that. She told me I had a very mature grasp of what was going on, of what made the participants tick, for someone as close to the situation as I was. She offered me an assistantship to work and study with her.

At Christmas recess, the nurse had left—my mother was up and around. I told my parents of the offer to change majors and have a psychology scholarship. My father would not hear of it. "In this family you finish what you start." If I wouldn't go back and do things his way (although it was on my mother's money), I could have two hundred dollars and get out. On my own. Or I could marry that local boyfriend.

Betrayed and abandoned, I knew I was in no position to "get out." I was not trained for any means of earning a living, and I had absolutely no desire to get married. I wished I could be somebody's child first, before I gave any thought to being somebody's wife. So I went back to school on my father's terms. At the end of the semester, he pulled me out of college anyhow.

Mother, who never dared protect me against his physical abuse, did rise to this occasion. She offered to send me, for a year, any place I wanted to go, in

147

order to learn to earn a living that could put me out of harm's way. I was grateful, but what could one do in a year? We settled on a business school. To me, it was like being doomed to a factory, but at least it was in a big city, away from Old GD. Perhaps I could use its potential to best advantage. I'd be on my own, living in a women's hotel. Now *that* was adult! Soon I'd be grown up and sophisticated.

My philosophy was to make the best of what I had, to make a life for myself with what I had to work with. My attitudes about myself were shaped by what little I knew of my mother's admirable family, her happy world before her marriage, and my determination not to lower my standards to anything approaching *his*. Good Christian principles and an elegant family heritage (my mother's family, that is) had to be invincible ultimately. Realistic or not, that's what kept me going.

I was a naïve, terrorized teenager, alternating between panic, despair, and blissful, supreme confidence that I was on the right path, that good things were now meant to happen just naturally.

Both moods proved valid. My life was not just a litany of cruelties. That *was* part of my life, true, and all my best efforts seemed to have no effect on changing it. But "victim" was not my only identity—and if someone strong would only believe me, and help me, I would soon shed that part of myself. What I wanted was goodness and fun in my life. That's what I reached out for and that's what I found. On any given day I could rejoice that I was out of his immediate grasp: Having twenty-four hours a day, day after day, with no violence threatening was an ever-present blessing. More than that, I could feel myself growing, growing up and growing outward, enjoying good people, good times, becoming a discoverer of the wonderful world around me.

In the midst of my determination and joy, however, Old GD pulled me out of school twice more, and cut off my income from my mother. All his letters to me included wild accusations of my being some sort of wicked woman, and when he finally banished me from his door forever, that's exactly what he insinuated to the church and the neighbors, to account for the fact that I wouldn't be visiting anymore.

Then, fortunately, I got to know my local minister and his wife, and I let them know me and my whole story. For the first time in my life—I wasn't yet twenty-one—I discovered loving, nurturing substitute parents. When my father cut off my allowance and my school funds, my minister let me do some paid secretarial work for him, however ineptly. He and his wife often invited me to dinner with them and their children. Just being in their home, in their presence, was the strength and warmth I'd always longed for, the tonic that kept me functioning and sane. Their supportive friendship became my life.

It was from this strong base of supportiveness that I was able to reach out to Buddy and try to keep him from the same fate Old GD had meant for me. Our father had begun to brainwash him with the notion that he would "never amount to anything." It looked as though Buddy might even give up the idea of college. I was afraid he'd never be truly independent of our father if he didn't first leave to go off to school.

I invited Buddy to spend a weekend with me, so we could talk. He could count on me to help him endure the few years left before college and escape, I told him. I urged him not to give up, to keep up his grades. I also showed him the town, enlisting my friends, pastor, and boyfriends to show him how good life could be out of our father's poisoned environment.

It was a poignant good-bye at the station. Buddy told me sadly, and with a look of surprise, "I like you, sis. I like your friends. You're not at all like daddy said."

Apparently our father was surprised, also, because soon after the visit I received the only nonhateful letter he ever wrote me:

Allow your poor father to personally congratulate you. You certainly did a remarkable job at entertaining your one and only brother. I hope that you two kids will always remain on the highest friendly relations. . . .

Buddy is a fine boy and is progressing rapidly. We work together wonderfully well. I think he likes me a little bit. I have been able to develop his personality magnificently, and as for culture, he is getting that, too. That is one of the reasons why I let him go to see you. Second is, because I do want you two to really know each other. . . .

You know, for the first time I think that I was jealous or envied Buddy. I don't have to necessarily envy or be jealous of most people. When he received that invitation to spend a weekend with you and see that Army and Navy game, I just felt that the whole world is unfair. After all, you perhaps don't know that your father was, once upon a time, quite a football player himself and hasn't seen a major game in ten years. Don't forget that if you are struck by an inspiration or have a little inclination to come home and say hello to your parents, that the door latch is always open.

He chose to ignore the fact that beyond the door latch, violence was waiting every time.

I was now working in New York. I saw Buddy from time to time during his college years. He was changing. He was no longer the cowed kid, coping with the violence by ignoring it. He was a young man who was going places. Wonderful! Another tribute to the resilience of the human spirit once free of a bad environment. And, of course, Buddy's size had long since prevented our father from beating him.

At commencement time, Buddy urged me to be very careful if I came to the ceremonies, because Old GD would also be present. "This is not a normal situation," he pointed out to me with great clarity. "I feel you recognize the situation for what it is and that there is some sort of understanding between us." He was worried that our father would retaliate against him in some way if I seemed too independent of his own dictates regarding the relationship between my brother, my mother, and myself. "Please don't make waves," Buddy said. "Just don't be overly solicitous of mother or overly affectionate to me. You should be polite to Old GD but reserved."

Acknowledging the reality of our lives and not taking

the easy way out by begging me to go along with Old GD's preference that I be absent from the celebration —these were acts of courage on my brother's part, and I appreciated the effort. I was touched. Well, soon he'd be free of Old GD, free to be friends, maybe even free to help end the violence. I looked forward to the time when the situation would be more normal.

Actually, I had been officially banished from the family home for several years by the time Buddy graduated from college. Old GD wanted me completely out of his sight. This is how the banishment came about: My mother believed a clergyman's wife should have no special friends, but be a friend to all humankind. Then a new church member, an attractive, vivacious woman I'll call Viv, began stopping at the parsonage regularly in the mornings, just to see my mother. I had come to know Viv and her husband on one of my visits and enjoyed their company. Urbane, sophisticated and fun-loving, they seemed to be on a perpetual honeymoon.

How grateful I was that at last my poor mother had a friend. And such a friend! Viv was the first not to be intimidated by my father. (He invariably broke in on the women's visiting—he did not want my mother alone with this particular person.) Viv even talked back to him and put him in his place, as if he were merely a rude, obstreperous human being instead of a feared almost-God. She teased him about his pretentiousness and dictatorial pronouncements to his face. I never saw anything like it!

One Thanksgiving, when I was there "on command" (the church might get suspicious if family unity did not seem intact), I stopped off to visit Viv and her husband before braving the parsonage. They began what I took to be a very revealing conversation:

"Your mother has a very hard life. . . ." True. "Living with your father isn't easy. . . ." "He's not the angel people think. . . ." "He can be very hard on her, really cruel. . . ." At last someone saw through him!

I was so glad mother had them for friends. Since they knew all about the family skeleton, they were in a position to help. I asked if they would speak to my father about his wifebeating. They were the only people who'd ever noticed or cared, and they would certainly have an influence on him. . . .

Back in New York, I received a mystified letter from mother, urging me not to confide in Viv anymore. Whatever Viv meant by her statements about my father, I'll never know—it seems that my mother had not told her about the physical assaults or how he terrorized us all. Viv ceased being mother's friend. Instead of the long-dreamed-of rescue of my mother, the one who was going to get rescued was my father! Rescued from his sick, lying, reputation-ruining daughter!

From then on I was considered to be virtually dead, or too wicked to mention. I was forbidden to come home ever again, or to store anything there. I wasn't to write letters, and mother was forbidden to visit me openly. My name could not be spoken (mother wrote in a letter she smuggled out).

Viv became a very special friend of father, to the point where the parishioners speculated, as the years went on, about the nature of the relationship. Buddy and I were curious too, but decided that compared to Viv's suave husband, Old GD was nothing, and the relationship couldn't be what it appeared to be. Otherwise, they wouldn't flaunt it so. . . .

Despite all my misgivings about marriage, I had met a man I felt I could trust in that delicate relationship. He was strong and tender, understanding of my deepest needs. With Old GD's banishment in effect, I never worried about leaving him out of our wedding plans. But I looked forward to mother's coming to visit us (under some pretense). I had always wondered if a loving marriage—enjoying both giving and receiving love—could be possible, given my unpromising background. But it was. My marriage became a wondrous revelation to me. And I wanted to share my very special happiness with her.

However, she wanted no part of the idea of visiting, because "it wouldn't be right" to exclude my father. And so, when my husband became fatally ill, I didn't turn to her for the parental comfort she could not give.

I didn't even tell her that he died until many years later. They'd never met.

After Buddy's graduation, I saw surprisingly little of him. At first we wrote to each other, but after a while he answered less and less often. I visited him once. Our conversations seemed to be clouded over by something—a loss of former understanding or closeness or friendship. This was a huge loss to me: I felt as though my state of orphanhood was now irrevocable. Here my mother didn't seem like a mother, my father wasn't a normal father . . . it was painful to see the dimming of the last hopes of salvaging a warm supportive family relationship.

Buddy flatly stated that he didn't want to hear anything about the parental situation and would not, could not, do anything about it. Today I realize I was putting too much of a burden on him, assuming he shared my standards. Buddy was coping with our problem in his way, as I was in mine. I thought of him as "unfeeling" then. Now I see he was self-protective, even realistic. His childhood conditioning had certainly not given him much strength to counteract a force like his all-powerful father.

In order to visit me, mother would say she was visiting the East Coast, perhaps attending a college reunion, and then she would secretly include New York in her itinerary. She stayed in a hotel, so she could truthfully claim she was not visiting *me*. She seemed to be aging fast, her anxiety-ridden life showing in all her gestures and attitudes. As her visits became infrequent, I pitied her captivity, yet the distance was less painful than the close contact had been. On one of her visits she wrote out a statement for me to keep in my safe deposit box in case my father ever went too far in his harassment of, or violence toward, either of us:

My married life has been marred by physical abuse from my husband. This has always horrified my daughter. As a little girl, she was always shielding me from my husband, but he would not only knock her down, but become violent to me as well. ...

The statement went on to detail some of the "humiliation and pain" Viv and my father were both causing her, events she'd never related before. She concluded with:

> The reason I did not leave my husband was that I realized that if the truth were known, it would mean the end of his ministry.

As partial protection from Old GD, I had an unlisted phone, and used a post office box for family mail. It had taken a lot of effort to get where I was professionally and I didn't want to risk his craziness damaging my career. But magazine editors (that's what I was) have their names on mastheads. So be it. I conquered my fear of his discovery by telling myself it represented a little gesture of proof that I felt no need to hide from him.

One day he wrote to the office, threatening to show up there "in my clerical collar to tell them what you're really like." This increasingly deranged man frightened me more than I cared to admit. And oh, how I longed to put an end to fear. I looked back at my life and thought, How could that little girl who was once me have been so brave? And why can't I have more courage now, and the wit to know how to deal with him?

There were answers, of course. But they were very discouraging. When I was little, the supreme merit of my crusade and my faith in my future kept me going. After all, soon I'd be grown up, and be out, and then everything would be all right.

But physically escaping this violent, vindictive troublemaker turned out not to be much of an escape at all. Absence did not reduce his vendetta. It only took new forms that permeated the basics of my life. (This was not his first attempt to interfere with a job, with housing, peace of mind, and he kept up a barrage of threatening, accusatory letters.)

My reserves of courage and coping were just about depleted. I was in therapy to try to regain my strength and direction. The dream of mutual supportiveness with Buddy was not going to materialize: He'd come to New York to live and work without letting me know, in accordance with his father's wishes.

It was lonely and frustrating having a secret like our family skeleton. It was too foreign a concept for most people's understanding, even in a watered-down version. It sounded like heresy—like not having a place to go at Christmas. A listener became uncomfortable, threatened, incredulous, bewildered. Families like mine surely could not possibly exist, especially not in the past of someone who did so well and enjoyed life as much as I did. Someone so friendly and outgoing couldn't possibly have anyone hate her . . . and a father? Why, a father would be so proud. Ministers don't beat their wives; the church wouldn't let them. Talking about the problem was only counterproductive. Now how was I going to explain Old GD if he showed up at work?

My therapist thought I might use this is an opportunity to free myself of his vendetta. If I could summon the courage to meet him, confront him—but out of the office, in a safe public place—and let him see I was an adult, a self-sufficient career woman, someone too big to be trifled with, then we might have a whole new ball game. And if I could keep the agenda to the one thing I had uppermost in my mind—that is, an end of his violence to my mother—and not let my own bitterness over his treatment of me get in the way, I might free myself of him forever.

My friend Flo offered her apartment/office for the confrontation, and suggested bringing along a big, strong friend to act as bodyguard. There I'd have the safety of witnesses, a ready hand on the telephone to summon police if necessary, and the privacy and comfort of her living room to have it all out in a thorough, calm, final way. "If you don't settle this now," she urged me, "and tell him how you feel, he may die before you get the courage to speak up. You'll regret for the rest of your life that you blew your chance to express yourself. You don't have to be afraid here. Show him you won't consent to oppression."

Okay, I'd try. This time I *had* to prove that I was

not only his peer but a stranger now, who simply did not lend herself to his sociopathic designs, but who would be thoroughly civil, listen to his grievances, and be fair.

He walked into the room and tried at once to maneuver me into a vulnerable position. "Sit *down,* young lady," he thundered. I, the gracious hostess, said, smiling, "Won't you sit there, father? It's a very comfortable chair."

It was surprising to both of us, I think, when he complied. (I'd arranged the furniture so we were on opposite sides of the room, his chair being the soft, low kind, awkward to get out of fast.) My bodyguard sat between us, near his right.

"You're living a very glamorous life," he began. "You've been to all those foreign countries. Now you're working with all those Hollywood people. I've never had a chance to know people like that. You've never offered to share your life with me."

"But father," I chided gently, smiling sympathetically, "I don't *know* them. I just write about them. It's just business."

"You're always on your mother's side," he went on without really hearing me. He was getting closer to his intended mission, I was sure. "I want you to reject your mother and let me into your life."

I remembered to hold on to the arms of my chair so my hands would not give away my anxiety. Then I began in my most adult manner: "Before I can think about letting you into my life, as you call it, we must discuss the way you treat my mother. Until you stop beating up my mother, we have nothing further to say to each other."

His eyes narrowed, his lips curled—the savage look I'd reacted to, outraged but helpless, all my life. Except this time, for the first time, I was in a built-in rescue situation. He moved forward in his chair, fists balling up, but he did nothing further. He paused. He stopped.

Wow! Just as my therapist had said. If I could be calm and grown-up, he would perceive me as someone not to be assaulted.

"What did I ever do to your mother? She made my life miserable all her goddamned life."

156

"You punched her and you kicked her. You still do."

"Show me some bruises. You can't pin that on me. Listen, I'll leave you all my money. I'll forget about Buddy. You can have it all."

"I really don't think it's fair to leave mother without a means of living, when she's old and can't support herself. You and I have nothing to discuss until you stop beating up my mother. Don't you ever pray that Jesus will help you stop your violence?"

There was elation in the unaccustomed feeling of not being afraid. Although I was on dangerous grounds, this might be my last chance to reach him.

"I . . . never . . . pray," he snarled in that exaggerated manner that used to subdue me instantly. "It's none of your business *what* I do. I'll beat her up whenever I want to."

Undistracted, he continued: "I want you to reject your mother and let me into your life. If you don't, I'll disinherit you; I always told you that. I'll leave it all to Buddy. He'll do what I say. He's a good boy, not like you. What's the matter with you, anyhow? What did I ever do to *you?*"

My years of struggle engulfed me suddenly, and I forgot my cool. "Father," I began, desperately serious to make him understand the reality of his experience, "you have made my life very difficult—" And my voice broke.

"Why, you little—" He lunged out of his chair.

My bodyguard moved toward him, and I retreated in paralyzed fear. I was the terrorized child again, the victim, as I always would be, forever and ever, impossible to cure. I shrank into the chair cringing, no longer a *person*. Defeated forever, I'd rather be dead. . . .

Hardly an instant had passed when I began to undergo an ineffable, changing experience, unlike anything I've ever known. A strength from beyond myself —not my familiar attempt at bravado—became a solid, dynamic thought which transformed my being, casting out fear: Enough! If he attacks me, this time I will fight back with all my strength, even if I die trying. And with this new credo, there was no doubt that the victimization was over. I felt light and free, calm and strong. Tall. It showed, that metamorphosis, I know it did, for the violent man came no nearer. My bodyguard resumed his seat. It takes longer to tell than it did to happen, but I would treasure the miraculous moment for years to come.

As if nothing had happened, he repeated his demand and bargain so many times it began to get boring. Imagine! I thought what an unaccustomed luxury it was to be bored instead of on guard.

Somehow the interview came to an end. I had been able to be more gracious and polite to him than ever in our relationship. It was the first time I'd been unafraid, and the first time he'd been in "my" house. The three of us were standing near the door, he ready to leave, when he suddenly turned to my bodyguard:

"My daughter's got guts," he said proudly. "She takes after me."

(That was unexpected. And I have to admit I was thrilled. I could have kissed him. For a moment, it was like having a real father. But I knew better and said nothing.)

His hand on the doorknob, he turned back for a parting shot. "Don't think you can escape me, young lady. I'll see you whenever I want. You'll never get away from me." And then he was gone. It was the last time I saw him.

Mother came to New York once more as his emissary. "Was that man with you a policeman?" she asked. "Your father thought he was. But he told me not to tell you."

I was astonished that he would have reported our confrontation to her. Whatever his version, his purpose was to send her to relay a message from me to him.

"Mother, I have no message for him," I said, running out of patience. "What can I possibly say that hasn't been said? We went over it all. He told me to reject you. I refused. I told him to stop beating you. He refused. Tell him you know he wants to cut you out of his will, and me too."

"Oh dear, you shouldn't be so disrespectful to your father." Winning smile, feminine, coy, ingratiating—who was this woman? "He wants a message from you. Let me tell him you send your love."

I was exhausted with this schizoid double-bind. Finally I knew beyond all wishful thinking that she couldn't change, just as poor Buddy couldn't. The wifebeater had conquered this human being, as he had tried to conquer his son and daughter. He had her just where he wanted her, vanquished in mind as well as body. She had to deal with her tragedy somehow. She chose denial, and I guess it worked for her. But as for me, now I would give no more of myself to their tragic nonsense.

Several years later nothing had changed, and the wifebeater and his wife were both dead. My mother never got a chance to live in peace.

What wasted lives.

Epilogue

Undeniably, it was a relief that there would be no more direct harassment. It was one form of happy ending. Yet I went through a strangely rough period after their deaths, for the parental attitude had prevailed through the last will and testament. Old GD knew he could crush anyone who dared disapprove of his need for wifebeating. Even in death, he made sure I would never forget it. High principles or hard-won courage did not count. None of my efforts had counted—and now I was crushed with the feeling that nothing would ever go right. The hopelessness left its mark on daily life, and my usual optimism could not be revived.

I had not realized how much I'd always assumed my father would become aware in his last days and repent, and there would be a different kind of happy ending for all of us. Now it was too late. Our family would never know a fearless, loving closeness. My fantasy of Buddy's wanting to be friends now that he was free of his bargain never became a reality.

I would have to come through that depression somehow if I were to get on with a worthwhile life. What helped the most, I think, were the following: Short-term counseling; leaning on good friends and appreciating their love; trying to reinterest myself in familiar work and consuming new interests—which little by little provided the needed sense of hope, the experiencing of small successes; and above all, regular meditation. I discovered meditation after months of trying to pull myself up by my own efforts—and it did, it does, make a difference. Life becomes a little easier, health improves, gnawing worries fade, a new outlook on life emerges. If I had known about meditation during my years of stress, coping would have been simpler. I could also say the same of regular Yoga exercises.

Eventually, I was able to get past bitterness and think in terms of forgiveness. For the three of them. And myself. Amazing, but I even came to accept the fact that Buddy's life choices were ones that had met his particular needs, had worked for him. So be it. I gave up wishing to re-create something that did not exist.

My outrage that the community did nothing took on an additional perspective when I discovered through my research that, until recently, doing nothing was the norm. But that is no longer the case.

There were no means then to bring exposure and relief to a situation like the one you've just read about. It could not change. The participants could not change themselves without expert help. In a world that preferred to pretend wifebeating did not exist, the victims were stuck; they had no choice.

I could not change them, could not help them. I could only change myself. And that, once more, became my intention—to move forward from the incapacitating past into the here and now and the good future. I had wasted too much of my life being drawn into the family madness. From now on I would choose to be free of it.

A few years ago, from that strong base of my freedom, it occurred to me that I had a contribution to make that would help today's victims of conjugal crime. Those harrowing early years were not necessarily wasted. Speaking out on the unspeakable is the first step toward public awareness. New laws are now ready to be passed; new shelters and hotline programs are ready to open. Once there is awareness, many good people in many communities will be ready to listen, understand at last, and help. There need never again be another family like the one in the parsonage.

A Personal Investigation:
One Week in the Life
of a Shelter for Battered Wives

One snowy Sunday morning a woman in middle America was fleeing the latest beating in five years of repeated violence. This time she was afraid it would be fatal. So the instant she could break free, tearing hair and wrist ligaments in escaping, she ran barefoot to seek help from a neighbor.

Fifteen worshipers on their way to church observed her urgency without any sign of awareness. A man shoveling snow continued shoveling snow. When she reached the haven of the neighbor's front porch, the lady of the house could not seem to open the door. The shivering, barefoot petitioner, pleading through the adjacent window, "Call the police, call the police," put her hand through the glass in her panic.

The neighbor looked at the spurting artery before her eyes. At last she called the police.[1]

The majority of people whose lives touch that of the battered woman do not want to become involved. And those people, from whom involvement is expected or asked, tend to do so little to help the woman that the effect is not merely ineffectual, but frequently harmful.

When the ugly fact of wifebeating first dawns in most people's consciousness, their psychological reaction is usually the defense of denial. There is often no room for empathy. However, later they may remember that someone knew they had that problem. Often the "someone" is a family member. But time and preference have pushed the incidents out of ready recall. These are some typical replies from well-meaning, law-abiding men, upon first hearing about the existence of shelters and the need for more:

"Oh, it can't be that bad."

"I can't sympathize with a grown woman in that situation. She's not a helpless child. Why should she be coddled? If she doesn't like her marriage, she could get a divorce."

"Why should there be these shelters, so a dissatisfied housewife can take *a cheap vacation from marriage?*"

The first and most famous shelters and hotline were started by women who were not battered wives. Rather than lapsing into dissociation, the instinct of these women was to try to do something constructive about it.

I visited a typical shelter for battered women and their children, and I was astounded by what I learned during my stay there. The concept of establishing a shelter "just evolved"; it did not begin with a plan or a long-held dream. This shelter was started by several women who met in a feminist consciousness-raising group in the early 1970s and noticed that emergency housing for women was badly needed.

Since there were no community resources, they began, individually, to take women with no place to go into their own homes and one-room apartments. Those who had the space took in their children as well. A large proportion of the women who came to them, it turned out, were fleeing from marital violence.

It soon became apparent that the need was far greater than could be filled in this informal, well-meaning way. In 1972 they formed a corporation. They dedicated themselves to advocating solutions to women's legal problems and established a telephone information and referral service. They sheltered 135 women and children in their own spare bedrooms and living room floors. They also began cooperation with other community agencies—a step that became essential when a house was finally found and staffed.

They discovered a big Victorian house for $34,000. The neighborhood was in transition. Within a few blocks there were private homes dating from the 1800s with lawns and gardens and backyards, rooming houses, apartment houses, small businesses, gas stations, supermarkets, lunch counters, and better restaurants.

In 1976 a prestigious magazine assigned me to do an article on wifebeating, written from the vantage point of a shelter. It would be a story about a house and especially the community spirit that made it possible. It would involve interviewing the local judges, attorneys, and police; social agencies, therapists; looking into funding and attitudes of neighbors of the house.

The assignment would include interviewing the residents, of course, and reporting on the ambiance of the house. I would try to get to know a child there and try to find a wifebeater willing to be interviewed. I would try to get the advocates to agree to my spending a night sleeping there, in order to get a sense of the action.

From New York I phoned one of the two names listed as contacts for the house, and developed a good rapport with S. (none of the names or initials used in this chapter are real), a very knowledgeable, interested person and one of the "founding mothers." She had sheltered many battered women and children in her own small apartment. She had been a college teacher of literature and history and a VISTA worker before this work drew her total involvement. I asked her to recommend a hotel nearby, and was about to request one night under their roof.

No, if I was to come out, S. explained, it was house policy that any journalist stay with the residents the entire time to experience their lives firsthand.

That was a condition I had not anticipated. The wifebeater's daughter in me did not want to do that. Not at all. The journalist in me countered with: what a superb opportunity.

I did not turn it down.

As a journalist I learned to keep my personal bias out of the stories I covered. So being professionally detached was very natural to me.

Nevertheless, the trip was bound to be a significant psychological upheaval for me. My face-to-face interviews for this book, on which I had already begun work, had not included sharing meals, sleeping space,

163

bathrooms, and "hanging around" with battered women and their children.

Now that I would be making that house my temporary home, would I not painfully have to see my mother in all those residents, and myself in those children?

I was very eager to meet the women who ran the house. Although they had no training as social workers, psychologists, or counselors, they had to perform the functions of all these professionals. They had to know all possible resources for local aid: legal problems of separation and divorce, the ins and outs of applying for welfare, job training programs, back-to-school programs, self-defense, and spiritual help. Each had to be a veritable encyclopedia of ways a battered woman might better her life. These women had an unquenchable belief in nondirectiveness: Their mission was to help the woman describe what *she* wanted to do with her life. They would help her gain control of her life. They would support, assist, and champion her freely made choices. They would not interfere with her decisions or impose their own values on her.

I knew these dedicated women to be exceptionally self-reliant and fearless, competent and concerned. But how did they deal with the inevitable emotional drain and with fears about wifebeaters who were known to retaliate and who might know where to find them? S. had said that she got a lot out of the work and had not thought to be afraid. No, she had not minded the lack of privacy when taking strangers into her small apartment.

I looked forward to meeting these admirable women, so different from myself. Now S. was not going to be there, since she was about to start off on vacation, but she would leave a list of the names and phones of the city officials I wanted to interview, and notify them I was coming. Further, she'd leave word for the other women about what I intended to accomplish.

The living conditions would not be very comfortable, so she had said. She offered to lend me her air mattress, to be set up on the floor outside the downstairs office. I could work in the attic. There was an office up there which locked, and had a noisy air conditioner ("you can't hear the phone with it on"), an old, semifunctioning typewriter, and a broken sofa ("so you can lie down and get away from all the confusion"). At times there might be over twenty women and children milling around in a house built for twelve.

This would be quite an experience, quite a Rorschach for me.

As I got off the plane, B., a first-year law student, came dashing up, friendly and welcoming. She explained, however, that my welcome at the house might be a little cool. It seemed that my confirming letter, mailed after the arrangements were made with S., had been tacked up on the office bulletin board. But it hadn't been read to the general staff until the day before my arrival. The women ran the house on collective principles, and all decisions were arrived at jointly. No one member, even a "founding mother" such as S., was empowered to give an approval for a journalist to come and live in. Many of the women felt they had not been properly consulted.

And, B. added, "We're shorthanded now, you know. . . . We have one large family of very disruptive kids. The new child consultant we just hired needs some time to deal with the problems the children are going through. But you're here now," she concluded brightly, "so don't worry about it. This house doesn't turn away a woman on the doorstep."

As we got out of B.'s car I looked up at the bulky Victorian house. Looming portentously, sagging a bit, the paint peeling, it looked like a Charles Addams cartoon house to me. A young black woman of Amazon proportions, in short shorts with a pale, pretty face, glided gracefully down the walk—my first resident. B. introduced me to Watusa and some of her kids. She had come from several states away and was expecting to move on soon.

The thought flashed through my mind, Well, that's not my mother. In the days ahead, I would struggle to keep my own personal identification out of my consciousness, and I succeeded much of the time.

B. and I trudged up the crooked concrete steps built into the unmowed grassy embankment, up the worn, wooden porch steps and into the cavernous house. It was dark inside for three in the afternoon. The shutters were always kept closed, for privacy and protection. Except for trips to social service offices, the women seldom ventured outside. Many of them were afraid to be spotted and did not dare let their children go out. Kidnappings by wifebeaters had occurred before.

The living rooms were dominated by six torn, faded, drooping sofas, placed wherever they'd fit and used for emergency sleeping. There was a lot of dark woodwork and pillars and fussy millwork, typical of the period. The downstairs bathroom opened right onto a living room, a few feet from a sofa. The toilet faced the door. It had no lock because of the little children. There was no shower, only a claw-footed old tub. The roller towel in the machine was used up. (It remained unchanged for several days because the staff believed in creating an environment where the residents would learn to help themselves, get used to not being ordered around or dominated or told what to do. They hoped the residents would consider the house *their* home during their stay, and would never give them directives. For most of these women, simply reporting the need for fresh toweling constituted an assertiveness they were not accustomed to.) There was no privacy available. Tears, anger, poor judgment in childrearing, all would have to be on view of everyone.

I felt overwhelmed with the depressiveness of it all. Yet this was the refuge, the safe haven. No one trying to escape from a man intent on maiming and killing could respond as I did, there only on business.

The place wasn't too bad, really. It was pleasantly cool and remarkably clean for all the children, teens, toddlers, babies, and mothers. There was never a cockroach. Except for the cigarette smoke constantly in the air, it even smelled clean.

The staff member on duty was a pleasant young woman who explained a little about the day-to-day operations. "If you have any questions, ask me," she offered. "Some of the others are not too happy about the press coming here at this time. Sorry I have to leave in a few minutes. But M. will be here overnight." How did M. feel? "Well, a little bitter that the press is exploiting us. When she heard you were coming, she said, 'The press is not my priority.' "

As if on cue, in came M., a maternal-looking woman with short iron-gray hair and an unsmiling, rotund face. She did not deny what she'd said. She expanded on it.

"Two networks came here from the East, spending days and days, disrupting the house, floodlighting everything we do, interviewing the residents. We gave them everything we could, and they never even sent any film clips we could use for fund raising.

"The media is all after a hot topic, exploiting us, and what have we gotten out of it? I don't see any more shelters being built. We still have to scrounge for every bit of funding and clothing and furniture. Is all this media interest going to help battered women? Do they really care about the problem? Or will it just be another fast sensation and then over with, with nothing accomplished? The media comes here and moves on and the battered wives still need help."

I had to admire her spirit. As a former magazine editor, I knew what she was saying was frequently true. On the other hand, without media publicity, how could the word spread?

"Don't you expect us to rearrange our schedule for you," she continued, still wound up. "You can stay if you try to fit in and observe and don't get in our way or make more work for us."

I had my choice of sleeping in the attic office or down there on the floor next to M.'s couch, a few feet away from where residents usually sat up, talking. The attic seemed the logical choice.

Then two gangling, streetwise older boys appeared, sidling near and drawling, "You the lady that's gonna sleep in the attic all alone?" They didn't make me feel awfully comfortable, I must admit.

I made a few preliminary phone calls from the long list of potential people to interview in the city. But everyone I called was on vacation or out of the office. No one was expecting to hear from me; no one had left a message for me; no one could suggest an alternative. In other out-of-town stories I'd covered before, the subjects were pleased at the idea of getting into print, recognized it as useful to their cause or growth, and responded cooperatively with information and a hospitable attitude. Now the lack of welcome got to me, as I worried about what would happen to my assignment for the magazine.

On the other hand, I could empathize with M.'s frustration. All right, I would keep out of their way and do my work . . . and somehow I'd absorb the house side by osmosis—later.

By suppertime all the residents were home. Babies and kids were everywhere, and over all the older boys, running, shoving, marching up and down, making their presence known. It was hard to tell which children belonged to which parents, as there was little evidence of relatedness or interaction. Little by little I distinguished individual children from the busy kaleidoscope of humanity.

There was one forlorn girl who approached any adult with a soft stroking on the bare arm, saying, "I love you." Then when the strokee was off guard, she'd suddenly lower her face, lunge, and bite—hard.

There was an undersized two-year-old boy who did something similar, except that he had no first phase. The only greeting I ever saw him make toward anyone, adult or infant, was a quick unpryable grab at hair or an attack of fingernails, clawing at face or arm. His cast-off navy blue short pants drooped from his small hips. His wizened, diminutive face seemed hardened into a permanent scowl, befitting his only word. *"No!"* No was whined indignantly whenever he was pried loose, or caught while trying to demolish someone's belongings, or when a child finally hit him back, or when he then ran to his mother, sobbing yet simultaneously rejecting her momentary attention and comfort. I never saw this little boy's face in repose. The only time I ever saw him smile was after he'd gotten a furious, pained response to one of his attacks. If a baby smile could be described as sadistic, his was.

There was an angelic-looking blond, creeping baby, with a deformed arm who played contentedly with a pull-toy. There was a sturdy black toddler, clad only in

Pampers, who padded about serenely, half crawling, half walking, smiling and trying out a word or two, oblivious to the clutter and cacophony enveloping us. The adults, too, advocates and residents alike, took it all in stride, paying little attention, involved in their own thoughts or conversations.

The staff did their work, with the door to the minuscule office left open: answering hotline calls; keeping the house log of every phone call, every visit, every crisis; counseling the women who came to have a look, wondering if they dared escape their own home situation; phoning various agencies for help for their own assigned resident-charges; answering emergency panic calls from former residents whose troubles were pursuing them.

Residents could feel free to come into the open office to talk; children, too. When the two little grabbers, whose names I discovered were Lawana and Bobby, came in to get some attention, two staff members were patient in disentangling themselves and gently removing them to the other room. There was a firm rule of no violence in the house. No mother could discipline her child physically (that rule was strictly observed). No children were to be violent to each other (that was less often caught). Most shelters have a firm injunction: Anyone who is violent must leave.

Out in the main living room, a woman sat clutching her pocketbook, looking weary and dazed, speaking to no one. One little black boy, about ten perhaps, was rocking a baby in a beautifully nurturing way, smiling and talking to him. I was to see very little nurturing of the babies by the residents in the house. Billy was an exception.

The other women in the room were all smoking, some staring absently, some deep in animated conversation. I'd get to know them all as separate persons in the coming days, but now they were only a part of the wall-to-wall confusion.

The whole scene seemed very foreign to me as I sat on the big, old telephone desk, up and out of the way, waiting for a call, absorbed by the chaos, yet viewing it from a great impenetrable distance. I'd done interviews from foreign locales, from Tokyo schools, from

Kahlil Gibran's primitive home in the mountains of Lebanon, from an Istanbul Turkish bath, from untraveled parts of Mexico . . . and somehow those environments seemed less foreign than what was before me now. This was a world I did not know; it did not seem real. A woman walked by my perch, shook her head, and said, "It's a regular zoo, isn't it?"

What *was* real was the problem of going to the bathroom. There were very few toys and very little to do, so the bathroom became a playground for some children. The minute an adult went in and closed the unlockable door, the kids began knocking on it. I was not about to attempt to take a bath in a tub used by twenty-five women and children and tough teen-agers, all of whom seemed to need the bathroom whenever I was in it. (How do they stand it? I thought, and felt immediately ashamed because I could leave for a hotel at any time. *They* don't dare leave the front door. I'd soon be leaving permanently, to a life where I felt at home, felt fulfilled, felt joy. When they left, they faced an unknown future.)

What was real also was that I had dozens of interviews to cover, and I wanted to get out of there as soon as possible. I would stay until I'd experienced a Saturday night, the night when violence is traditionally at its height. . . .

That first night, however, I wanted very much to get some sleep. I waited for the teen-agers to be safely in bed themselves before I ventured up to the second floor sleeping quarters, and then alone, up the dim steep attic stairs. The only light in the attic office was overhead, with a string I had to stand on tiptoes to reach; I walked halfway into the dark room before I could find the string or could shut and lock the door. My suitcase was up there, still unpacked. Tomorrow I'll take a hotel room, I decided.

As I started up the stairs a voice stopped me:

"You the lady that's gonna be sleeping in the attic all alone?"

"Why do you ask?"

"Oh, nothin'."

"It seems to be on your mind. Why do you ask?"

"It's very scary up there."

All right, who was I trying to prove my nonexistent bravery to? I'd sleep downstairs on the floor, but the two violent toddlers were still up. When did these people go to bed? I was so exhausted I could sleep with the racket, lights still blazing, if only I could be assured of safety of person and possessions.

When there were finally just a few women left awake, talking earnestly, sharing problems and solutions, I folded the torn, unironed muslin sheet on the air mattress and tried to fall asleep. I thought of the comments, back in New York, about shelters being "a cheap vacation from marriage." Surely no woman would choose to live like this if her marriage had not made her desperate. . . .

By Friday, a lot had changed. I had spent much of my time in the attic office getting my interviews set up, away from the downstairs hubbub. I had asked the staff for nothing. I kept out of their way during the day and kept them company during the night watch. I'd given up the idea of moving to a hotel. Too much went on in the house to miss any of it.

I would be interviewing a wifebeater on Saturday, courtesy of a therapist who had agreed that it was important to the story that a perpetrator have his say. The man himself wanted to tell his story. Then I could leave, thank God.

Downstairs among the people, I was no longer the enemy "press" coming to bother the house. I was now accepted as a person. I was feeling comfortable and friendly with several of the staff and some of the residents. We were exchanging life stories, or bits of them, with ease. No, I did not say anything about my personal involvement. In my consciousness, I was there solely as a concerned journalist who had been helping the movement in New York and writing about it.

I'd begun taking residents out alone for a drink or dinner, to give a worried woman a break from the drabness and to listen to her privately. To relieve the total immersion in the problems of her existence, I'd tell her about some of the celebrities I'd interviewed

171

—Joanne Woodward, Glenn Campbell, Shelley Winters. For once the gossip was out of the house and on to people without the terrors of the battered life. Each woman was interested in hearing what my research had turned up on the dynamics of a husband like hers, marveling that I had actually interviewed some of these men. And that I was not afraid. Some could see their own situations in the studies; many added new dimensions. Most, however, simply could not fathom their lives and spouses at all.

No one staff member, I was told, had ever spent as many consecutive overnights as I was now doing, sleeping there outside the office, waking up with the staffer on duty whenever any emergency, small or large, occurred. I guess I had "won my stripes."

I'd solved the bathroom problem and the privacy problem by asking volunteers and interviewees, whomever lived within walking distance of the house, if I could come over and wash my hair or use their clean carpet and quiet home for a half hour of meditation and Yoga. I was beginning to feel very good about my assignment. I could see it was going to shape up, despite the original obstacles. I was beginning to feel very good about the community, admiring it for the concerned and practical action it had taken to overcome wifebeating in this generation.

By Friday after dinnertime, however, I sensed that something was going on. Something ominous. I couldn't put my finger on it, but something seemed very wrong. The noise level was lower. Mothers kept their children close to them. Nervous glances were exchanged.

"What's up? Is something wrong?" I asked the residents. At first there was general silence. Then someone said tentatively, "Um, well, you remember what Debbie said?" Debbie had come to my first daily house meeting with a report from her mother. (Among the few house regulations was mandatory attendance at these brief meetings. There, all problems were aired, input from all residents was encouraged, and house chores were assigned.)

Debbie was a child who'd lived in the house some time ago, and now lived nearby. It seemed that there was a petition going around the neighborhood to close down the house. The reason? Some older boys from the house were vandalizing the property of homeowners and were suspected of setting a nearby apartment fire.

The staffer on duty met the news with the usual composure. The residents joined in the discussion of how to cope. There had never been any problems with neighbors since the house opened. In fact, I'd been searching for a story on opposition to the house and found out that there had been general acceptance from the community.

Together, residents and staff decided that two steps were necessary and possible. One, each mother must be more responsible for the discipline of her own children. Two, money must be raised to build a secure fence around the backyard so the children could work off their energies outdoors and still be safe from vindictive wifebeaters waiting to grab them. The newly hired child advocate could devise some inexpensive way of occupying the older children, perhaps a club in the basement playroom away from the toddlers.

The vandals and suspected pyromaniacs were Watusa's children, the gangly teen-agers I'd felt so uneasy about.

Tonight the entire house was uneasy because of them. Watusa had gone out for the evening, leaving her brood in charge of one of the residents. It was a house rule that any mother absent must put her children under the responsibility of a specified resident, and she had selected Holly, a tall redheaded college graduate and concerned and nurturing mother, who had one well-behaved little boy. She'd protested that she simply had no luck, ever, in getting Watusa's kids to mind her. She reluctantly accepted the task because Watusa had once minded her Charlie for her.

"Don't you worry," boasted Watusa. "I tell those kids to sit and watch TV until I come back and they'd better obey me. Or else." It had been her custom to enforce obedience with a strap. When the nonviolence house rule was enforced, she'd protested that they had "taken away my means of discipline."

The kids were not sitting watching TV. They were all over the house, defying Holly to make them obey. They weren't doing anything in particular, but there was the gnawing suspicion that all controls were off, or rather, had passed from the adults to Watusa's six streetwise offspring.

The staffer on duty, D., was a strong black woman who had first learned the job in a prison work-release program. She was devoted to the first legitimate job she'd ever had, and she was very effective, very growing. She also understood the world Watusa's family had come from. Lately, however, the boys, and sometimes their mother, were accusing her of "siding with the honkeys." They didn't quite regard D. as an authority figure anymore.

The state-of-siege night ground on as our apprehension escalated. I really wanted to leave for a hotel.

One of the women got my attention. It was Bobby's mother, Mary Martha. She had divorced her policeman spouse, remarried him on his promise of reform, and Bobby was the product of that second violent honeymoon. "Don't you agree, Terry," she began, "that it's not fair that *we* have to suffer because Watusa can't discipline her kids? I don't understand the idea of being so patient with her when she was supposed to leave here weeks ago. She hasn't made any effort to help herself."

"Why not tell the staff how you feel?" I suggested.

"I can't say anything to them. They're so good, they believe everybody is as good as they are. They'd never understand me. They'd think I didn't have a heart. And *they* don't have to live with them day after day. Watusa has been here six weeks."

Holly joined us. "It's bad enough I can't go home because I'm scared of my husband. Now do I have to be scared to live here because of those kids? Don't you agree it's not fair?"

"Understand, I've got nothing against Watusa," Mary Martha said. "She's had a hard life. But she won't go looking for an apartment the way we're all supposed to and she just isn't any good at making those kids mind anymore. I can't even get my own kid to mind so well these days after he sees the way they act. . . . Why don't *you* say something to the staff, Terry?"

I'd been wondering the same thing myself. I understood the staff's dedication and compassion, their beautiful belief that no woman in need should be turned away. I saw them as stronger than most mortals —stronger than these residents, of course, but also stronger and better, better able to deal with crises than I was myself. What was my role here? Surely not that of critic. I was only a writer without a stake in the house, yet I was noticing something that perhaps they hadn't seen.

"All right, this is what I think," I said finally to the women around me. "I really think your own voice will have more meaning than mine. The founders want you to take a part in the house. They believe in not imposing their values on you, so nothing will happen unless you speak up. They *want* to know how you feel—that's the whole purpose of this place."

We sat there in a silence that was increasingly weighty.

Suddenly something made me look past the other sofa, about six feet away. The oldest boy was moving fast. There was a flash of long metal. He had a butcher knife! D. was there in an instant. "Give me that knife."

Unreal; unreal; this is not happening, my brain signaled to my motionless body, and I felt no fear. The knife was safe in D.'s possession now. She said something inaudible to him.

For the next hour, Watusa's boys and Lawana sat in a row on the long sofa. They refused to go upstairs to bed, but they no longer prowled the house. A standoff. Everyone was still. Tense. Waiting, waiting.

D. made several terse, low-voiced phone calls, her sensitive face reflecting a great deal of anguish that did not show in her manner. I went over to her. "You were very deft. Very cool," I said in admiration. She began telling me some of the incredible complexities of the situation. "Am I right? Am I right?" she'd say, wanting confirmation of the way she saw her role.

Watusa came home. D. had some hushed words with her. The kids went up to bed. The residents went upstairs. The crisis was over.

Downstairs, D. and I talked through the night. Despite her cool in emergency, she was very much concerned. For the last several weeks, she told me, one of Watusa's family, just out of jail, had been threatening D.

Each staff member always takes a new family as her special, personal charge. D.—with another colleague as backup—was Watusa's counselor. She had been the family's spokesperson when others could not comprehend their way of life. She had helped arrange a parole for a son. "Now they're turning against me for thinking like a white person. I don't care what color a person is. Right is right." D. was not afraid, but hurt and angry. "I know how to stop them, put a scare into them—the only way they understand—and end this mess. They don't understand this soft way of dealing. The founders don't believe in retaliating. Now those kids think *I'm* soft."

At daybreak, D. said, "Thanks for listening. I'm glad you were here when it happened. I'm going to ask you to speak at the staff luncheon meeting and give your recommendations about what you've seen here." And I decided it was time I spoke up myself.

I doubt that it was my testimony that swung the decision; after all, they'd had D.'s report. But a very smooth, decisive action now took place. Two staffers went upstairs to speak calmly and firmly to Watusa. The house "needed a breather for a few days."

They had found a motel room for the entire brood that an emergency housing agency would pay for. Watusa was told to be out of the house by three o'clock. She was welcome, however, to phone for counseling or visit (without the children) at any time. Her preference, though, was to move on to another state.

After the taxi pulled away, residents discovered the boys had scattered garbage in the basement playroom, smashed everything smashable, and sprayed the chemical fire extinguisher over all the donated clothing stored in the attic.

Everyone felt sadness and pity for Watusa, but no blame or anger. The staff called a work meeting to clear out their damage and losses. Their heartfelt credo was not to deny the house to any woman in need. "If we get ripped off in the process," they said, "well, perhaps the woman had a need met while living here and so could grow from it."

That evening the house came alive with a new sense of camaraderie, serenity, festivity. Everyone seemed exhilarated with relief from present danger. Everything that is implied in the terms *shelter* and *refuge* was in the very air that night. Hope and relaxation had touched the tense shoulders of the residents. When eyes met, there was a smile now, instead of the old wariness. The children played with a new contentment. The place no longer looked so forboding to me. When I went into the bathroom, for some reason there was no knocking on the door. When I went into the communal kitchen, heretofore such a mess, it seemed cheery and hospitable. I even found an untorn sheet in the cupboard, a pretty, blue-patterned one. Mary Martha got out the big, donated industrial vacuum cleaner. Holly got out the furniture polish. Soon the drab, threadbare living room was looking alive and cheery.

Two little girls, one white, one black, good friends, sang "Happy Birthday" to their mother, and gave them pretend-presents—although it wasn't anyone's birthday. The black child was the daughter of Thelma, a gospel singer who paid her few dollars a day room and board by working as an aide in a nursing home. She would not go on welfare. She kept praying a miracle would change her husband's recent, unexpected behavior. She still loved him, would say nothing against him. The sturdy, happy baby in diapers and Billy, the nurturing boy of ten, were her other children, all of them a joy to have around. She ran a tight ship with her kids.

The new feeling of solidarity embraced everyone. All the mothers wanted a better life for their children, wanted them growing up with love and discipline and safety.

For dinner the big kitchen table was actually set, and graciously. Heretofore, everyone had just grabbed a plate and tried to go off and ignore the confusion. Tonight Holly carried in the long, low coffee table and set it up so the children could eat there together, "like a party."

The staff instituted a new rule they'd long been considering: to limit the shelter to women who were presently battered, in immediate danger, and to limit the age of the older boys.

The residents stayed up until early morning, smoking and talking around the kitchen table about how they would solve their problems, enjoying the sense of friendship and supportiveness. This Saturday night turned out to be the most joyous and restful the house had known in ages. This women's shelter was indeed a place where the weary and troubled could lay down their burdens and get some peace. I felt as if I had embarked on a second visit.

The next day, a staff member who'd been away for several days returned to the house. "You still here?" she asked me, surprised. "I didn't think you'd stick it out."

In the days to follow, there was a lot to stick out. I was there when a bruised and broken woman stumbled through the door, her face swollen and blackened until her features were virtually destroyed, her hand inhuman in shape from being stomped on by her husband's shoe. And I was able to help her. I was there on overnight, when one of the women phoning suddenly panicked and shouted, "The phone lines have been cut!" I was there when two burly policemen appeared at the door at 3:15 A.M., asking was so-and-so in residence, her husband is looking for her. A complexity of problems was now set in motion, and I suggested we three women confer before we went back to sleep, while the details were still fresh in our minds. I had some ideas we could use, from interviews with another police department.

How good it felt to be in a position to help. I had not wanted to come to this place. Now I couldn't seem to leave.

In thanking me for my ideas, one staff member told me, "You seem very different from when you first came." I *felt* so different. Despite my intended firm "objective," I had begun to feel at home here (here in

178

these uncomfortable surroundings? These difficult conditions? I couldn't believe it).

I felt close to several of the staff members. I valued the chance to get to know them better as people, and admired what they had done with their lives. I was very much impressed by the people I met in the community who were not only morally dedicated to ending the problem of battered women in this generation, but were also coming up with innovative, workable plans to actualize it.

I felt concern—but more than concern, *admiration* —for some of the residents, the ones I sensed would pull through, the ones who were trying to create as good a world as possible for their children—and for themselves.

One warm and lovely evening, some of the younger residents dared to sit out on the porch and talk. It was risky for that's when a retaliatory husband could try to make trouble . . . yet they discovered their strength lay in numbers. I found them there when I came back from an appointment, and they asked me to join them. It felt so natural being there, enjoying, like any neighbors, the simple pleasure of conversation in the evening breeze, instead of a daring glimpse of the normal world by troubled, injured women.

I no longer thought about moving to a hotel. To my surprise, I stopped wishing I were back in New York. One more interview, one more story, one more day. Or two. I could not believe it, but I was not looking forward to leaving.

On one of my last overnights there, the staffer on duty and I were awakened by screaming and scurrying from the second floor. "A man broke in!" was the cry. The staffer, cool and reasoning, countered with, "That's not possible with this security system. We'd hear the alarm. And you know about the panic button. . . . Oh, all right, I'll go up and check."

Was someone really up there? According to the pit of my stomach, that lifelong barometer of my fears, no. According to my logic, maybe. If there were, I guess I'd think of something. I didn't notice that I was not afraid, but now I recall it with pride. Husbands *had* tried to break in before. Before the new, excellent, security system, one had come brandishing a weapon—which the staffer had talked him out of using. One had come with a shower of broken glass scattered over sleeping children. But this time a fan had fallen out of a window, creating the sound—to anxiety-ridden residents—of a break-in.

Suddenly a little figure in a bathrobe came rushing blindly by my air mattress. I couldn't recognize the child's face in the dark. I sat up and held out my arms. "Sweetheart," I called out, "what's the matter?"

"I've got to get out!"

It was Charlie, Holly's little boy. I held the trembling little child close to me, crooning and stroking the shaking shoulders.

"My father's upstairs," he said frantically. "My father's upstairs!"

I would not deny the reality of his fear. While I was fairly certain there'd been no break-in, Charlie had every reason to believe he was right, every reason for terror. He had seen his mother whipped, kicked, thrown down the stairs. I would not make an expedient mockery of his fear by denying it.

(Did I think it through then? I doubt it. But I know now I was comforting my own little brother who had never asked for comfort, who had reacted with blankness to what was going on in our home, who never showed any fear, or any emotion, who accepted our father's brutality and never wanted to hear about it. And I was also mothering the child that had been me, weeping hysterically to my battered mother, "I'm afraid of my father, I hate him, I'm going to tell . . . ," only to get the denial of denials: "There, there, how can you talk that way about your father? You know he loves you.")

"I don't blame you for being afraid, Charlie," I began, stroking back his red hair from his eyes, "but I think this time no one broke in. I can see how you thought so, but I think it's a false alarm. If someone did break in, it's probably not your father. Even if it is, there's more of us; we'd outnumber him. And the panic button is right there on the wall. A couple of policemen would be here in a minute. . . ."

When nothing happened from upstairs and Charlie felt more secure, he drew away a little and said earnestly, "My father can do anything he wants. He could climb up to this roof if he wanted to. I'm more afraid of him than anyone."

I smiled and said, "That's all right, Charlie, you had every right to be afraid of all that fuss upstairs. But it's okay now, and things are going to be better from now on." We began talking about what he was going to do the next day, and soon he was sleepy enough to go back to bed.

I wandered out to the kitchen. For once, no one was up. A poem tacked to the bulletin board caught my eye.

Learning to live with a person you do not love and
    respect,
Learning to live with a person who neither loves
    nor respects you,
Is merely learning how to die,
How to walk around as a shell,
How to deny what you feel,
How to hate without showing it,
How to weep without tears,
How to declare that the sham you live
Is the true reality and that it is good.

The poem was attributed to a "J. Henry," but neither the staff nor the residents knew who tacked it up or who had written it. No matter, it spoke for everyone.

What to Do, What to Avoid:
Guidelines to Help for Battered Wives,
Wifebeaters, Children,
Friends and Family,
Counselors and Clergy

Once a battered woman realizes, possibly for the first time in her life, that she's not a freak with an unspeakable problem, she may be ready to take some kind of action. People are at different stages, and any one individual may not be ready to do what another does. The battered wife is probably in one of three stages:

1. *She is resigned to her fate, and longs for help to endure:* This woman is often the wife of a highly placed professional man or a well-connected, conservative businessman. She may be trapped in her marriage by her belief that her religious duty demands she endure her cross. Her social position or family pressure may demand that she remain married, never exposing her tormentor. Perhaps her children would lose their right to quality higher education and a top spot in the pecking order of the community. Or her husband's career would be ruined and then he would ruin her. She may have weighed the desirable exteriors of her role as Mrs. X against her conviction that she has become too old and inept to attempt anything unfamiliar. This woman, although she is the despair of those who want to help her, still needs help. And there are guidelines, even for her.

2. *She is anxious to change the wifebeater:* The greatest percentage of longtime battered women, according to the shelters and the counselors, will be too beaten down emotionally to take the drastic step of

leaving forever. But many women will finally be ready to cease denying and begin acknowledging that there is a problem—that they have a right to a better life. Such a woman is ready, though timorously, to try with tools she never before knew existed, to change the wifebeater. She needs guidance to take what, for her, is an enormous step forward.

3. *She is eager to change her own life:* At last recognizing that the established system won't change her husband, at last acknowledging that the marriage is not salvageable, now unwilling to endure any more, this woman is ready—no matter what the risk, danger, and loss of former living standards—to make all the moves necessary toward freedom from her oppressor. She needs help to change her own life.

For ease of reference, this chapter is divided into sections. However, don't let yourself be limited by the sections; there may be ideas that also apply to you and that suggest new approaches you might never have thought of otherwise.

Guidelines for the Woman Who Is Resigned to Her Fate

If you ever think of a future for yourself different from your present life, it is with ambivalence. It's possible that you keep reminding yourself of your assailant's good points and lean on heavy denial between assaults. You may long to forgive. You may tell yourself you still love him. You may even believe that a part of him still loves you. I understand where you are coming from. This is your life.

Now, what can you do about it, within the terms you can accept? Although you feel helpless, you can free the children, and you can increase your own stamina and clearheadedness. But first you should understand the probable progression of tolerated, unchecked wifebeating. More and more your husband will feel justified in his behavior and attitudes toward you. After all, nothing stops him, not police, not community pressure, not you. His deviance is protected because his victim won't tell. You try even harder, don't you, whenever he threatens or assaults? Why should he change?

He will never be satisfied. No human wife could be what he thinks he wants. There may be times when his genuine disgust at his behavior and consequent making-up will bring you together for a while. But it will wear off. You will become a thing to him, deserving no rights. Violence is a way of life, increasing as you are less able to cope or please, as your physical and emotional health weakens. He may tell himself that you wouldn't know any other way, that you like it. He may tell that to the children. More and more, he loses respect for you because you take it. The children, at first terrified and disgusted, begin to wonder if perhaps their father is right. They may grow up to become the next generation of wifebeaters and battered wives because of their conditioning.

Before that happens, this is what you can do for the children now:

1. *Realize that their father will never change unless he gets psychological help or is intimidated into nonviolence by exposure and punishment.* It is possible that your suggestion of psychological help for him, or for both of you together, will only enrage him. On the other hand, some men have accepted it. It helps if the wife has gotten herself to a position to give that ultimatum, or the man is able to relate the children's problems to what happens at home.

2. *Stop devoting 100 percent of your energies to trying to please your assailant.* It's an impossible feat. Instead, use your energy to help the kids. Think of what they are learning about marriage, about victims and victimizers. Some women in your predicament feel they must minimize the reality by somehow defending the father, reminding the kids that he loves them. If that's you, stop deceiving yourself. You can't fool them. You are creating a schizophrenic situation where they see one truth and are told another—by you as well as by him. Your child is unlikely to understand your noble motivations. From whom can the child seek comfort if mother keeps saying everything is all right when it clearly is not? Let the children have every chance to view the relationship *objectively,* as an out-

sider would, and not repeat the patterns in their own lives.

3. *Don't complain to the children about their father.* It don't do you or them any good in the long run. Despite the very real difficulties of leaving, what they will see ultimately is a complainer who, nevertheless, does not leave. I understand your need to talk to someone. But for best results and least damage, it should be to a level-headed, sympathetic adult. A counselor in this field would be ideal. But there are other potentially good listeners, too. You can find out if the person is receptive by showing her/him this book first; if (s)he doesn't believe the problem is real, try elsewhere. Try a favorite teacher, perhaps—yours or the children's. Most schools have a school psychologist or guidance counselor who is no stranger to real problems, no matter how unique, or the need to keep secrets—although there's no guarantee.

Probably any woman who is active in the National Organization for Women (NOW) will be a good choice as the right listener. NOW made this problem the focus of their national activities in 1976, and many local chapters became the impetus behind the hotline and shelter movement in America. The local chapter may have a task force on the battered wife, or at least a marriage and divorce committee.

4. *Help your children get free of the worst influences at home.* Have a frank talk with them. Explain your decision to stay, and tell them that you don't want it any harder on them than necessary. Encourage them to find wholesome outside interests and stable, happy, nonviolent friends. Encourage them to get to know other adults, both men and women, whom they can trust, admire, and have as models. You don't want them to have only the one image of marriage, do you?

5. *Bring the painful topic of intervention out into the open.* Wifebeating families like yours tend to live on denial, thus perpetuating and reinforcing the problem. Whether you talk about it or not, some children instinctively rush to intervene. Others never do (but later admit they agonized over it). Some wifebeaters are shamed into stopping momentarily when their little child tries to take the grown-up role of intervening. But men

185

who feel no guilt harm the child first, then continue the intended mayhem to the wife. Such men may never cease their retaliation against the peacemaker.

You may be hoping that after the children are grown and more of a match for your husband, they will shelter you or have him stopped. The trouble is, this seldom seems to happen. More often, their guilt has turned to anger against the once beloved mother who stayed in this sick relationship; finally it surfaces into loss of respect for her. Many girls give up in disgust. Many boys even imitate the father in violence toward the mother. These are painful facts, I realize. But now you know what you've got to work with.

6. *Find out the address of the nearest shelter,* and the procedure for getting there—just in case. Although you believe you must never tell, and never leave, realize this: Wifebeaters' violence has been known to escalate into murder, and battered wives have accidentally killed their attackers while trying to defend themselves. And, given the escalating nature of violence, wifebeaters are often increasingly savage to children, especially those they decide don't love them enough. Battered wives, in their torment, have even turned on their children and passed the violence along.

Here are some things you can do for yourself, to keep up your stamina and your sanity. Or to stretch your mind to the possibilities of unexpected growth, or undreamed-of approaches.

1. *Plan ways of dealing with the next time.* That awful period when you wait, wait, wait . . . the silence, the thumping heart, the helplessness. Listening for the awful sound of his car driving up—*What is he going to do to me this time?* Trying to arrange your face in some neutral way, trying to show welcome instead of fear, stomach in knots, almost crazy with anxiety. . . .

If you don't want to use the next incident as evidence against him, there is not much to say to comfort you. You cannot change him; only he can. But weigh these possibilities: What if the neighbors knew and were ready with a tape recorder? Or a camera? Or a knock at the window? Or a call to the police? Or if they were willing to testify? What if someone were there, someone he respects, waiting with you? Could that person spend the night? Stay through the coming bad times? He won't start anything with a respected nonfamily witness around. What if you simply were not there? What if you left a note that you are afraid you'll die under his hand, and so are giving you both a chance to avoid the consequences, and left a copy of the note with someone trustworthy?

He is involving you in a kind of *folie à deux*. He expects you to cooperate in your own downfall. If he should be caught in the act, he'll expect you to deny it, say it's okay—the way a hostage has to obey a terrorist. If you need hospitalization, he'll expect you to lie about the causes—as you probably do now. But what if you didn't? You know how dangerous he is, so I can't presume to advise you, but it's something to talk over with someone who knows your case . . . or to ponder yourself.

The most important suggestion I can give in a book is *talk to someone*. Until you acknowledge the problem, and speak of it, *he* won't do anything about it. And neither will you.

Perhaps you have difficulty having friends over. A sensitive friend will understand that she must arrive as a nonenemy of your husband. If she flatters his ego and doesn't seem to extol you too much, and certainly doesn't pity or favor you, then you will have more chance for extending your friendships. Tell her to say hello to him when she phones, or give her regards. This is so he won't try to cut you off from an outside contact —a typical wifebeater device.

Sometimes friends and neighbors have brought a primitive, frontier justice to an otherwise hopeless situation. In America's early history, occasionally some wives would take matters into their own hands, using quite radical methods. There was once a church sewing circle, attended with great interest by all the wives in the neighborhood. One, however, was married to a wifebeater who didn't want her to have friends or leave the house. He used his usual methods of enforcement. When the other women found out, they all dressed up in their husbands' clothes, waylaid the wifebeater outside in the dark, and beat him up. After that, the wife-beater mended his ways.

And I have heard present-day versions, where the vigilantes were the battered woman's brothers.

If you are not ready to try any bold steps, the following will help you in the meantime:

2. *Learn to relax or meditate, and practice regularly.* Here is a simple technique for relaxation: With eyes closed, simply sit quietly in a straight-backed chair, or lie on the floor (not bed). Concentrate on your breathing, observing the breath as it enters and leaves the body. Gradually, your worried thoughts will begin to fade. Do this for at least ten minutes twice a day.

Some people, after learning the breathing technique, like to add a *mantra* along with their breathing. Mantras are special words that can be learned from a Yoga teacher or book. Or you could use a word like *love,* or *peace,* or the ancient Christian prayer, "Lord Jesus, Have Mercy Upon Me." Try to use the same one each time.

Once this kind of relaxation-meditation habit is firmly established, you could begin to repeat your special word at any time—when you are doing something that doesn't require much concentration, such as doing the dishes or taking a walk. Or when you are afraid. I have found it to be very calming.

3. *Build up your health.* Constant battering is damaging to emotional and physical health. You need all the extra stamina you can develop. Try to keep your weight normal. Keep your muscles working for you. Doing something for yourself will give you a new focus for your life and make you feel better and better about yourself. Hatha Yoga movements are excellent for this, available in the least expensive classes and illustrated paperbacks. Yoga also teaches breathing exercises that promote either energy or calming (any deep, slow, full breathing will aid calming). Walk briskly in the fresh air. Cut down and try to cut out smoking (smoking seems to be a common denominator among the battered wives I've met). Confine your drinking to beer and wine, and not much of that.

Avoid those foods that contribute nothing to your

health—the empty calories of junk food, packaged snacks, overprocessed foods. Coffee and sugar, for example, have many harmful side effects. Substitute herb tea, water and lemon, broths, and honey. Beef is restricted or forbidden by doctors in treating many diseases that have to do with stress. Try chicken and fish instead. You will note that the nonrecommended foods are expensive, while the suggested foods cost less. Fortunately, there is an additional fringe benefit. Healthful eating will also provide a hidden way to save some money for your escape (not that you have to leave if you are not ready, but knowing you could is comforting) or some counseling or medical attention.

4. *Attach less importance to your material possessions.* Some middle-class battered wives weigh their standard of living—their home, cars, clothing, furniture, vacations, status in the community, and advantages that naturally accrue to the children—and decide it is a trade-off. They find it hard to leave these behind as they ponder leaving the man who provides them along with the brutality—living at welfare level is unthinkable.

Try an experiment. Could you look as good with careful shopping on a smaller budget? Learn about public transportation or car pools? Try a wash-and-wear haircut, which doesn't require frequent trips to the hairdresser? The idea is to learn to value yourself more than your possessions. To know that you are still *you* —no matter what your exterior conditions.

Even if you intend to stay and endure, remember that attorney Marjory Fields says that of the two thousand divorces she obtained for battered women, "Not one ever expressed any regrets, even though she had many doubts before and during the process." The self-respect of living without fear and injuries has been worth the lower standard of living. Practicing flexibility now will give you the self-respect of knowing you could live differently if you had to.

5. *Learn independence skills.* Even if you are not ready now, not sure you will ever be brave or secure enough to try the unknown, or risk your husband's wrath, you can consider the possibility that he may die

before you do. Or he may find someone else who is more appealing to him.

Now is the time to know something about the details a woman alone handles. Decision-making, finances, dealing with landlord or mortgage, repairs, creating a social life or entertaining yourself, making new friends. There are adult education classes available for many of these, in high schools, colleges and women's centers, and at the local chapter of NOW. Before you need it, find out if there's a branch of the Family Service Association of America in your locality. It can be helpful with information about many of these areas.

Brush up or learn job skills, just in case. You needn't actually get a job. Volunteer work is a pretty good introduction to a paid working situation.

6. *Immerse yourself in the dogma that sustains you.* Ambivalence is an uncomfortable state to remain in. If you really feel beyond self-help, if you are committed by your religion or other strong pulls to the marriage you've got, then you may as well devote yourself to the philosophy that created it. Give a lot of thought to it. Let it fill all your time between assaults.

In seeking help, you've got the *wrong* person or agency if the following happens:

1. You are not believed.

2. You are made to feel guilty.

3. You are told you don't feel or think the way you say you do.

4. You are not asked what *you* want to do about the situation.

5. (This applies to agencies.) You are not helped with the "environmental" problems affecting your situation—legal and bureaucratic procedures.

6. (This applies to psychiatrists or clergy.) You are prescribed tranquilizers or prayer *only* to endure the situation, instead of being referred to concrete means toward possible change.

7. You are told that reconciliation is the only alternative; that a woman "ought to" be happy just being a wife and mother, ought not to have desires, sexual preferences, ought not to argue or compete.

Using the Directory at the back of this book, contact the nearest shelter. Phoning doesn't mean you have to *go* there: your decision not to will be respected as your choice. But you will be given or directed to good counseling, geared to your needs. If there are no specialized services near where you live, you may get some ideas or help from the local chapter of National Organization for Women or the nearest office of the Family Service Association of America. Failing that, you may have to make do with the traditional "helpers" who have often proved so sadly inadequate for this problem.

This inadequacy very much concerns the devoted workers in this field. Many are starting workshops to reeducate or retrain the traditional therapists who knew only one method: keep the couple together, blame the woman, and get her to adjust to whatever male orientation suggests.

I put the question to the best, most effective counselors I know: "What can I tell a reader who lives too far away from effective help?" Their answers follow.

Janet Geller, the psychiatric social worker who designed the method of couple counseling in use at the Victims Information Bureau of Suffolk (VIBS), Hauppauge, Long Island, New York, says: "If it were me, I would try to find one friend who really believed in me, to whom I could take my troubles, someone who would not say, 'You must be a bad person if you had that kind of marriage.' Someone who believed the violence was beyond my control. Then I would take her with me on the first therapy appointment, because I don't think I could withstand being abused at home and in the therapist's office, too. I would need her to validate my feelings until I found someone who said, 'What a terrible situation you are in. Let's see how we can make it better for you.' If you get one person who understands, then it is easier to tell it to ten. . . ."

Nancy Lynn of VIBS says: "Most battered women were shaped by traditional societal values. Most are not feminists, not interested in the women's movement.

191

But that's what they've got to seek out—concerned women who understand a woman's problem and will help, and where they are not looked on as crazy."

What if your only possibility of a counselor is your clergyman, and what if he is a man who still believes a woman has no rights over her own body? Nancy Lynn suggests: "Maybe she could arrange for someone from the nearest shelter or woman's counseling group to come and talk with her church group. Or show her pastor this book before she talks to him."

How to find a counselor who will really help you: Elizabeth Farrell, director of the Battered Wife Program of Washington, D.C.'s House of Ruth, says: "Start with a hotline, preferably one for battered women, but almost any hotline will know how to direct you to women's groups. If there seems to be nothing in your community, try looking up a rape hotline. [Even police departments often have rape units.] Most of these are adding services for battered wives. That's usually the core of the women's groups really doing something."

Counselor Margaret Allen Elbow, of the Family Service Association (FSA) of Lubbock, Texas, discusses the ideal goal of such counseling: "The battered wife needs to build her self-esteem. She needs to realize that she is not the *cause* of the violence. She may play a role in some way, but she does not cause him to hit her. Counseling can help—either with her mate or alone. She may even have to go secretly. [FSA agencies have a sliding scale of fees, so financial problems are kept to a minimum.] Check with the counselors to determine if they will work with a wife without her husband's knowledge, if that is necessary. Some won't. Counseling for marital problems is much more effective if both partners are working together, but we need to recognize that in some situations this is not possible. The woman needs to sort out what is most important to her for the present and in the future, and what are her options. This is difficult if she is depressed."

What can you say when you phone a new counselor? Carol Victor suggests: "State the problem and then ask, 'What do you think I should do with my life . . . *now?'* If the therapist doesn't express concern for your safety and ask if you are in danger *now*, then he doesn't understand what wifebeating is all about." And I would add that these days, if he has read nothing on the subject, hasn't made it his business to find out where the nearest shelter or services are, then he is not keeping up with his profession and is not the right one for you.

Now that wifebeating is being exposed as a wide-ranging admitted problem, many traditional agencies are becoming aware and helpful. I think it is symbolic of the trend toward growing consciousness to hear what W. Keith Daugherty, general director of the well-respected, long-established Family Service Association of America, has to say.

"Marriages cannot be viewed as more important than the individual mother, father, and children that compose the family. It is important to try to save the marriage because divorce plays havoc with the family and the individuals contained therein. However, there are times when the marriages cannot be salvaged: The price to the individual marital partners is too great and consequently destructive to all the family members including the children. Family counselors will then work toward helping the partners separate and build their individual lives again with consideration to the needs of the children."

If you are the battered wife who hopes somehow to end the wifebeating but not the marriage itself, you must first realize one stark fact: Without some co-operation from your husband, nothing you do will significantly change his behavior. You are beaten simply because your husband decided to express his frustrations and angers that way, and because until now, society has let him get away with it. And because the family conspiracy of silence compounds the problem.

You deserve a nonviolent life. It's possible you deserve your husband's anger for something, but no human being deserves *violence* from anyone. It's even possible that something in your childhood conditioned you to take this treatment without taking action against it. Perhaps you care more about the institution of marriage than about your own safety or the psychological damage to the children. Perhaps the thought of the neighbors knowing is enough to ensure your silence. (But they know. So far, they've pretended not to.) The right kind of therapy can help you know what you prefer and why.

Margaret Elbow warns that the battered wife "should not make threats to leave, to go to counseling, or to hit back, etc., unless she intends to follow through and *can,* in fact, do so. I would advise against hitting back, although some clients have reported that the wifebeater stops when his wife takes that action. It is a dangerous situation in that it could enrage him further. Threats to tell family or friends, etc., only exacerbate the man's feeling of powerlessness and increase the potential for more violence.

"She should determine what, if any, pattern exists in the violence—when does it occur, what tends to set it off, so that she can try to avoid situations that are potentially violent. This is not always possible, and it places considerable responsibility on the woman.

"She should not accuse or put him down, particularly in relation to his violence. This is not to say that she should never assert herself, but *how* she does it is important."

Carol Victor sums up guidance for the battered woman at this stage of awareness:

"1. Recognize that the violence is an indication of problems within the relationship and not acceptable behavior.

"2. Clarify communications. Many men complain that women don't communicate, but chatter or nag. Don't put him down verbally, but, in a straightforward way, express anger at the violence rather than at him, at his character. Of course, this is very difficult for any human being to do when enmeshed, without professional help.

"3. If you love him, tell him so, spontaneously and frankly, and that it's the beating you hate, not him.

"4. If you don't love him, why not leave?"

If you intend to get out before the next attack, you will find the most immediate help in a crisis shelter. First, call the hotline, get counseling, and learn what the admittance procedures are. Some shelters won't turn away any woman in danger who makes it to their doorstep. Others strictly observe their space limitations, and there may not be room.

Remember, these shelters are *crisis* shelters, not meant for permanent living. Or coasting. Most have time limits in order to save as many endangered women as possible. The staff will help you with your next step, such as getting income maintenance, job training, and cheap living quarters. Helping does not mean doing it for you. You must help yourself, too.

You may bring your young children with you. Some shelters limit the ages of older boys. There is never storage room for more than a suitcase per person. You will be living, eating, and sleeping under crowded, noisy conditions, without privacy, surrounded constantly by strangers whom you will get to know and sometimes love more than family (or be irritated with more than family), in an old rundown, but clean, house.

But you will be safe. And respected. And understood. And cared about. And listened to. And given every opportunity to grow and regain (or achieve for the first time in your life) your self-respect and dignity as a worthwhile human being with rights and responsibilities. You will deal with your ambivalences. You will be allowed—and expected—to make your own choices about what to do with your life, and given referrals on how to accomplish the first steps.

How to find supportive services in a nearby community: See the list of over fifty shelters in the back of this book. I personally called each one for the latest information. In addition, if you have time, and dare to receive such mail at home (or can get a friend to do it for you), send for Betsy Warrior's "Working on Wife Abuse," a mimeographed listing of a variety of services in operation across the country. It is updated periodically. (See Recommended Publications at end of this book.)

But check any shelter first to see if it is still operating and will take someone out of its own "catchment" district. Some do; some can't, depending on their funding.

There are other ways to find out yourself. Without exception, any shelter during its planning stages enlisted the cooperation of the local police department, hospital emergency room, and social service agencies—such as counseling services, community mental health clinics, legal and feminist clinics, hotlines. Often the local Family Service Association has a battered-wife program. It may be a waste of time calling most traditional organizations, such as the county medical association, psychotherapy training institutes, and churches. However, a few have at last discovered the women's groups' efforts against wifebeating and are beginning to institute programs. (See chapter 10.)

An almost guaranteed source of information is the local chapter of the National Organization for Women (NOW). Almost every chapter has a task force on the battered woman as part of the marriage and divorce committee.

Your husband's explosive temper may have brought you in contact with the police already; or you may meet them for the first time in your search for shelter information.

I have some advice about dealing with policemen, passed along by very frank officers in various communities. You may not like it, but at least you'll know where you stand. One helpful detective said, apologetically, "We bring our male viewpoints with us when we deal with domestic calls. It's *his* house. We can't ask him out of it. Myself, I'm changing as I learn more about this movement, but a lot more reeducation is needed. It's not easy to change a lifetime of attitudes. I'll admit it; I'm probably a male chauvinist."

Another added: "Everyone badmouths the cops. But we have a side, too. With civilian review, we are wary of being sued. We can't come into the home without being asked. We must leave if we see no reason not to. If the woman seems in distress, we may stick around long enough to find out, but if we are asked to leave, we must leave. It's the law. Many husbands say 'get out.' His home is the man's castle."

Another detective who worked directly with a battered-wives program revealed that, "When a woman is hysterical and disheveled, emotional and yelling—which she is after a beating—she doesn't make as good an impression on police officers called to the scene as if she could be well-mannered and calm. Yes, I know it's rather irrational, but couldn't you tell your readers not to make the officer think she's crazy or the kind of wife he'd hate to have?"

So, if possible, visit the station house on a calm day, well dressed. Makeup, a dress, stockings, and heels have proven to meet with more favor than what many policemen call the "women's lib look" of pants, no makeup, and no bra. (I'm not telling you what's right, just what works.) It's good to bring a similarly "feminine" friend along, partly as witness to any runaround you may get, partly to establish your credibility psychologically, partly to give you moral support and refresh your memory on details.

The community relations officer may have a broader outlook, be more sensitive to people's needs and aware of community resources than a random person at the desk. But all are supposed to know what's available and tell you. If you're not satisfied, return. It won't hurt for a few of the policemen to have met you and seen you at your best, when the patrol car stops at your door after a battering.

Some women's groups used to make the suggestion—born of frustration over nonhelp from police—that a wife phone that "a man" is assaulting her, not "my husband," to ensure that the police would actually show up. Or that a gun is involved. But realize that the professionals are wise to this amateur ploy by now. It's counterproductive.

Getting out for good is not just a matter of walking out, or fleeing. There must be a record left behind of your attempts to get help from police, doctors, etc. Suffering in silence is counterproductive. If that's what you've been doing, you must rectify it before you make your escape. Otherwise you'll be in legal trouble. When you start reporting, include past history and why you didn't leave or report it earlier.

Says Marjory Fields, of South Brooklyn Legal Services: "You should be prepared not to come back, if necessary." This is because a high percentage of violent men will become even more enraged, intending to maim further or even murder. They think: "How dare *she* do this to *me?*" To the wifebeater, her leaving indicates that he is not as desirable to her as he needed to believe he was, seldom that it's in reaction to his violence.

To other wifebeating husbands, the leaving becomes the first shock of reality. The man sees that she really means it, she doesn't intend to participate in her own destruction, and she suddenly becomes valuable to him. His sorrow for the brutal night before no longer brings forth the same old promises or denial. If she really wants to try again, she should secure his agreement —not merely his promise, but his actual *appearing* for several sessions—to enter therapy with a counselor experienced in this problem.

Thousands of case histories have proved that if a wife returns immediately, or even shortly after his begging or demanding, the violent patterns will not change and may get even worse. The wifebeater sees how thoroughly he controls her, with no effort on his part. He sees her as stupid, masochistic, needing to be taken in hand. She embarrassed him; inconvenienced him. She deserves to be punished. Every dangerous thought he had before is reinforced.

Many other women have learned these harsh facts the hard way. You can give some thought to your future now. You can guard against the possibility of being charged with desertion in retaliation by knowing your state laws. You can find out from NOW, feminist legal clinics, and sometimes Legal Aid.

Attorney Lester Wallman, chairman of the Committee on Legislation of the Family Section of the New York State Bar Association, and a panelist of the NOW New York Divorce Clinic says: "In a divorce action, I'd prefer to get the husband out of the house, instead of the wife, if she will also agree not to charge desertion. If she takes an unmerciful beating, however, and must flee for her safety, she should immediately report it to the police, her doctor, or hospital emergency room, so she will have proof against a possible charge of desertion."

Guidelines for the Wifebeater Who Wants to Change

When you discover that you do want to change, your life will open up to greater pleasures and opportunities and self-respect. You don't have to be a slave to out-of-control impulses. Your marital violence may not have been observed as criminal when you began, but it is today, more and more. The furious energies you now expend against your wife can be transformed into energy available for furthering your life's goals.

Recognize that you get angry and frustrated, as all people do (even your wife), and that there are other ways of dealing with it. (These methods won't work, however, if you're drunk or stoned.)

1. *When you feel anger taking over, get away from your wife.* Leave the room, the floor, the house. Then, when you are away from her, telephone a good listener and talk out how you feel. (Don't go to a bar.) Or, alone, yell at the top of your lungs, muffling the sound with the radio or TV turned up loud. Or yell in a long shower. Or in the car in the garage (this is no time to drive, remember, you are much too worked up emotionally to drive safely), with the engine off and the windows closed. Or near a noisy factory or construction site. (If you say you can't because you're too embarrassed, figure out why it's less embarrassing to hit someone smaller than you. Write it down. Keep your reasons and study them. See if they change over a period of time.)

2. *Get exercise immediately.* Adrenalin builds up in the body when anger is as strong as yours is, and it should be burned off to make anger more controllable, and you more comfortable. Pound a pillow. Kick a bed or padded furniture. Buy an old-fashioned leather punching bag and punch it. Try jogging. Run up and down the stairs or run in place. Get a jump rope, a

fast, easy, inexpensive way to work out wherever you want to.

3. *Pay attention to what's going on in your mind and body when your destructive emotions start to build.* Learn your own warning signals. Learn to apply your own brakes before you escalate out of self-control. Try deep, slow breathing. Applied properly and long enough, it's guaranteed to produce some calm. Just stop whatever you're doing or saying and concentrate on breathing in to the count of 3, slowly, holding for 12, and then exhaling slowly to the count of 6. Repeat until you feel calmer.

4. *Talk out your feelings.* Get an inexpensive tape recorder and talk into it about what is bothering you at the moment. Let it all out—all your angers, even your feelings of inadequacy.

5. *List the pros and cons.* In a calm moment, think over what your wifebeating has accomplished and at what cost. Has it been worth it? Divide a piece of paper down the middle and draw up a list of pros and cons on wifebeating as a way of relating, a way of running a marriage. Make another list. What is there about it that you would recommend to your son? To your daughter?

Be specific. Rather than saying, "All women like it or need it," try saying your daughter would like some guy to do the same to her.

6. *Communicate.* There are so many ways of communicating, or expressing your opinions and emotions. If it's difficult for you to do this by *talking,* without using violence for emphasis, try writing it out. Start with a heading, such as "How I Feel About Money" (or about sex, or about disagreements, or about meals and housekeeping, or about the children). Then express what you feel and why. Tell your expectations. Add, if you can, things that happened in your childhood to create this viewpoint. Add other possible viewpoints you haven't explored yet. Add what you would be willing to contribute to achieve your ideal and what you would not. Take as long as you like with it. Then ask your wife to read it. Ask her to write out her viewpoint, following the same format. Make a pact that this time you will not resort to physical abuse, no matter

200

what you read. (Very likely you won't even feel so inclined. This is a less violent method. Eventually you may even graduate to writing what you appreciate most about each other.)

When you've tried this experiment with all the present disagreements, perhaps you'd like to try a new one, perhaps, "I want to continue this marriage because _____" or "I don't want to because _____." If you really hate your wife, why stay?

7. *Think what you're doing to your children.* Your children are affected by what goes on in the house, whether they actually see it or not. They *know*. (Didn't you know the things your parents were trying to keep from you when you were a kid? Today's kids are even more perceptive.)

One repentant wifebeater, whose wife and children had to flee his violence for good, was painfully aware of how he had estranged himself from those he loved. He wrote: "One single act of violence is as damaging, creates as much lasting fear, impresses a watching child, as a hundred years of repetitive acts." He wrote of living alone, "very much withdrawn, with few visits from children or friends, with remembrances as punishments. . . . That I am deprived of making direct atonement is in itself the greatest punishment." There was remembrance of "the shame and remorse which I used to experience after the madness of an incidence of violence: the renewed determination of 'never again.' My sense of compassion or wisdom used to black out and die in an explosion of frustration in the moment before the blow was struck."[1]

Children of wifebeaters, unless they are very strong, or very lucky, or *helped,* tend to repeat the pattern of victimizer and victim in their future relationships. It is urgent that they have other caring adults—men and women, but especially nonviolent men they can trust —in their lives so that violence triumphant is not the only image they have of men and marriage.

8. *If you've been blaming alcohol for your uncontrolled, unremembered violence, join AA.* Your behavior during drinking is putting you in danger of a murder rap.

9. *Develop outside friends and interests in things*

that make you proud of yourself. It could be community work, helping underprivileged children, handicapped people, the elderly, volunteering in a hospital. Meeting new people will give you a broader outlook on life, help you see yourself in a new light—and introduce yourself to some of your good points which you may have been overlooking. For the time being, avoid the company of groups of men whose main conversational theme is putting women down and whose social life centers around drinking.

10. *Get counseling.* Changing your violent behavior will be easier if you, preferably together with your wife, are in counseling with someone who is specializing in this work. (Not all therapists know what to do with the wifebeating problem. A call to the local chapter of NOW—there are men members, too—might give you some leads. The nearest Family Service Association may have a special program for your problem.)

In the right kind of counseling, you will discover that you are not *blamed.* It is not like going before a judge or to prison. The counselor knows you have a problem and is there to help you understand it and solve it, not to shame you or put you down. Your terrible anger is, for once, *understood.* And yet if you cooperate and don't give up, you will be able to discontinue the violence. In addition, you will discover that many half-forgotten hang-ups from earlier years, or in your life outside the home, get resolved. Things you felt guilty about from your past you may discover you are *not* guilty about after all. And what a relief that is!

You'll learn how to express your feelings as they come up, rather than bottling them up until you explode with them. You may discover that it's all right for a man to cry: There's no loss of respect or manliness involved. You'll gain much more than the relief for the original problem you came for—in general, a happier *life* as well as marriage, a higher opinion of yourself. And all those things you so long wanted to say, and couldn't communicate, now become possible in the warm, accepting, neutral, nonjudgmental environment of the counselor's office.

This is the very best thing you could do for yourself.

One thing more, it might be an eye-opener to explore the thinking of men's liberation groups. The participants are enhancing their own lives, and their relationships with women, by freeing themselves from outmoded stereotypes. A few groups are beginning to add a special kind of rap group open to men who are troubled by their out-of-control impulses toward violence against those weaker than themselves. Even in a group that does not include this, the liberated man *listens*, tends not to be judgmental, believes in respecting confidentiality. A good book on this is *The Liberated Man* by Warren Farrell. (See Recommended Publications.)

Guidelines for the Witnessing Child

I know what it feels like, how excruciating it is to sit and watch and do nothing. Yet it is probably best not to intervene until you are strong enough to *win*.

From reading chapter 7, you know I went through my own childhood and young adulthood intervening, trying to stop the violence. I'm sad to say it didn't work.

Would I do it again if I could live my life again? I still could not sit idly by and tolerate such cruelties without reacting. But today there are more effective ways of helping both your mother and your father. And yourself.

1. *Helping your mother*. There are laws being passed or enforced to help people like your mother and to force people like your father to change. There are even psychological programs that may cure him instead of punish him. A better way of helping your mother, instead of ineffectually trying to fend off a stronger adult, would be to start by showing her this book and suggest that she may want to do something. Then, whatever her decision, you all know exactly what you're dealing with.

2. *Helping your father*. Only if you *know* it won't backfire, would I suggest showing this book to your father, too. You know how dangerous he is. If you decide to, try to make it very clear that you are risking this gesture out of love and hope for a happier family.

203

3. *Helping yourself.* You deserve having someone to help you, too. When you look for someone to discuss the problem with—and you really must, for your own sanity—make sure he or she knows that wifebeating exists and knows how difficult it is to prevent or punish. The ideal person would be working in the anti-wife-beating movement, such as a member of NOW. Someone who knows, even before you tell your story, that whatever you relate is *real*. And that you are putting yourself in serious danger, and your mother as well, if your revelations are divulged to your father. Confiding in the wrong person can have terrible consequences.

How can you find someone who will respect your confidence—someone who will be concerned about protecting you and your mother, rather than your father's public image? As a group, I believe these people would be trustworthy: people in NOW, in Alcoholics Anonymous, in men's liberation groups—as well as anyone working at a shelter for battered wives (see the list in the back of this book). Whoever it is, she or he should be someone who fully understands the dangerous consequences of betraying your confidence.

Most therapists feel committed to the client/patient: If you are the client, even if your father is paying the bills, you are probably safe. But experience suggests caution. I'd insist on a promise first. And don't get distracted by "Why do you want to know?" or, "Do you have trouble trusting people?" School psychologists ought to be safe: They are not beholden to your father. But to ensure confidentiality, you might bring this book to a session so they can take a look at it and better understand the problem.

Maybe you can trust your family doctor or clergyman, but before confiding in him, you should first consider what you know about him as a *person*. If he is automatically on the side of the breadwinner, if he is a traditionalist who believes marriage is absolutely sacrosanct or children have no rights of their own, or feels strong allegiance to your father or to any male head of a household—try elsewhere. Again, I'd get a commitment of nondisclosure first. And test for knowledge of the subject.

Too many family attorneys in wifebattering cases have proved loyal only to the husband and manipulative of the wife, so a child seeking guidance can be fore-warned.

"What can witnessing children do? Get out of the way!" says therapist Carol Victor. "Anything you do will be inflammatory to one parent or other. Seek out an adult you can trust—maybe a clergyman, school counselor, or favorite teacher—realizing at the same time they might not understand. Extricate yourself from your homelife as soon as possible. Save yourself at least, since you probably can't save your mother."

Victor suggests a way to stand it, while you are living through the terror, unable to do anything about it. "Try to use it as a learning experience. Observe what happens objectively, then you could be more helpful. Get some of the emotion out of the situation, the hate and pity, your pain and possibly your feeling of guilt. Think in terms of the process, of what's happening be-tween these two people. Why he does it. Why she accepts it."

Counselor Margaret Elbow has worked with the children of violent marriages. Her evaluation is, "Chil-dren should not accuse or attack either parent. If they attack the father for beating their mother, they only alienate him further and increase his potential for violence. They cannot help but feel anger, disgust and fear, but—for the child's own safety—those feelings should not be expressed to him in accusatory terms. I would advise that children not attempt to intervene during a beating *unless they can actually stop the violence.* Calling the police is appropriate, but should be done unobtrusively."

I am concerned that you not become *overwhelmed* by the devastation in your house, and manage instead to make your life as good as possible for now and for your future. I was often overwhelmed myself. It often seemed that my father's endless violence and threats of more violence obliterated everything else in the whole world. And that is rough . . . especially if you don't have any trustworthy person outside the family to comfort you. And give you another perspective on life. And believe you.

I want to pass along some of the things, the saving graces, that worked for me, plus some I wished I had known about.

1. *Meditate or Practice Relaxation Exercises.* What you need now is something to counterbalance the insanity around you so the rest of your life is not permanently scarred by it. I promise you, it *is* possible, with hard work and determination, not to be another statistic, drowning, marked and struggling forever. Regular meditation will make it all easier.

2. *Fortify yourself.* Don't get into the habit of poor nutrition. You may have to take the responsibility for yourself. Tobacco, sugar, coffee, and empty calories (the overprocessed snacks you munch while watching TV) don't help you. And drugs or alcohol will make your difficult adjustments harder than need be.

3. *Make plans for the future.* Please don't, by your own neglect, let your life go to hell now, before you have a chance to get out and really make a decent life for yourself. Many of us in your position have felt self-destructive, but I want to reach out with love and say hang in there. It will be worth it. Make plans that can actually be fulfilled. Career plans, moving-away plans. Learn all you can to broaden your future acceptability for a good first job. Get all the medical care you need now—have your teeth fixed, physical checkups. Don't get bogged down in a young marriage or a pregnancy. You'll be amazed how your needs and ideals will change after you are free of the violent homelife, and again after you have put the first adjustment years behind you.

4. *Get to know some good, solid, sensitive, trustworthy adults.* Here I'm not necessarily referring to the one(s) you seek out to confide in. You've got an amount of time to put in—almost like living through a prison sentence—so use it to your best advantage. Now is the time to learn to feel comfortable with adults (who are not in the victim/victimizer relationship), to like them and be liked by them. It will be a valuable tool if ever you are forced out on your own, or when you first go job hunting. Learn all you can

about what careers there are in this world. All this will be more effective from home base, while you are still in school.

5. *Get to know the parents of your friends.* Whether or not you decide to reveal the family skeleton, a relationship with a strong, healthy married couple can add some needed warmth to your life. Ditto with the staff at school. Ditto with some church personnel. If none of them appeals to you, well, forget it. But give them a chance first. It will be very good to see another kind of marriage, another kind of parenting. It won't hurt to have a substitute family.

6. *Join a self-help group.* You might find some supportiveness in Ala-teen, the branch of AA (Alcoholics Anonymous) for children of alcoholics. You can find out a lot from them, about making your own life count while you share an address with a sick, troubled, terrifying parent.

7. *Learn how to keep your own house.* Whether you are a boy or girl, learn how to cook, shop, clean, fix things. Then you won't be thrown when you are on your own, or be stuck living in a furnished room with cheap lunch-counter meals because you can't fend for yourself.

8. *Don't waste time with anguishing over "Why me?"* It's possible there's no reason at all, just meaningless luck of the draw—except that it is not your fault. On the other hand, there is an ancient philosophy that says we have chosen our parents because we once believed (but don't remember) we could handle the life they gave us and would naturally be rewarded later by the strengthening that comes from living through the tests with grace. Although I cannot use this philosophy to explain the sufferings of others or the villains who cause the pain, I personally find it beneficial, a far better alternative to anguish.

9. *Be aware of the good things in your life.* Here is a little ritual of Appreciation Awareness which is guaranteed to make these years seem less inundated with horror. Every day when you awake and before your evening begins, close your eyes and say to yourself, "I give thanks for _____." You'll discover there will always be something, however small. Perhaps

beautiful weather, the taste of a particularly favorite food, perfecting a sport, a new or renewed friendship, understanding a tough subject, the sound of live music, a period of peacefulness, enjoying a show or a book or a hobby, avoiding a crisis—or meeting one well. There is a possible continuum of responses to life, ranging from the high of feeling "my cup runneth over," to the depths of experiencing only the dregs at the bottom of your busted cornucopia. After a few months you'll see how effective this daily ritual is in changing your outlook from "half empty" to "half full."

Best of luck. The statistics say you may be doomed to repeat the pattern of your parents. I say you can rise above it, and respect women, men, and yourself.

Guidelines for the Woman About to Marry

When daughters of wifebeaters consider getting married themselves, they wonder how they can avoid choosing someone like their father. Records show that most battered wives knew little or nothing of several significant facets of the mentality of the husband-to-be. There was never much premarital discussion about important issues.

Is any given man likely to claim a "right" to future wifebeating? The key is in his attitude about himself, about women, about the marriage relationship, about what ideal sex would be like, what turns him on, what turns him off, and whether violence or use of force play a part. And whether he knows or cares what the woman thinks about sexual pleasuring.

Does he believe woman was born to serve and service man? Does he "own" her? Is he born to give her "orders"? Is she supposed to "obey" him?

Is woman innately "dumb," without opinions worth listening to? What are his attitudes about shared responsibilities, about decision-making, household and child-rearing chores, job-holding and how the money is used? If dinner isn't on the table at 6:02, will he help, or will he hit?

How secure is he? Is he so insecure that he's got to devalue his mate in order to inflate his ego? Does he make a show of being supersecure, taking command of situations and people? And the woman in his life—does she feel that as long as she's nearly perfect, everything will be all right? What will happen if she's herself? What is he like when he's angry? When he hears a differing viewpoint?

What is known about violence in his family? Ask. Are you afraid to? Records indicate that many battered wives knew nothing about that sort of family history. And nothing about personal history, such as military service and how much money he makes now.

If the young couple does not feel comfortable about communicating their goals and expectations of married life beforehand, there are bound to be occasions for anger later.

Because many cases of wifebeating begin only after the onset of the first pregnancy, it would be useful to have some clues to identify the man's potential for marital violence. Two therapists experienced in dealing with wifebeaters share their early warning signals.

Margaret Elbow divides his personality traits into four types:

"The Controller may manipulate, and if manipulation fails, then demands and force may follow. He must have his way. He must control situations. He seems to know no limits.

"The Defender cannot tolerate budding independence of his mate. As long as she is dependent, that is, seems to need him, he feels fairly comfortable. He resists counseling, because he believes—and tells her so—'I'm all you need' (for himself or for her).

"The Approval Seeker tends to belittle any performance or skills or talents of his wife, particularly when he feels inadequate himself. He tends to feel that others are nagging, blaming, or putting him down inappropriately, and often says so. He is easily hurt, often depressed.

"The Incorporator is an intense man, characterized by irrational jealousy and extreme possessiveness. However, he doesn't necessarily see his wife as a possession to control, but rather as a part of himself. He is enmeshed in a stormy relationship of 'I-can't-live-without-you-and-can't-live-with-you' syndrome. But he can never sever the relationship or alter it."

Therapist Carol Victor says, "In addition to possessiveness and jealousy, other early warning signs are: any physical violence which is combined with 'playfulness' or lovemaking, such as a slap, or throwing the wife across the bed on coming home high from a party. Breaking things. Throwing things. Being savage to animals or children.

"Furthermore, verbal warnings about beatings to come should not be ignored. If the husband says, 'The next time you do that, I'll break your neck,' the wife should say, calmly, unaccusingly, without provoking, 'What do you mean by that?'

"And remember, a beating followed by apologies and promises should not be ignored. It's not a guarantee it won't happen again. It probably will."

Guidelines for Concerned Friends and Family

You can be a great savior, the best and only helper your battered friend has. Or you can add to her burdens. First, realize that the chronic stress the woman lives under makes her very uncertain of her capabilities. And the treatment she was dealt by traditional "helpers" adds to her feelings of powerlessness. Many battered women believe no one cares. And many are right. If you can't actually follow through with your help, despite her sometimes exasperating ambivalence, and her chronic habit of giving her violent husband yet another chance, don't raise hopes that she has at last found someone she can count on.

Actual intervention at the height of the violence has often proved disastrous, even fatal. It would be better to help by either *deflecting* the violence or by *providing a means of escape* from it. Your friend needs a safe place to stay, with the children if necessary, where there are people who will care about her.

"Really listen. And *believe* her," suggests therapist Carol Victor as a first step. "No matter how gallant he seems, believe her. If she were making it up, she'd still need help, too! Search out resources for her. They may not be within the community. She may not dare to on her own. [I would suggest your sending for Betsy Warrior's *Working on Wife Abuse*—it's safer if it arrives at your address for her—and also Women's Policy Studies' *Response* newsletter, which lists a number of recently funded groups caring for rape and battery victims. See Recommended Publications in the back of the book. Rape counselors often know of services for battered women, or plan to expand to provide them.] If you talk to the husband, let him know that it's his *behavior* that's unacceptable, not he himself. Wifebeaters are already insecure, so he must have an out, be able to save face somehow. Convey the idea that violence is only an outward manifestation of anger and frustration, which everyone has."

Counselor Margaret Elbow has found that friends and family sometimes make the situation worse by making counterproductive efforts. "They should not urge her to leave unless she is ready," she cautions, "but rather, offer support and help if and when she is ready. By telling her she *should* leave, they are only setting her up to feel inadequate if she cannot bring herself to do it at that time. Making the option possible is very helpful. But setting up an expectation can be harmful.

"Friends should also realize that a woman's leaving can precipitate a more dangerous situation unless precautions are taken. If a man has threatened to kill a woman if she leaves him, the threat should be taken seriously. Great care should be taken to protect her, not only with legal injunctions, but everyone should be alerted—the police, those with whom the woman is staying, her employer and whoever will be in a position to take precautionary measures."

Perhaps you've sensed that your friend or relative is in this predicament, but you don't know how to offer help or indicate you'd be willing to listen or offer shelter. Here is a workable opening approach:

Refer to the problem, whether to the evidence of her bruises, apparent fear of her husband, or simply that you've noted the movement against wifebeating appears to be the fastest-growing international social movement. Then, according to Gary Schoener, of the Walk-In Counseling Clinic in St. Paul, "If you get little or no response, say, 'It sounds like you really don't want to talk about it.' Stating that actually reduces

211

reluctance and shows your concern. Say, 'Is it something you'd feel like talking about to *me?*' Or, 'It's none of my business but I am concerned.' Explain you are not prying, but as a human being feel concern and moral obligation."

You can also help by becoming part of the movement working toward a solution. Many of the anti-wifebeating groups welcome new members, supporters, volunteers. Support is needed for proposed legislation which is now accelerating around the nation. Connecticut, for instance, is appropriating money for shelters and proposing modification of the restraining order to prevent the wifebeater from returning home for a time when he's caught in the midst of his violence.

The reason this crime is so widespread, particularly among the middle class who found it so shameful they kept it a dark family secret, is that it has been reinforced by the conspiracy of silence. The silence made the crime tacitly acceptable. Now is the time to speak out publicly against wifebeating. Otherwise it will take too long for help to reach all the isolated victims.

Guidelines for Mental Health Professionals (and Clergy)

Be forewarned that your client may be frustrating to work with, for three main reasons:

1. *She's in grave physical danger.* If your psychological help does not include support systems, shelter and advocacy with the bureaucracies, you may find a client who is ready psychologically to take charge of her own life—yet with all the environmental and societal odds stacked so severely against her that she winds up brutally maimed or even dead. Those odds may seem Kafkaesque but they're real.

2. *She may have very mixed feelings about getting help.* The battered woman herself may be struggling with ambivalence. She may be so battered emotionally that she is fatalistic and apathetic. She has been so thoroughly indoctrinated that she is a failure if she isn't *in* her marriage, pleasing her husband, that she may utilize help just to get through the present crisis

and then go back to the assailant, pathetically eager to believe his promise of reform. Or she may be motivated by terror of displeasing him—a perfectly realistic attitude for many a woman. For another, the mere fact of admitting to herself that she has a problem, and actually coming for help, is the giant step beyond which she cannot progress. Societal and environmental pressures combine with threats from the assailant to keep her from rocking the boat.

You, as counselor, may do your best work and feel the problem is getting resolved, and then the woman's past conditioning takes over and the good work is undone.

This sometimes exasperating client has often tried to practice the same four A's that Marabel Morgan preaches so successfully: Accept, Adapt, Admire, Adjust (to husband), even though it backfires for her. When she believes her salvation lies only in serving her husband better, she often cannot see her responsibility to others. The Ann Arbor NOW began with a system of volunteer safe homes for the battered wife. And they discovered, they told me, that not every client could be trusted to keep her part of the bargain. The Svengalian pull of her husband was too strong. In return for emergency private sheltering, she was to promise not to reveal her refuge to anyone. This precaution was, of course, for the safety of the host home and future refugees. One hostess left for a previous appointment, trusting the battered guest alone for a few hours. When she returned, she found the woman had contacted the assailant himself, and there he was, in her home, while his victim was busy making dinner for him!

3. *There may be some danger to the helper,* although much more is perceived than really exists. The retaliation from a husband-assailant is usually against easily intimidated family members who are reinforcing the conspiracy of silence, not against an agency or therapist or private person known to be working to counteract wifebeating. The key is in the shame of public exposure any retaliation would incur.

In Britain, with its network of shelters, only the secret-address ones have experienced such problems;

the open, publicized ones have not. As for counseling the wifebeater, Erin Pizzey told me: "No violent men have ever troubled us because we go into the violent home with *love*. We say, 'I'm sorry about what's happening.' Within five minutes he breaks down and cries. We never send the male staff. The wifebeater doesn't want people to be afraid of him."

She adds: "If the battered wife believes you are just as frightened as she is, she'll be a paranoid refugee for the rest of her life."

Margaret Ball, area director of Family Service of Detroit and Wayne County, recognized the problem of fear in the counselor's dealing with the wifebeater. In a paper presented at the Metropolitan Detroit Chapter of National Association of Social Workers on December 3, 1975, she stated:

". . . We respond to the client's emotional reality and demonstrate the caring and understanding aspects of a helpful relationship. . . . We reinforce the rational aspect of the functioning adult toward self-understanding and self-control. . . . We provide optimistic but realistic expectations that each person can develop more control over his own life toward greater fulfillment."

Among the specifics she included: "Identifying the client's feelings which go into the violent behavior . . . Timing here is important, and eliciting the client's participation in this . . . is crucial—so as to avoid regression and more violence. Also to be avoided are techniques to uncover more primitive or repressed emotion—the difference being the control of the cognitive component in the person. The handling of explosive or panicky feelings with the goal of integrating them is a longer treatment goal, and depends much more heavily on the diagnostic picture presented than the other 'crisis handling' techniques."

The counselor—and the clergyman—should remember that the woman's children are living in a senseless, crisis-ridden, apprehensive environment, with few or no strong supports or good models. The children greatly need a compassionate, empathic, trustworthy adult in their lives—particularly a male image different from the one they know so well.

For any counselor new to his work, the most pertinent guide I can recommend are the two training manuals created from experience by the Ann Arbor NOW. (See Recommended Publications at end of this book.)

A Question and a Proposal for Mental Health Institutes, Theological Seminaries, and Law Schools

What can be learned from the frustrating experiences of battered wives trying in vain to get protection from the professions presumed to be humanitarian?

The traditional therapies have not been responsive to the needs of our changing culture, as the proliferation of self-help groups attests. Freudian-based therapies—women of today's consciousness complain—bear little or no relevance to their lives or goals. These therapies have almost uniformly been counterproductive in the case of battered wives.

The clergy preaches a male-oriented theology and structure of the marriage relationship. The clergy has not been in the vanguard of help for the battered wife. Instead, its attitudes about woman's place, duty, and nature, have added to the problem. Even now, with few exceptions, the silence from the churches on the issue is profound.

The law, whether as written or as practiced, has upheld the married man's "right" to unpunished felonious assault upon his wife. The court bureaucracy and judges have guaranteed the woman an unspeedy and unfair hearing.

Clearly, the training grounds for the major professions require some reevaluation, if they are going to be responsive to the needs of over half the population.

There is always welcome room for more and more involvement from all professions. (Dentists, for instance, could be case finders, could have literature in their offices on local supportive services. Physicians, it goes without saying, could help immeasurably.) The crusade has grown so far-reaching that it won't be long before academia will have to acknowledge the problem and make plans to incorporate it into the curriculum. Schools are already beginning to invite speakers and workshops from the field of personal involvement for an enlightening learning experience. Research grants will be available.

The opportunity is there for adding university resources, support, and cooperation to the struggling grassroots movement for amelioration. Professional groups who take off on their own without consulting with the people actually working on wife abuse find they are missing out on the fundamentals and the reality. Women working on wife abuse from coast to coast have a message they are trying to deliver: Please *help* the battered wife, don't just study her. It's the wifebeater who needs to be analyzed.

10

The Future:
The Fastest-growing
Social Movement in America

There has been so much progress since I began research on this subject that I feel very encouraged. When I began, no librarian had knowledge of the subject. Most magazines were certain the subject was too ugly and irrelevant for their middle-class readership. Every fact, every statistic, every interview was very hard won. There were only a handful of shelters in America, none of them publicized outside their own locality— if there. AWAIC was the only agency devoted exclusively to helping battered wives. Growth & Life Center was the only private counseling service that dared treat wifebeaters and their children as well as the woman, and it got little publicity.

Today it seems that most educated, concerned persons are at least aware of the problem, although there is some resistance to believing it happens in the best of families. The media report on it with increasing frequency. It is a "hot" topic. There is a Library of Congress catalogue listing: Under Conjugal Violence, "Wifebeating" was recently given its own number.

A national network of communication has sprung up which also publishes a newsletter (see Recommended Publications), and the number of shelters is growing rapidly. A directory of over three hundred shelters appears at the end of this book.

A number of groups are now counseling couples in the Minneapolis/St. Paul area. For example, the Walk-In Counseling Center in Minneapolis treats wifebeaters whose wives are in one of the shelters and are afraid to risk seeing them again. A men's liberation group is now seeking funding to provide consciousness-raising and rap sessions for wifebeaters to gain a new perspective on roles in marriage. A volunteer male counselor offers therapy for wifebeaters via Woman's Survival Space, Brooklyn, New York.

By 1980, in several cities, sensitive counselors, women and men, established programs of eight to twelve weeks, to reach out to the wifebeater and help him understand himself (often for the first time in his life) and then effect change in his attitude and behavior. Some attendance is voluntary; some is court-mandated. A list of these rehabilitation programs is in the Appendix of the book.

More and more supportive services are developing across the United States—140,000 programs is the estimate from the Center for Woman Policy Studies, as of December 1977—and attitudes are changing, albeit slowly. The Family Service Association of St. Paul, Minnesota, now routinely asks *all* clients whether physical abuse is part of the family problem, since one of the well-known battered-wife patterns is hiding the fact that beating goes on in the home. One by one, autonomously, YWCAs have developed services for battered women until, by 1980, more than a third of the nation's Ys offer shelters or programs.

A most heartening statement comes from Yolanda Bako, a pioneer in the New York shelter movement, and presently the Director of Volunteers Against Violence Technical Assistance Program: "The National Coalition Against Domestic Violence now has a network which connects shelters in 37 states, with more to come. And it looks as if Congress finally acknowledges the need for shelters."

Across the land, concerned citizens are becoming aware of the problem and are beginning to take responsibility for reducing it, sometimes without waiting for the slow-moving judicial system to act or reform. In Brooklyn, New York, for instance, the Park Slope Clergy Association began an innovative "Safe Home" project, worked out with Kathryn Conroy of the Family Reception Center of Children and Youth Services. The idea was sparked when a clergyman drove around with night-patrol police and found that 60 percent of their calls for help concerned family violence. Now

218

families within the twenty-five congregations of the three major faiths in this ecumenical group will volunteer to stay home for three days each, to provide refuge for a local fleeing woman and her children. The woman would receive counseling and information; similar help would be available to the husband-assailant.

Although churches have been slow to join the movement against wifebeating, some are beginning to come through now. For the Ann Arbor, Michigan, project (which moved to Ypsilanti), and for the referral center for the many shelters in the state of Washington, churches are providing low-cost space. And the American Friends Service Committee in Manhattan provided a significant step forward with its conference for six hundred concerned men and women of all faiths (and those not affiliated with any religion) from several neighboring states. Next the AFSC provided meeting space for the New York Coalition for Battered Women —the smoothly running information and resource sharing exchange of former smaller coalitions and interested individuals, staffers and volunteers from shelters and counseling services, community and private agencies and individuals encountering the problem.

In March 1979, I was keynote speaker at a Lubbock, Texas, weekend conference on family violence, held in facilities donated by a large downtown church. In the workshop co-led with Ann Chrisman of the Women's Protective League, many of the clergy attending expressed eagerness to understand a problem which admittedly had long been left unexamined.

In Crown Heights, Brooklyn, a group of Roman Catholic clergy and nuns met in October to discuss wifebeating, and the idea that they might provide churchly Outreach through the parochial school. Many of them had read an article in *America* (July 30, 1977), a Jesuit weekly magazine, "Wives, Mothers and Victims," by George M. Anderson, a chaplain at Rikers Island prison. They asked me to address their group, as did the Safe Home project.

The new Hartford, Connecticut, shelter was a project of clergy, doctors, and their wives. A church women's group donated $2,000 to Women's Advocates House. The American Baptist Church of metropolitan New

York, numbering 145 congregations, now has a Task Force on Battered Women. Its women's mission societies have begun to request speakers or workshops. The Reverend Sarah L. Darter, convener of Task Force, is also a practicing psychotherapist, and in October 1977 instituted an eight-week seminar of volunteer counselor training. Some thirty women and men attended. Rev. Darter has written the foreword for a Presbyterian proposal on why the church should work with battered wives, and plans to write programs for the National American Baptist office. An ordained minister and a feminist, she is also a Ph.D. candidate at Union Theological Seminary in ethics, where the first course dealing with wifebeating was given in the spring of 1978, "Violence and Violation."

Rev. Darter speaks of agencies being "very surprised that churches are interested in battered women's work. Their stereotype of us is that we don't care and that we only tell women to go back home to their husbands, regardless of how psychologically or physiologically harmful it is to them and their children. Though this is part of the church's embarrassing history, it is not the whole picture . . . I would like to develop a national, ecumenical network of people in religion who are working on these issues." (See Recommended Publications and Useful Addresses.)

Ellen Kirby, of the Board of Global Ministries of the United Methodist Church, said in December 1977, "The abuse of women . . . should be a major focus of concern for religious institutions in the next decade or until this terrible problem is eradicated from our society. . . . Unfortunately, . . . the institutional church either through its blatant sexist theology, which has blessed the subordination of women, or through its silence, blindness, or lack of courage, has allowed itself to be one of the leading actors in the continuing tragedy of abuse." Nevertheless, in 1977 the 1.5 million-strong United Methodist Women set a goal "to work to end violence towards women." Though its focus had been rape, not conjugal crime, the church held a national conference in 1978 on responding specifically to battered women. As I outlined the low-cost and costless help a church could provide, I was impressed by the dedicated concern and leadership abilities of the women intending to implement the suggestions. In Minnesota, a Roman Catholic nun bought a house and created a shelter. (See the shelter directory.) It is very heartening to see how the numbers of caring people are increasing, and how even small support can effect larger changes when enough good people are behind the effort.

In New York City, concerned citizens lobbied to provide services for the battered woman. There are now two shelters, opened during the summer of 1977. A coalition of several women's groups, the Center for the Elimination of Violence in the Family, found a soon-to-be-vacated maternity hospital building in Brooklyn and bought it for a shelter with state funding through the former State Senator Carol Bellamy. It is called Women's Survival Space.

The city-run shelter in Manhattan might never have come about had it not been for city councilwoman Miriam Friedlander's resolution to aid battered wives and their children, introduced on May 9, 1975. It had been designed not to cost the near-bankrupt city additional money, but rather, to take advantage of its already existing facilities and use them for informing battered women of their rights, the service available, and mandating agencies to provide concrete plans for assistance.

However, this resolution remained stalled in committee. Susan Maurer and Enid Keljik, of the New York NOW Task Force on the Battered Wife, began enlisting support and exerting pressure for a hearing. They organized a meeting, which was well attended, to provide a forum for the emerging authorities in the field. Jo Sutton, of the National Women's Aid Federation in England, was one of the guest speakers. Now there was more pressure to get that hearing scheduled.

On October 14, 1976, there was full media coverage of the hearing. A city task force was formed as a result, and from then on, there was no more stalling. Soon the Henry Street Settlement House, HRA, and AWAIC announced the opening of a shelter, complete with a mini-school, in Manhattan.

The two shelters required a face-to-face extensive

screening process with an experienced admitting counselor, to avoid conditions the staff was not equipped to handle—alcohol or drug dependency, for example, or psychiatric problems. So admission was not necessarily instantaneous or on demand, and space was limited.

Some months later, Candice Butcher, coordinator of the new HRA Battered Woman Program, was able to cut through massive red tape to provide refuge for fleeing women who could not be accommodated at the time of the emergency, at the shelters. She secured a floor in a hotel where open-ended admission would be offered to an apparent battered woman in flight, upon referral by police via the welfare office (to which women sometimes turned when they left their pocketbook behind in escaping, and which in the past was not authorized to give emergency assistance). Five days' emergency Income Maintenance (to be repaid when possible) was now available, along with a bed that evening. Follow-up services would begin in the morning.

Making Sure of Justice

It was a group of concerned women who helped make sure justice was done, possibly for the first time, when a habitual, boastful wifebeater finally came to trial. He had been beating his wife all fourteen years of their marriage. Elvia Elias was kept virtually imprisoned in her house, busy bearing babies (seven, plus a miscarriage caused by an abdominal beating), not allowed to go out, even to church. Her husband was indoctrinating his older boys that a woman's role was to be a slave of man. He encouraged them to participate in violence against their mother. The last assault proved nearly fatal, requiring skull surgery. Then Elvia discovered two women's organizations: South Brooklyn Legal Services and the National Congress of Neighborhood Women (NCNW), both part of the Center for the Elimination of Violence in the Family coalition. South Brooklyn helped her get a divorce, although she had no money of her own. NCNW provided supportive services so she could start afresh with the goal of being a self-supporting woman, no longer dependent on a wifebeater or welfare. Elvia Elias was one of the women who had conscientiously tried to help herself throughout those fourteen years—via police, courts, social work agencies—and at every turn had been stymied by the traditional system set up to refuse help to a battered wife. Her husband was aware of this as he shouted to the arresting officers, "You can't arrest me —that's my legal wife."

The day of the trial for attempted murder (which had been plea-bargained down to assault), volunteers from NCNW, South Brooklyn, and other women's groups showed up at court to monitor the proceedings. Brooklyn Supreme Court Judge Larry M. Vetrano asked his secretary who were all those women, law students who had come to observe? He appeared intimidated by the reporters the women had alerted, angrily accusing them of trying to "blackmail" him into a harsher sentence. Judge Vetrano did agree to meet with women who could provide the history of Mr. Elias's brutality—something judges have ignored in sentencing many similar cases.

The possible sentence could be one to fifteen years. The NCNW believes that the sentence—three years— would have been the usual insignificant amount had not one of the volunteers run out to phone more women to come and add to the crowd of observers. The comment from South Brooklyn Legal Services, disappointed because the assailant could get out on probation in only a year, was, "It's probably the first time a wifebeater has gotten more than ten days in jail, so it's a victory of sorts."[1] The greatest victory will be if it sets a precedent for more and more just punishment for the crime, and if other women are thereby encouraged to monitor judges.

In another court case, in Queens County, New York, on December 17, 1976, some forty concerned people came to the support of a battered woman. And this time the judge was light-years away from the chauvinist approach. In most cases where the habitually attacked woman fights back in self-defense and happens to hit a vulnerable spot, the pleas of longtime provoca-

223

tion and self-defense have carried little or no weight with male judges. The husband's history of endangering her life is ignored.

Sandra Lowe was married to a vicious, habitual wife-beater. She was recovering from surgery when her husband, John, went at it again on the night of September 10, 1975. The kitchen knife she grabbed to defend herself contacted his chest and he died several hours later in the hospital. Supreme Court Justice George Balbach, on the bench for sixteen years, noted that he had received about forty letters of support for Mrs. Lowe from relatives, neighbors, a clergyman, local school officials and community leaders. Mr. Lowe's own mother and sister petitioned the court to be lenient to their long-suffering in-law. Assistant District Attorney Randall Eng, who handled the case for the state, said he didn't believe she had intended to kill. She had suffered enough, and had three children at home, including an emotionally handicapped twelve-year-old son.

Judge Balbach said he saw no purpose in incarcerating Sandra Lowe. He allowed her to go free with five years' probation.[2]

Battered wives themselves are becoming concerned citizens on behalf of their sisters. Once they have extricated themselves from their husbands' dominion, many have found that they are able to speak out in public—despite the fact that they may have been shy and self-effacing in their marriages. Encouraged by support from the new women's counselors, they have felt moved to take a risk in order to further the cause. Over and over again I've seen these real-life testimonials move the indifferent, hostile, or stereotypic thinking of an audience of politicians, press, and others. Those who believed wifebeating to be an exaggeration find their minds opening and their resolve to change the system emerging.

Because of this courage, protective legislation is in the works or already passed in Arkansas, California, Colorado, Connecticut, Florida, Maryland, Massachusetts, Minnesota, Nebraska, New Jersey, New York, Oregon, Pennsylvania, Virginia, and Washington. In New York State, a woman who flees marital violence, with or without the children, can no longer be sued for desertion or abandonment because of it. And, in New York, a married woman now has a choice of having her assault case heard by criminal court—a privilege that a woman merely living with a man already has—or by Family Court, which is infamous for not prosecuting. By law, the children may now remain with the mother if she has to flee to shelter, instead of being farmed out by officials. Also planned by former State Senator Bellamy and State Senators Burstein and Winikow, are a family court reporting act, to ensure accurate statistics on wifebeating in the future, and a procedure to keep a copy of the order of protection on file at the local precinct, so the cop on the beat can act quickly.

PRECEDENT-SETTING REVERSALS

The Eschevarria divorce-for-cruelty case was fought through appeals by attorneys Marjory D. Fields and John C. Gray, Jr., and won precedent-setting reversals. A trial judge decided that two fierce beatings of face, head, and body in four years of marriage, of severity enough to cause Mrs. Eschevarria to flee for her life, were not enough for divorce on grounds of cruel and inhuman treatment. (Mr. Eschevarria agreed: He did not want the divorce.) Four of five justices of the appellate division affirmed. The lone dissenter, Justice Marcus G. Christ, held that "One beating may provide the ground for divorce," and subsequently, his colleagues on the Court of Appeals agreed. They ruled in favor of Mrs. Eschevarria—that one beating is sufficient grounds for divorce. This action marks great progress. It will reverse the customary fate of many a battered wife to come.[3]

We are seeing the beginning of a trend toward legally overturning traditional practices against the battered wife. One landmark lawsuit is the class action brought against the New York City Police Department and the Family Court by twelve battered wives. These women were unlawfully denied assistance by police who refused to arrest, and by Family Court personnel who denied them access to judges to seek orders of protection.

The opposition asked the Manhattan Supreme Court

to dismiss the lawsuit, claiming that their actions were legal. In what is believed to be the first judicial declaration of the rights of battered wives, the court in July 1977 ruled that the justice system has the obligation to protect battered wives, just as they do other victims of crime. (To follow the case, see Recommended Publications & Useful Addresses.)

The class action lawsuit was filed by MFY Legal Services, Inc., Brooklyn Legal Services Corporation B., the Center for Constitutional Rights, and the Legal Aid Society's Civil Division, all organizations representing indigent or public interest clients. It was undertaken "on behalf of all wives in similar positions," and is the first comprehensive challenge to a legal system that has been remiss in justice for victims of marital violence. It won't be the last. Many legal groups and women's groups around the country are monitoring this, waiting to use the precedent to help their own people.[4]

At this writing, although Family Court has not lost the lawsuit, it has improved somewhat unofficially, because of the exposure and publicity. The Police settled, and agreed that battered women should have their protection. A special course in understanding and effectiveness has been added at the Police Academy.

Raising the Public Consciousness

All this activity has laid the groundwork for a significant increase in public and private consciousness of the existence of wifebeating among all classes and for the need to end it. The Detroit Family Service Association conference on marital violence, mentioned earlier in the book, was the first of its type. It has been followed by many others, in many states, with many more on the calendar. Each one gets good press coverage. The result is that more wives now dare to reach out beyond the old taboo of family silence and get help. The need for reeducation was overwhelming; now it has begun. From Yale University to the University of Georgia there are symposia. The U.S. Commission on Civil Rights published a report on its January 1978 two-day consultation, "Battered Woman's Issues of Public Policy."

Here and there, even the traditional groups which had not been in the forefront of this movement are at last awakening and coming through. I foresee a trend inherent in two examples from religion and psychiatry/psychoanalysis.

On February 12, 1977, the American Friends Service Committee in New York held an all-day conference on the battered woman. About 10 or 15 percent of the six hundred participants from several states were men. Some participants included therapists, friends and relatives of wifebeaters and their wives, and former wifebeaters. At the meeting's close, it was determined that part of the group would evolve into a form of consciousness-raising group offered for husbands caught up in the pathology, and some would reach out to the city's clergy, to help them understand. The emphasis, obviously, had changed from a help-the-victim mentality to a treat-the-sick-criminal approach.

And then there is the example of the Karen Horney Clinic program of Psychological First-Aid for Victims of Senseless Violence. It is headed by Dr. Martin Symonds (once a policeman), a psychiatrist known and respected for his work in victimology and police training. When I began my research, I contacted the Victims of Violence program, hoping for some findings gleaned from the battered wives they were helping. But no. Their program was only for victims of rape and mugging—in other words, violence by *strangers*. There was no call for *home* violence, I was told. In the winter of 1977, however, the program added a battered-wives proposal.

True Community Spirit

There are other antiwifebeating programs now operating around the country that involve smooth cooperation and sensitivity from the community, police, the justice system, and the social agencies. Pima County, Arizona, has an excellent program, a harbinger, I hope, of a national trend. A discretionary grant from the federal Law Enforcement Assistance Administration

(LEAA) set up a Victim Witness Advocate Program, and included battered wives among the population of crime victims. A unique judicial process was instituted. In the Superior Court's Pre-Trial Release Program, a judge may release the abuser to a friend or relative's residence, and not permit him to contact his victim via telephone or in person during the proceedings. In contrast to the prevailing situation, the woman is kept informed at all times. Many a victim has requested treatment for the husband for alcohol or emotional problems, more so than punishment. And these treatment programs are widely available in the community.[5]

Communities showing the most progress have invariably also shown wide coordination of services. In St. Paul, there is cooperation instead of competition among the many social agencies, toward the goal of ending wifebeating in this generation. Says Gary Schoener of the Walk-In Counseling Center, who helped organize the consortium of these agencies: "We would like to teach other professionals who may come into contact with the problem how to spot it—dentists, for example—as case finders, how to communicate instead of sitting by and watching. Coordinating the hospitals, police, courts and social agencies has really paid off here."

This spirit has fostered many a creative program. For example, assault complaints are screened by a sympathetic investigator for the city attorney's office, Sgt. Dave Hubenette, who makes sure the woman understands her rights. In contrast to other communities where she has neither lawyer nor friend in court, here the investigator presents her case to the judge. Assault charges are never dropped—so a wifebeater cannot intimidate his victim into saying everything is all right now. There is always a follow-up. If the woman is too frightened (or too compassionate) to press charges, there is an alternative: Sgt. Hubenette will write a letter on official stationery, warning the wifebeater. Although "it has no legal teeth," it has "a good effect."

Assistant Attorney Rick Enga proposed the new Citizen's Dispute Diversionary Program, which went into effect in September 1976, patterned after a superlatively effective program in Kansas City. Enga says: "It provides the assault victim with immediate emotional support and gives the assailant an alternative to jail—choices of counseling or chemical dependency programs—all at an earlier stage, before actual prosecution. After the police arrive at the home, the assailant is told, 'Your options are arrest now or the Program.' It clears the air, avoids further hostility. If there is a repeat violation, then there will be a prosecution."

The St. Paul deputy police chief is also a state senator. William McCutcheon proposed legislation to authorize police on domestics call, where evidence of wifebeating is obvious but not witnessed, to order the assailant to leave the home for a specified amount of time—three hours or overnight, to guarantee the beating is stopped instantly and to cool off the assailant. (This is a form of the "shelters-for-men" concept, allowing the battered wife to rest in her own home, attending to her injuries, instead of fleeing.) This is not an arrest. The Department's goal is to be able to go to a domestics call just once, instead of the usual ten to fifteen times a year per family it is now. Hawaii has a similar procedure, which has indeed cut these calls drastically.

State Senator John Lewis also introduced legislation for pilot programs, community education, data collection, a legislative study commission, and appropriating money.

The county hospital emergency rooms are now documenting the wife assaults for what they are, not evading the crime by recording them as just "fractures." Then the victim is referred to a social worker who can explain her rights and options. Educational and training workshops are being presented by the consortium members to various disciplines. There is now a speaker's bureau. The police are equipped with a "domestics card," listing community resources, to be handed to the battered wife when police answer a call.

Shelters for Men

The concept of shelters for men began in an innovative program of Erin Pizzey, the British pioneer of the antiwifebeating movement. Her Chiswick House complex of refuges for battered wives had included a Boys' House for children of the wifebeater, and a Men's House.

The boys learned carpentry and other building skills, taught by volunteers who were, by their very caring, also giving one-to-one therapy influence. And a moving business was being planned, to keep the teenage boys profitably occupied.

Erin Pizzey speaks of the results: "All of the boys had been in trouble with the police for violence against other people before they came into our care, and . . . since that time they have not mugged anyone."

The Men's House is staffed by two men who are "experienced in dealing with acute problems of stress behavior." The house offers both sanctuary and meeting place to disturbed men. These men, who have mostly come from backgrounds where "violence was . . . a means of enforcing dominance or expressing need, can attend group therapy meetings or, indeed, be residents at the house."[6]

New Therapies

Innovative forms of therapy are being designed to reach the recalcitrant husband. Janet Geller, ACSW, center director and therapist at VIBS (Victim's Information Bureau of Suffolk) in Hauppauge, Long Island, evolved a method which, so far, has stopped the husband's violence as soon as the couple's counseling begins. The husband signs a contract for delaying the impulse to strike. Training Coordinator Nancy Lynn explains: "The therapist helps the couple identify when violence usually starts to escalate, to examine what point they have to look out for. The man then contracts to do something else to rechannel the anger. . . ." He can also call the VIBS twenty-four-hour hotline, and talk out the anger, a procedure "very much like an alcoholic's calling his supportive friend in AA when he feels his need for a drink is escalating."

VIBS is also making innovative strides in working with the children of these marriages. While the child is playing in the child-care room during parental counseling, its behavior and personality are noted and charted.

A more detailed study is planned; meanwhile, this information is often used to urge a reluctant father to join his wife in counseling.

The International Movement

All over the world, shelters and services are starting up. There is one reference (and only one at this writing) listing the activity in the nation and the world: Betsy Warrior's pamphlet, "Working on Wife Abuse" (see Recommended Publications).

Today there are shelters in Australia: Glebe, Sidney, Melbourne, Victoria, Brisbane, Hobart, Launceston, Perth, Queensland, Tasmania, and Western Australia. In Belgium: Brussels. In Canada: Calgary, Alberta; Victoria, British Columbia; Vancouver, British Columbia; Aldergrove, British Columbia; Windsor, Ontario; Saskatoon, Saskatchewan; and two in Toronto. There is a shelter in Paris, at least one in Scotland, Switzerland, and Denmark, and four in Germany. There is a halfway house, combined with rape crisis shelter, in Auckland, New Zealand, and several in Holland. Amsterdam has an excellent one, mentioned in chapter 6. Inquiries come to Betsy Warrior from all over the world.

Erin Pizzey wrote me that since her book *Scream Quietly or the Neighbours Will Hear*[7] was published in France, "it sold out to groups of French women trying to establish refuge." It looks, she said, as if soon "there will be refuge all over."

The world's established church image of the woman as subservient to the man is changing. In Norway, for instance, the Lutheran Bishops' Conference has resolved that women can no longer be asked "to be submissive" to their men. "The Apostle Paul's admonition merely reflected the mores of his time and . . . is not eternally binding for the church, the bishops declared," reports *Trinity Parish Newsletter*. "With the advent of the women's liberation movement, the patriarchal social order is more and more being questioned by an ethical consciousness in accord with the Christian understanding of the value and rights of all mankind. Today the Christian Church must realize this basic view by working towards women's liberation to the best of its Christian understanding."[8]

Federal Legislation

Perhaps the best news of all is this: Awareness of this social phenomenon has reached Congress. Legislation that seems to stem from a sensitive understanding of the problem was drafted in cooperation with sociologist Dr. Veronica Maz and the House of Ruth shelter in Washington. The proposed bill was sponsored by Representatives Lindy Boggs (Dem.-La.) and Newton I. Steers, Jr., Republican from the affluent, socially aware Montgomery County, Maryland. In the Senate, Edward Kennedy (D.-Ma.) and Wendell Anderson (R.-Min.) introduced a similar bill. Co-sponsors are Senators Humphrey, Javits, Abourezk, Hatfield, Matsurnaga, and McIntyre.

I was invited to say a few words at a luncheon at the Speakers Dining Room in the Capitol on March 15, 1977. The occasion, well covered by the media, was "to raise consciousness," according to the sponsors, who sensed the Congress might be ready to consider the problem of conjugal crime: "Remember child abuse legislation—it took so many years for it to pass, although the public seems to be more aware these days."

The bill, dated June 21 and entitled "Domestic Violence Prevention & Treatment Act of 1977," authorizes the Department of Health, Education & Welfare (HEW) to establish a grant to develop methods of prevention and treatment, using not less than 60 percent of the money for the actual work (shelters and hotlines) itself. An information clearinghouse would also be established. Appropriations will be $15 million for the fiscal year 1979, $20 million for 1980, $25 million for 1981. NIMH (National Institutes of Mental Health) would coordinate an effectiveness study of state and local laws dealing with domestic violence.

The bill was modified in various ways over time and attracted many additional sponsors. The shelter movement was shocked when the bill lost by only a few votes. Some legislators who usually cared about humanitarian causes did not vote for it—simply from lack of awareness. Toward the end of 1979, a new Domestic Violence bill, HR 2977, with a modest amount of funding to be processed through state bureaucracy before reaching the direct-service providers, came up for a vote again.

On September 7, Representative Barbara A. Mikulski (Md.), who had attended the March luncheon, introduced her "Family Violence and Treatment Act," to use supported volunteers at the local level. Her bill would establish within the existing agency ACTION (which covers the Peace Corps and VISTA volunteers) a new National Center for Community Action Against Family Violence. Its purpose: to train and place volunteers in community organizations against family violence, act as a clearinghouse for information, and maintain a national toll-free hotline for instant help or information. The existing child abuse reporting systems would also be used to obtain wifebeating data. The Secretary of HEW would contract with a coalition of National Private Voluntary groups with a demonstrated interest in family violence for a two-year evaluation of how HEW-assisted programs are actually working at the local level.

Congresswoman Mikulski read into the Congressional Record, "I am convinced that the programs that work best are those initiated by citizens of the community. . . . By using the existing administrative structure of ACTION, we avoid creating a new federal bureaucracy."

The two basic differences in proposed legislation are explained by Congressman Steers: "My bill would be administered by the National Institutes of Mental Health. Ms. Mikulski's would be administered by ACTION. The basic thrust of my bill for which 60 percent of its funds must be spent is a provision for the contracting out of demonstration grants to be used for testing out ways of preventing and treating domestic violence [spouse abuse]. . . . The main thrust of Ms. Mikulski's measure would be to provide training and stipends for volunteers working in the emergency shelters. The intent of my bill is for the demonstration grant money to go to those working directly with battered spouses. . . . I believe that both the demonstration grant and volunteer training and stipend components are necessary to further the existence and expansion of the emergency shelters for battered wives. As is usually the case, a committee will hold hearings on several measures relating to the same topic and then take the best provisions from those measures coming up with a new committee version. In addition, I should note that I anticipate the introduction by other members of Congress of other bills relating to this topic." Hearings will begin winter/spring 1978.

Problems

Despite the encouraging progress that has been made, the crusade has a long way to go. Three problems stand out.

The most universal one is concern for the future direction of the movement. The other two relate to the occasional strong negative attitudes, both organized and individual, expressed against helping. These are lessening, but when they occur they can be devastating.

Women's groups that have struggled to provide services for the battered wife, from the days when there was no public education, are concerned that people who never knew or cared about the crusade will turn it into a pork barrel, much as happened with the Medicaid-paid nursing homes, or with rape programs in which money went into research grants instead of services for the victims. They are concerned that the same traditional social services that kept the battered woman where she was will seize the advantage and install themselves again.

Betsy Warrior expresses that concern: "The attitude toward this issue . . . by professionals and bureaucrats administering these traditional institutions . . . I believe . . . is being seen by [women's groups] as merely a new way to obtain funding and jobs, a new area to exploit for profit and sinecures."

An example of this occurred in New York City, just as the various hardworking women's groups had joined forces in the New York Coalition for Battered Women. Mayor Beame announced, a few weeks before elections, that his Task Force on Rape had secured a $300,000 CEDA grant for counseling battered women in four city hospitals. But the women's groups had been excluded from the grant-writing process, they charged, and the grant might easily take the major share of money available in the field, thereby closing out any independent efforts of women's groups to obtain funds.[9] And the Coalition was never consulted or informed or offered job descriptions. Neither was the Care and Treatment Committee of the Task Force itself—the one that had recommended women's groups could do the job better. Instead of hiring from the many experienced, dedicated personnel available in the Coalition, the salaries quickly went to new, inadequately screened people without a background or even sensitivity to the problem.

There were additional charges from two women. One taped the brief training session and then resigned with a well-circulated letter of protest at its sexism and insensitivity. One of the male Counselor Advocates, for example, insisted that "some women enjoy being beaten." The trainer, whose background was not in this field, agreed that some women are masochists, and other trainees agreed. One of the counselor trainees, it was charged, admitted to having been a wifebeater himself for fifteen years.

Betsy Warrior explains another "establishment tactic, which is . . . to obtain thousands of dollars to do a study to see if the problem exists or if a shelter is needed. If this money were simply used for a refuge, evidence of the need would be quickly demonstrated through use of the facility."[10]

Beyond the expected apathy, there has been some actual hostility to shelters, surprisingly enough from women! Often an organized, fundamentalist church group was behind it. In one city in Texas, for instance, $50,000 was proposed in the city budget to help the one thousand wifebeating cases per month. But it was sent down to defeat by strong antifeminist women who believed the wife should "just get up and leave. The city has no business interfering in the private lives of families."

An attorney with the shelter group told me, "We weren't prepared to handle the unexpected red herring. The opposition was economic, political, and religious,

235

claiming, 'If we give money to feminists, they will encourage women to leave their homes and destroy the Christian family.' What is sorely needed now is people who are in religion saying, 'But the church doesn't support wifebeating. It's the batterer that destroys the family.' "

The humanitarians were stunned by the refusal of the city council to help fund services for battered wives. But they managed to keep the good work going despite the obstacles, by setting up a women's help hotline.

Then there is the minority of unfriendly hecklers who often disrupt radio and TV talk shows on the subject. One or more of the following responses from listeners are predictable: A man bragging that "all his women like it"; a man asking what's being done for battered *husbands;* a woman defiantly claiming that she needs a hit now and then; a woman protesting furiously that other women are not as amiable as she, or as self-sufficient, and so they deserve what they get.

I find that if the guest speaker can question the heckler to detail what he or she really means, it becomes evident it is not actual wifebeating as defined in this book that is being argued for, but rather a philosophical exercise in power struggle. I have noticed lately, however, a continued trend toward awareness of the problem and less need for callers to joust defensively with antiwifebeating speakers. Recently, the very worst type of heckler is a man that insists defensively his particular provocation was surely worth meting out a beating, wasn't it?

Susan Maurer and Enid Keljik, from the New York NOW Task Force on the Battered Wife, both veterans of the call-in radio program, suggest the following in rebuttals:

1. Don't get angry.
2. Make the heckler repeat the hostility. It will be toned down.
3. Acknowledge that you hear the other viewpoint. Pick out something you can deal with.
4. Then go on to mention the four to six points you want to get across.
5. Come prepared. It would be good to have docu-

mented several examples of the runaround battered wives have received from the local system, which have displayed attitudes similar to those of the caller instead of giving the woman her legal right to protection. Point to dramatic proofs as to why the woman who wants to leave is, in fact, prevented from saving herself.

6. This is an argument for the most hardened anti-woman heckler: A program to save battered women will also save the heckler and friends from another generation of violent teenagers—teenagers who, having learned that people consider wifebeating acceptable, will extend the violence they learned at home to strangers.

Potential

The significant impetus evidenced by this growing social movement in 1978 seems to augur far-reaching beneficial effects.

This one, small, brave movement, which initially fought so hard against such odds, has the potential of reforming all the many systems that made wifebeating the most unreported crime in America, systems that touch the lives of everyone. The complacent establishment is now being forced to reexamine itself, as the great imbalances in the treatment of criminal versus victim are being exposed, publicized, and even taken to court.

As Enid Keljik testified at the New York City Council hearings, the façade of services and protection generate confusion for the battered wife, her husband, and community, who prefer to believe that the issue is being taken care of.

The church can hardly avoid taking a second look at the façade of Christian caring it extended to the battered wife. Of the thirty pastors known to be responsive to social issues, first contacted by the American Service Committee (AFSC) Clergy Outreach, only seven were caring enough to respond.

In affluent Westchester County, 700 invitations went out to religious professionals for an ecumenical conference on what the church can do about wifebeating. Only 30 people responded, most of them nuns. One cathedral has postponed its conference for three years for fear of lack of support. A major church's regional office had allotted a few thousand dollars for outreach to its many congregations and rescinded the pittance. Changing the wifebeating pattern among Christians, it seemed, was not directly related to the work of the Lord. But that notion calls for prayerful rethinking. The greatest potential would be realized if the church revived its ancient tradition of safe refuge on behalf of the fleeing victim and her children.

As this problem is increasingly aired, more and more middle-class victims will dare to speak out, which is in itself enough to end much of the middle-class wifebeating because such a man is so bound up in his reputation as a "nice guy," a civilized being. As he learns that society no longer looks the other way, that he is considered psychologically sick and a criminal, he will have to change for the sake of his own self-respect.

Even the nonwifebeater, as he realizes this pathology exists, may be inspired to give some thought to his expectations of the man-woman relationship and of dangers of clinging to a rigid, role-bound stereotype of uncommunicating, macho masculinity. He may begin to explore the pleasures of tenderness, nurturing, and freeing his emotional life.

The wifebeater counts on the battered woman's state of helplessness. Traditionally, she has been helpless. He also counts on the traditional noninterference and noncastigation from good people and good institutions. However, concerned citizens are changing this, and the movement, I predict, will continue to flourish.

Recommendations

The pathology of wifebeating could so easily be lessened if only everyone would take a small step toward correcting it. Change for the better could result from supporting the new laws that are being proposed, or announcing a personal stand that marital violence is wrong and not a matter for embarrassed laughter, or making as committed a step as giving supportiveness, time, or money to a shelter project.

I call upon the churches—where the acceptance of wifebeating has been fostered—to realize that even today the churches have not been in the vanguard of the antiwifebeating movement. Determine to form a group of volunteers from within the congregation (perhaps banding together with other congregations to ensure anonymity and security) who will give emergency overnight shelter to a battered woman and her children fleeing from marital violence. As a start, to interest volunteers, invite a women's group offering services to battered wives—legal, advocacy with courts, counseling, or an overworked shelter—to come and give a workshop. Your local YWCA, Family Service Association or chapter of NOW could undoubtedly direct you to these groups. If there is nothing at all like this in your community, there is practical help in the Recommended Publications at the end of this book.

Concerned clergymen might preach a sermon verifying that Christ did not endorse wifebeating and neither does he. Speak out from the pulpit and face to face that wifebeating is sinful. And when a battered wife comes to you, don't exclude her husband from your pastoral counseling.

Guarantee help for the offspring of wifebeating unions. Publicize a phone number such a child can call and be assured anonymity if desired, and confidentiality, where the child can unburden itself about the horrors in its household. The daily nightmare will be somewhat eased if there is a nurturing, trustworthy adult the child can talk to—and be believed by.

As documented earlier in this book, in many violent homes babies were the result of forced sexual relations after an assault, of sex used as brute power, not love or communication. In significant numbers of case histories, wifebeating became a serious problem with the first pregnancy. The unwelcomed child's presence then ensured continued violence.

Every baby has a right to be wanted by both parents,

239

who are both interested in and able to give care and love. Every woman has a right not to be pregnant if those conditions do not obtain. I commend society's recognition of these facts.

The need for reeducation of inhumane attitudes is vital. A common refrain among wifebeaters is that "woman is supposed to serve man." If household chores were perceived as shared responsibility he'd have almost no excuse for anger and assault.

A recent University of California pilot study on household and mental health[11] showed that the vast majority of women still do the bulk of household work, with "quiet resignation," even when they have outside jobs; that, in addition, many do the "men's work" of mowing the lawn, keeping accounts, and shoveling snow; that many find it less trouble to do their husbands' and children's share of chores than "to go after them."

Professor Murray A. Straus, specialist in family violence, has observed the "antagonism between the sexes engendered by sex role differentiation and inequality."[12] He also notes that sexism contributes to the frequency of wifebeating because society puts the full burden of childrearing on women, denying them equal job opportunity, perpetuating the myth that wife and mother are the only roles worthwhile for a woman, and that raising a child without a father in the house is necessarily damaging.

What is needed, according to Professor Straus, is recognition that "both women's liberation and male liberation are necessary to effect a substantial reduction in wifebeating."

Specifically, I would like to make recommendations in the following areas:

COMMUNITY INVOLVEMENT

The most effective helping will come about through community action, whether on an organizational or concerned citizen level. I highly recommend the consortium idea in use in St. Paul or the Coalition project in New York City to coordinate activities and minimize wasted time and effort.

MONITORING JUDGES

A precedent has already been set for the effectiveness of representatives from various women's groups appearing at court, in a nondisruptive manner, to monitor the judiciousness of the presiding judge when sentencing a wifebeater. Although an entrenched chauvinist or lenient judge might be annoyed at being unexpectedly exposed to public awareness, in this democracy it is every citizen's right to monitor him.

If enough serious citizens show interest in this procedure, a local newspaper may be interested in following the results, naming names and publishing photographs, ensuring justice for victim as well as assailant.

HOUSING THE WIFEBEATER INSTEAD

It is ironic that the wounded victim must leave home while the assailant remains to enjoy its comforts. Once the victim is assured that society has a means of protecting the woman, it seems sensible to turn attention to the one who caused the need for protection. I recommend alternate housing for the man, not a jail, not on his record, but removed from his target. A place to cool off and get psychiatric or consciousness-raising help. Other types of criminals have access to rehabilitation programs, why not this one?

SHELTERS

I believe the best way to start a shelter is to get in contact with the women who are already running an effective one. Arrange to visit one. Talk to staff and residents. Realize that each community will present different problems to overcome. Know your own community.

Some shelters have compiled their history of beginnings, wrong moves and all, complete with samples of all the legal and tax forms necessary, intake forms, budgets, public relations, etc., and will make them available for a small fee (see Recommended Publications). Concerned feminist groups should make sure they have a part in the planning stages of shelters, and a place on the board of directors.

In addition to learning from others, I suggest the planners of a new shelter consider the following:

1. Effective public relations and reeducation, community understanding and cooperation are essential. Those include police, hospitals, social agencies, graduate schools, concerned legislators, and the neighbors.

2. The lack of precise documentation is one reason there were no wifebeating statistics for so long, and therefore no acknowledgment and no help. Useful records include places where the battered wife sought help previously and their effectiveness; where the shelter sought help for her and the effectiveness of that help; the resident's evaluation of the shelter and her suggestions; follow-up. Fund-granters always want statistics. Government always wants "research," and will allot monies for it. With thoughtful intake and follow-up forms, you can provide this "research" without diverting funds for actual protection of the battered wife.

3. A useful service adjunct is a regular meeting schedule for women (anonymous, if preferred) whose marriages have not yet become regularly or severely violent but where there is still marked apprehension. This will add to the required "research." Cooperate with a counseling service, located elsewhere, which can provide violence-preventing couple counseling. Consciousness-raising for husbands will be helpful, too.

4. Announce through the school system the availability of anonymous telephone counseling for frightened children of battering marriages. This will also constitute "research," practically cost-free, which has never been done and is urgently needed.

5. A priority in your budget is child advocacy. Older children can be very disruptive to both staff and residents. Some shelters have learned from experience the maximum age for boys must be ten or twelve. Some have found alternate temporary shelter for boys over this age elsewhere. There must be space for children's energies away from the adults, under guidance of a

secure, concerned play leader accustomed to troubled youngsters.

6. A useful staff or volunteer person is a house mother who mothers the mothers and (re-)introduces them to nurturing and baby care. There is so much battered out of the battered mother she may have little left to give.

7. Inner peace. Someone on call who can teach meditation is a great blessing for both staff and residents in reducing stress and habits of stress, such as reliance on cigarettes, tranquilizers, and coffee. Hatha Yoga can also be a good focal point of the day in an otherwise grim, boring, or crisis-ridden existence. In some communities, volunteers also teach martial arts.

8. Inner growth. One of the great inner obstacles preventing the battered woman from daring to risk independence is her dependency and dread of loneliness. A fringe benefit to meditation and Hatha Yoga is a new perspective on loneliness. It can be welcomed solitude. Any opportunity for alternate ways to old habits will aid her inner growth. I also recommend a book, for its practical chapters on overcoming depression, loneliness, and inertia: *The Book of Hope*. Psychiatrist Helen De Rosis, who is also a training analyst at the American Institute for Psychoanalysis of the Karen Horney Psychoanalytic Clinic, is co-author with Victoria Pellegrino.

9. I would like to see a version of the old underground railroad, to spirit away the victims of the most tenacious assailants. Perhaps through the new shelter network, women can move far enough away to assure safety and anonymity.

LEGISLATION

A way must be found to guarantee protection and anonymity for battered women who have escaped from their tormentors and started new lives. There is too much history of well-meaning but ignorant people who decided the unregenerated assailant was "sorry" or "rehabilitated" and so cooperated with him in his relocation of the victim. When the wife needs references for credit, jobs, welfare, or child care, or further education, there is always the danger that the information may get into the wrong hands. Back in the 1880s the feminist Mrs. Cobb suggested that alimony/child support be paid by the former wifebeater to a central office, which would get the subsistence money to the former victim in confidentiality. Child support or separate maintenance should be scrupulously enforced, because the woman who separated from her husband because of wifebeating dares do nothing about enforcement herself.

All agencies that encounter wifebeating in their regular work—doctors, dentists, public health nurses, hospitals, social service agencies, courts—should be mandated to report the crime for what it is, not "family disturbance" or "felonious assault." Continued identification is necessary.

Some of these suggestions may become law in New York State in the 1980s. Governor Carey appointed a 25-member Task Force on Domestic Violence, headed by former State Senator Karen Burstein, now on the Public Service Commission, and Marjory Fields, an attorney often mentioned in this book. Pertinent legislation is expected to result from their recommendations. Concerned women's groups and humanitarian groups should contact their legislators and give information necessary to draft responsible bills, and then support the proposed legislation. It is a basic human right to be free from any sort of violence. Each concerned community can shape its own legislation regarding shelters and supportive services.

Among the most serious and immediately feasible political action that can be undertaken now is to correlate the relationship between unwelcomed pregnancy and wifebeating. The wife who finds her husband displaying his feelings about pregnancy by beating her has the legal right of *choice* of terminating the pregnancy as well as the relationship. She should not be disenfranchised if she's poor. People who are against wifebeating should let Ms. Patricia Harris, secretary of HEW, their senators, and the White House know how they feel about this discrimination against women, against poor women, by those who would legislate to deny them access to their legal right to safe abortion, or at the very least, a choice.

It's very possible that some well-intentioned people will object to Medicaid termination of pregnancy, saying that a woman should have considered alternative methods first. But they don't realize that wifebeaters typically do not allow birth control, frequently conclude their violence with a marital rape, and that the onset of pregnancy frequently is provocation for continuing the wifebeating. It is essential, if the idea of wife-beating is to become unthinkable, that all women value themselves—and that society values them—as full human beings, with right of choice over body, life and destiny, and not solely as child bearers subjected to their husband's violence or society's whims.

If we do not convey this understanding to our legislators, a terrible trend may worsen. Those who would impose their private belief in enforced pregnancy upon everyone, regardless of *their* private beliefs, have become increasingly militant in the last few years, and are heavily funded by powerful organizations—one powerful, prosperous church in particular. The pro-choice people are nonviolent and depend on small contributions from private citizens. The anti-choice faction has used threats, violence and vandalism, even initiated a move to overturn the Constitution. Their unrelenting pressure upon legislators is seen in continued attempts to pass restrictions on Medicaid and other programs affecting women.

Happily, there is legislation that will greatly aid the battered wife who escapes and wants to start a new life, not dependent on welfare or infrequent charity. *The NOW York Woman,* a newsletter, reported in its March 1977 issue: "Senator Birch Bayh (Dem.-Ind.) recently introduced the Displaced Homemakers Act of 1977, S.418, to aid homemakers who, through death, divorce, or other loss of family income, find themselves in the labor market with no training or marketable skills.

"The bill provides for (1) the establishment of multipurpose service centers to offer job training and placement services, (2) counseling and referral services in health care, legal problems, and financial management, and (3) outreach information services to

245

acquaint these women with existing assistance problems. More than 2.2 million women are estimated to fall into the categories covered by this bill. Congresswoman Yvonne Braithwaite Burke (Dem.-Ca.) has introduced a companion bill in the house." This is legislation that became reality.

An innovative means of funding certain existing shelters is now law in the states of Florida, Montana, Ohio and Pennsylvania. An additional tax of from $5 to $10 is added to marriage licenses. Presently Connecticut, Kansas and West Virginia are working on similar legislation. Write your senators and representatives. If you don't know their names, call your local newspaper or the local League of Women Voters.

On a local level, what's needed is simplification of the process of getting basic protection.

These are some procedures which might be explored: A Bar Association review of the competency of judges to publicize the proviolence, antivictim ones; educational programs for police; a separate domestic violence section in court, operating around the clock; baby-sitting facilities in court; penalties for the wife-beater's ignoring the hearing, and some means of not requiring witnesses to keep coming to dismissed hearings; allowing the battered wife to have a lawyer and/or a friend with her in court; victim-advocates who will clearly explain the complex procedures as well as the victim's rights. (See Marjory Fields's booklet, Recommended Publications and Useful Addresses.)

FUNDING

Three of the pioneers in the crusade against wife-beating are either without funding or with inadequate funding. The Women's Advocates' House, in St. Paul, Minnesota, struggles along from crisis to crisis, funded but not adequately or permanently. AWAIC can operate only limited hours. Growth & Life Center has operated with no funding at all. These groups, which began the movement in America, should not have to struggle to keep going with their good work.

Groups seeking to get funds are always asked for

statistics and for proof of need. I hope this book will reduce the need of scurrying for the usual nonexistent statistics. The proof of need is echoed in Erin Pizzey's and Betsy Warrior's statement, "Just open the shelters. They'll fill up."

Before funds are used to make "studies," shelters and supportive services should be established. Their records are built-in studies. Money doesn't have to be appropriated for this as an additional expense. It would be more valuable to study the perpetrators and the system that devalues wives and encourages the crime, in order to help society become nonviolent.

Areas of worthwhile study are: why traditional supportive services fail and how they can be rehabilitated; why the public attitude has been embarrassed laughter, how that is changing, and what it takes to raise public consciousness; the effect of sexual counseling (away from sex as a means of domination) on domestic peacefulness; follow-up studies on wifebeater's future relationships; what is most effective in changing the wifebeater's self-righteousness about his behavior; what makes for survivorship in former victims; and how best to help the children of these marriages.

We are past the point of researching whether the wifebeating problem exists or whether the battered wife is a true victim. If a woman wants help, she should be able to get it at last.

It is time this loyally hidden family skeleton be taken out of the closet everywhere. The exposure has begun. Society, down the ages, has left the full responsibility for a solution up to the victim and refused to help her. The problem is still up to the victim to resolve, but increasingly now she will have a way to help herself. In enlightened communities, society is beginning to cooperate with *her,* not with her assailant.

Now there is the beginning of a happy ending to this grim history of man's inhumanity to woman—happier than I ever imagined when I undertook this work. My avowed intention had been to try to wake up the public, the helping professions, and the legislatures, and spur them to plan immediately to make up for lost time, and so prevent the next beating, the next killing, the next generation conditioned to repeat the tragedy of their abused and abusive parents.

As time has moved forward, however, this chronicle has also developed encouraging evidence that these audiences are beginning to be reached.

As I sat in the historic old Friends Meeting House, in the midst of some six hundred caring women and men gathered for the Conference of Concern About the Battered Woman, I was so moved. I felt joyous. Here were people who acknowledged that the problem was real, and serious, and who cared enough to intend to do something about it.

Let us continue. Join us in furthering this good beginning. Count yourself among the increasing numbers whose purpose is to put an end to marital violence in this generation.

Appendixes

Directory of Over Three Hundred Shelters for Battered Wives and Their Children, Including Hotline Telephone Numbers

Some numbers given are not the shelter building's actual number, but the answering service or connecting referral service—necessary for screening and security. Some shelters do not want their addresses publicized, and this need has been respected.

All shelters accept a battered wife's young children accompanying her—with a few exceptions, as indicated. Most give priority to local residents, but won't turn away a terrorized woman who makes it to their doorstep—with some exceptions, as noted.

Most shelters were started by devoted feminists who struggled long and hard to answer this need, and include comprehensive supportive services from specially selected, deeply understanding, experienced people. You can call them for information or counseling and legal service, even if you are not planning to stay there. Caution: If a need for refuge in the near future is anticipated, do not wait until the emergency to contact. Phone numbers and admission eligibility conditions may change. Any correspondence with a shelter should include a self-addressed, stamped envelope, and, if possible, a small donation. Shelters tend to be understaffed and underfunded. It is indicative of the growing change in awareness that some shelters listed here are traditional refuges for other categories of needy people, which formerly excluded fleeing battered wives and children.

New shelters are being created every month. To find

a new one nearer you, contact the closest one in this listing and inquire.

ALABAMA

MOBILE: (205) 471-1771. Penelope House, Inc. P.O. Box 6871 (zip 36606).

MONTGOMERY: (Contact police or social services for phone). Domestic Abuse Shelter, Inc., P.O. Box 4752 (zip 36606).

ARIZONA

GLENDALE: (602) 939-6798. Faith House, 4506 West Citrus Way (zip 85301). Capacity: twenty-one. Special requirements: residents must need the Alanon program (husband has problems with alcohol or drugs) and attend the Alanon house meetings.

PHOENIX: (602) 263-1113. Rainbow Retreat, 513 W. Latham (zip 85003). Capacity: Thirteen to fifteen. Women have fled here from as far away as New Jersey. This shelter was originally for victims of alcoholic husbands only; now that restriction is lifted. Effective program of counseling for the wifebeater; 64 percent have requested it. If wife plans to return, a mutual meeting is arranged away from Retreat. Next priorities: Outreach and child counseling.

PHOENIX: (602) 258-5344. Sojourner Center. P.O. Box 2649 (zip 85602).

SCOTTSDALE: (602) 949-7256. Friends-of-the-Family, 6825 E. Osborne Rd. (zip 85251).

TUCSON: (602) 792-1929. Tucson Center for Women and Children, P.O. Box 942 (zip 85701). Capacity: eight. No sons over age twelve. One-week limit. Women with other problems also admitted. New Outreach Program, under CETA, Title VI, reaching those who feel "cultural barriers to using agency-type services in times of crisis." Bilingual, male-female teams, "unidentified as either welfare or law-enforcement connected," will offer community education, counseling and crisis intervention in the home. . . . From the brochure: "We have certain expectations of anyone who stays at the Center. If someone is not comfortable with these general terms for living and working together, we will talk and work out agreed-upon changes. If attempts to encourage a person to assume more responsibility for herself lead nowhere, the woman will be asked to leave. If you disagree with this policy, you are welcome to raise objections at any meeting." I have found that this philosophy typifies the thinking of many shelters. The following food philosophy is unique, though, and I heartily endorse it: "The mind and body are not only related, but a person's physical health directly influences her state of mind. We do not advocate the use of sugar or caffeine within this crisis setting. We do not supply foodstuff with additives, chemicals or sugar. Since all of these affect the body and mind negatively, we also do not want these stored in the house."

CALIFORNIA

APTOS: (408) 476-1489. Mariposa House—Battered Women Shelter Project, P.O. Box 1123 (zip 95003).

AUBURN: (916) 885-8406. Women Encouraging Enterprise & Development (WEED), Station A, Box 111 (zip 95603).

BERKELEY: (415) 849-2314. Berkeley Women's Refuge, 2134 Allison Way (zip 94704).

CANOGA PARK: (213) 887-6589. Haven Hills, Inc. P.O. Box 66 (zip 91305).

FAIRFIELD: (707) 429-HELP. Solano Center for Battered Women, P.O. Box 2051 (zip 94533).

HAYWARD: (415) 881-1244. Emergency Shelter Program, Inc. 24518 Mission Blvd., (zip 94544).

LIVERMORE: (415) 433-1955. Tri-Valley Haven for Women, P.O. Box 188 (zip 94550).

LONG BEACH: (213) 437-4663. Women's Shelter, P.O. Box 4222 (zip 90804).

LOS ANGELES COUNTY: (213) 681-2626. Haven House. P.O. Box 2007, Pasadena (zip 91107). Ruth Slaughter, director. This pioneer shelter for victims of alcoholics has added ten new beds for battered women without that restriction. Stay extended to thirty days.

MERCED: (209) 726-7549. Merced County Commission on the Status of Women: Friends of Battered Women, 2150 M Street (zip 95340).

MONTEREY: (408) 649-0834. YWCA Women Against Domestic Violence, P.O. Box 1362 (zip 93940).

NORTH HOLLYWOOD: (213) 781-2722. Rosasharon, P.O. Box 4583 (zip 91607).

PLACERVILLE: (916) 622-1235. Women United Against Battering, P.O. Box 893 (zip 95667).

OAKLAND: (415) 444-7233. A Safe Place, P.O. Box 275 (zip 94604).

ORANGE COUNTY: (714) 992-1931. Women's Transitional Living Center, P.O. Box 6103, Orange (zip 92667). Susan Naples, director. Capacity: eighteen. Thirty-day limit. Multiservices: child psychologist, psychiatrist, individual and group counseling, legal aid, advocacy through bureaucracy. Center sells a booklet on details—mistakes and all—on how it got started, including samples of necessary red-tape.

RIVERSIDE: (714) 686-HELP. Coalition for Alternatives to Domestic Violence, P.O. Box 910 (zip 92502).

SACRAMENTO: (916) 446-7811. Mother's Emergency Stress Service, 2515 J St., (zip 95816).

SACRAMENTO: (916) 446-7811. Womanspace Shelter for Battered Women, P.O. Box 106994 (zip 95816).

SAN FRANCISCO: (415) 626-9343-4. La Casa de las Madres, Box 137 (zip 94102). Capacity: thirty.

SAN FRANCISCO: (415) 431-1180. San Francisco Women's Center, 63 Brady St., (zip 94103).

SAN JOSE: (408) 251-6655. The Women's Alliance (WOMA), 1509 E. Santa Clara St., (zip 95116).

SAN LUIS REY: (714) 757-5300. Women's Resource Center, Inc., 4070 Mission Ave., Rm. 220 (zip 92068).

SAN MATEO: (415) 342-0850. San Mateo Women's Shelter, P.O. Box 652 (zip 94401).

SANTA BARBARA: (805) 968-2556. Violence in the Family Project, Community Action Commission, 735 State St. (zip 93102).

SANTA MONICA: (213) 399-9228. Sojourn, c/o Ocean Park Community Center, 245 Hill St. (zip 90405).

SAN PEDRO: (213) 547-9343. Harbor Area YWCA Refuge and Services for Victims of Domestic Violence, 437 W. 9th St. (zip 90731).

SAN RAFAEL: (415) 924-6616. Marin Abused Women's Services, P.O. Box 2924 (zip 94901).

COLORADO

COLORADO SPRINGS: (303) 633-4601. Battered Women Services, 12 N. Meade (zip 80907).

COMMERCE CITY: (303) 289-4441. Women's Assistance Services, P.O. Box 385, 6571 Kearney (zip 80037).

DENVER: 303) 832-7826. Brandum Guest House, 1260 Pennsylvania (zip 80203).

DENVER: (303) 399-0082. Columbine Center, 1331 Columbine (zip 80206).

DENVER: (303) 338-4703. Safe House, 1264 Race St. (zip 80206).

DENVER: (303) 333-6626. York Street Center, 1632 York St. (zip 80206). Dr. Kathryn Saltzman, director. This is not an actual shelter building but a service that will arrange crisis housing in volunteer homes and other facilities for up to two weeks for residents of the city and county of Denver. "We have not had to turn anyone away." If wifebeater is willing, couple counseling is available.

EVERGREEN: (303) 232-0996. Women in Crisis, P.O. Box 1955 (zip 80439).

GRAND JUNCTION: (303) 243-0190. Battered Women Project, c/o Women's Resource Center, 4th & Rood (zip 81501).

GRAND JUNCTION: (303) 242-0190. Battered Woman Project, 205 N. 4th (zip 81501).

LAKEWOOD: (303) 232-0996. Women in Crisis, 1426 Pierce St. (zip 80214).

CONNECTICUT

BRIDGEPORT: (205) 334-6154. Women Helping Women Shelter, c/o YWCA of Greater Bridgeport, 1862 East Main (zip 06610). The YMCA is planning counseling for the wifebeater.

HARTFORD: (203) 527-0550, hotline. Hartford Interval House for Battered Women, c/o 814 Asylum Ave. (zip 06105).

HARTFORD: The Salvation Army Emergency Shelter, which has been taking in a variety of homeless people, is now also accepting battered wives and their children. However, it does not want its phone mentioned, "because our capacity is limited and all local social services know about us."

MERIDEN: (203) 238-1501. Meriden-Wallingford Battered Women's Task Force, Box 636 (zip 06450).

NEW BRITAIN: (203) 229-6939. Prudence Crandall Center for Women, P.O. Box 895 (zip 06051). Capacity: a six-room apartment with three bedrooms, not exclusively for battered wives and children. Funding requires serving only a small area of the city.

NEW HAVEN: (203) 789-8104. New Haven Project for Battered Women, P.O. Box 1329, (zip 06505). Accommodates twenty women and their children. 60-day maximum stay. Child Day Care Worker. Gentle male volunteer.

PUTNAM: (203) 928-6569. Screening number of United Social & Mental Health Services, Inc. Shelter will begin with a donated town trailer in safe location, patrolled by constables. Serves twenty-one-town area.

NOTE: A useful reference for future shelters is Connecticut Task Force on Abused Women, c/o YWCA, 135 Broad Street, Hartford, CT. 06105.

DELAWARE

ARDENTOWN: (302) 475-8424. New Beginnings, Arden House, 2210 Swiss Lane (zip 19810).

MILFORD: (302) 422-8058. Families in Transition, 121 S. Walnut (zip 19963).

WILMINGTON: (302) 658-3555, c/o YWCA, 908 King St. (zip 19810).

FLORIDA

FORT LAUDERDALE: (305) 761-2143, approx. 8:00 A.M. to 11:00 P.M. (answered by the Victim Advocates Office, 1300 W. Broward Blvd., zip 33312) and (305) 761-2415 (answered by the police, who will locate a victim advocate). There is no shelter for battered women as such, but two alternatives: Women in Distress, funded by Broward County, can shelter about twenty-seven women (not exclusively battered) but no children. The Salvation Army can take about five or six battered women with children for a few days. Says Jim Fogerty, civilian member of the police department: "Awareness of this problem is increasing. As problem manifests, there will probably be additional help available."

JACKSONVILLE: (904) 345-3114. Hubbard House, 1213 Hubbard St. (zip 32207). Capacity: eighteen to twenty beds, plus couches. "For women in active danger of physical abuse, with their children, from anyplace in the country." Offers group and individual counseling, including for the children.

JACKSONVILLE: (904) 354-6681. YWCA of Jacksonville, 325 E. Duval St. (zip 32202).

ORLANDO: (305) 628-1227. Spouse Abuse, Inc., c/o We Care, Inc. 112 Pasadena Place (zip 32803).

MIAMI: (305) 576-6161. Safespace: Battered Women's Shelter, P.O. Box 186 (zip 33137).

TAMPA: (813) 835-4471. The Spring, Inc., P.O. Box 11087 (zip 33610).

WEST PALM BEACH: (305) 833-2439. YWCA Domestic Assault Shelter, 901 South Olive Avenue (zip 33401).

GEORGIA

ATLANTA: (404) 572-2626. Council on Battered Women, 45 11th St., NE (zip 30309).

MARIETTA: (404) 973-8890. YWCA Crisis Center, 48 Henderson St. (zip 30064).

ROME: (912) 235-4673. Hospitality House for Women, 216 S. Broad St. (zip 30161).

IDAHO

BOISE: (208) 343-7541. Emergency Housing Services, Inc. P.O. Box 286, 815 North 7th St. (zip 83701).

POCATELLO: (208) 232-HELP. Women's Advocates, YWCA, 454 N. Garfield (zip 83201).

ILLINOIS

CARBONDALE: (618) 457-0346. Women's Center, 408 W. Freeman (zip 62901).

CHICAGO: (312) 275-9383. Salvation Army Emergency Lodge, 800 West Lawrence Ave. (zip 60640). Captain Joy Wessel, director. This perceptive woman has a good understanding of the problem—a grasp which has not been true of all religious-oriented crisis shelters. Unlike the usual shelter policy, the social worker will try to talk to the husband, if desired. "He is encouraged to get in touch with his alcoholism, his sadism. He can be helped with financial aid or advocacy with red tape. We've found the wife holds a valuable weapon, because if she leaves him, he realizes he needs her and the children; he can be convinced to seek counseling. We are not trying to build a picture of utopia, but of what's meaningful. The woman can get a better look at herself and her lack of ego." Also offered: child care, menu planning, family budgeting, legal aid, rights re separate maintenance and divorce. No limit on stay, "as long as she's taking a meaningful approach to the problem. We are the only service in this area which can offer privacy. Board of Education teachers are assigned to two classrooms here—a solution for the women and children afraid to appear outside. We've found wifebeating exists even on the Gold Coast of Chicago, among doctors, attorneys. We've been fortunate to have leadership to recognize this problem."

CHICAGO: There are also two smaller, Bowery Mission–type institutions which will accept battered women and their children, but offer no supportive services:

(312) 922-1462. Pacific Garden Mission, Women and Children Division, 646 South State St. Capacity: dormitory of thirteen beds, eight baby beds, "and we can make pallets on the floor if they're full. I suppose some of them are battered women: The Mission is for anyone who needs shelter. Our purpose is not just lodging, but bringing people to Christ, rescuing them from sin. We supply food, clothing, and medicine. There's no limit to their stay—until they get situated —unless they refuse to cooperate. Yes, some alcoholic men do hang around outside on the sidewalk."

(312) 243-2480. Gospel League Shelter, 955 W. Grand. Rev. and Mrs. Taggert. Capacity: dormitories for forty-five men, women, and children. No limit on stay—"until people get on their feet, or public aid. Our purpose is to teach people about Jesus. We supply food, clothing, and shelter as secondary to religious devotions—as many as three nights a week, and two services on Sunday. It is compulsory to attend. It may seem cruel, but they need the discipline and they enjoy it. We urge the wives to go back to their husbands—."

Here I protested, "Back to a wifebeater?!" "Well, unless he won't change his violence."

EAST MOLINE: (309) 797-4220. R.I. County Council on Alcoholism/New Hope League, RR #2, P.O. Box 288 (zip 61244).

ELGIN: (312) 697-1093. Community Crisis Center (zip 60120). "Please don't give our address." Capacity: up to eleven. "We serve Elgin township and several surrounding counties. Or, if a woman is referred from other townships, it's $25 a night [this is the highest fee I've encountered; most are a few dollars, and waived if penniless] including food and counseling. We are not involved in welfare [many others are, which helps lower rates]. We also do counseling by phone."

PEORIA: (309) 674-4443. Tri-County Women Strength, 301 NE Jefferson (zip 61602).

PEORIA: (309) 674-4443. Women's Crisis Service, 1101 Main St., #306 (zip 61606).

ROCKFORD: (815) 962-6102. Coalition Opposed to a Violent Environment (COVE), 630 North Church St. (zip 61103).

SPRINGFIELD: (217) 544-2484. Sojourn Women's Center, Inc. 915 North 7th St. (zip 62702).

URBANA: (217) 384-4390. A Woman's Place, 505 West Green (zip 61801).

INDIANA

FORT WAYNE: (219) 424-2554. YWCA Shelter for Women Victims of Violence, P.O. Box 5338 (zip 46805).

SOUTH BEND: (219) 232-3344. Women's Shelter Advisory Committee of YWCA, 802 N. LaFayette Blvd. (zip 46601).

IOWA

AMES: (515) 292-1101. Story County Sexual Assault Care Center. P.O. Box 1150, Iowa State University Station (zip 50010).

CEDAR RAPIDS: (319) 363-2093. YWCA Women's Emergency Shelter, c/o YWCA, 318 5th Street, SE (zip 52401).

CLINTON: (319) 243-3611. Gateway YWCA Women's Resource Center, 317 7th Ave. South (zip 52732).

DECORAH: (319) 382-2989. Helping Services for Northeast Iowa, Abused Women Program, Box 372 (zip 52101).

MASON CITY: (515) 424-0971. The Door Opener, 215 North Federal Ave. (zip 50401). Note: There is also a branch, same phone, in ALGONA: at 106 Moore Street.

SIOUX CITY: (800) 352-4929. Council on Sexual Assault and Domestic Violence, 722 Nebraska St. (zip 51101).

KANSAS

LAWRENCE: (316) 864-3506. Women's Transitional Care Services, P.O. Box 633 (zip 66044).

WICHITA: (316) 263-9806. Wichita Women's Crisis Center, 1158 N. Waco (zip 67203). Capacity: ten. Sons must be under age fifteen. Opened August 1976, not just for battered women; for transients, evictions, some former mental patients.

KENTUCKY

FORT CAMPBELL: (502) 798-2103. Social Work Service, US Army Hospital, Ft. Campbell (zip 42223).

LOUISVILLE: (502) 584-4024. Mission House, 1305 W. Market St. (zip 40203).

LOUISVILLE: (502) 585-2331. Spouse Abuse Center, YWCA, 604 South 3rd St. (zip 40202).

OWENSBORO: (800) 482-7972. Green River Comprehensive Care Center, P.O. Box 950 (zip 42301).

LOUISIANA

NEW ORLEANS: (504) 866-7481. Crescent House, 2929 South Carrollton Ave. (zip 70118).

SHREVEPORT: (318) 222-0556. Women's Resource Center of the YWCA, 710 Travis St. (zip 71101).

MAINE

AUBURN: (207) 783-2042. Abused Women's Advocacy Project, P.O. Box 713 (zip 04210).

BANGOR: (207) 947-0496 during business hours; (207) 947-6143 during evenings and weekends. Tenant Union, Spruce Run Association (zip 04401).

BIDDEFORD: (207) 282-4435. Caring Unlimited, P.O. Box 955 (zip 04005).

MARYLAND

ANNAPOLIS: (phone unlisted; referral must come through police). Good Neighbors Unlimited, 208 Duke of Gloucester St. (zip 21401).

ANNAPOLIS: (301) 268-4393. YWCA Women's Center, 167 Duke of Gloucester Road (zip 21401).

BALTIMORE: (301) 889- RUTH. House of Ruth, Baltimore, 2402 North Calvert St. (zip 21218).

BETHESDA: (301) 656-9161. Community Crisis Center, Abused Persons Program, 4910 Auburn Ave. (zip 20014).

COLUMBIA: (301) 997-CASA. Citizens Against Spousal Assault (CASA), P.O. Box 915 (zip 21044).

CUMBERLAND: (301) 777-1509. Women's Refuge. Seton Plaza, Suite 201, 952 Seton Drive (zip 21502).

HAGERSTOWN: (301) 739-6000. CASA, Inc. 101 Summit Ave. (zip 21740).

LA PLATA: (301) 645-0001. Family Abuse Program, c/o General Delivery (zip 20646).

MONTGOMERY COUNTY Social Services Abused Persons Program. (301) 279-1331. Cynthia Anderson, supervisor. 5630 Fishers Lane, Rockville (zip 20852). No shelter building yet, but emergency shelter is available in various facilities. Crisis intervention; family —including wifebeater—counseling; medical, dental, psychiatric and day care; information and referral for those not in need of immediate crisis housing; Outreach. This program shows sensitive understanding, as exemplified in a procedure worked out with the Income Maintenance Unit of Social Service: "A client who is visibly battered and embarrassed about her appearance is able to fill out the public assistance application in privacy. She is then seen by appointment with an interviewer aware of her situation." The counselors are trained to realize that "often what the client is saying is true: that both options open to her—i.e., remaining in the current situation or facing a life where she will be alone with her children, probably in a strange place, and almost always managing at a very reduced standard of living—are bad."

N.B. Montgomery County is one of the most affluent counties in America. Public assistance is below the poverty level as defined by the state.

UPPER MARLBORO: (301) 529-0611. Assisi, P.O. Box 203 (zip 20870).

WESTMINISTER: (301) 848-5060. Battered Partners Program—Carroll County Department of Social Services, 95 Carroll St. (zip 21157).

WESTMINISTER: (301) 848-3111. Maryland Children's Aid and Family Services Society, 22 North Court St. (zip 21157).

MASSACHUSETTS

BOSTON: (617) 262-9581. Casa Myrna Vazquez, 425 Shawmut Ave. (zip 02118).

BOSTON: (617) 536-4652. 5:00 P.M. overnight to 8:30 A.M. Rosie's Place, 1662 Washington St., near Boston City Hospital. Capacity: ten beds. Sons must be under twelve. "We are not connected with any religion or agency. There never was a 'Rosie,' it's just a noninstitutional-sounding name, probably from Rosen's Meat Market, which used to be at our first shelter. Free food, clothes, beds, not just for battered women. We don't offer counseling, just friendship. We'll refer—although there's not much available that's good."

CAMBRIDGE: (617) 661-7203. Transition House. Secret address; can be contacted via Cambridge Women's Center, 46 Pleasant St. (zip 02139). Capacity: five to thirteen women, twelve to fifteen children, bunk beds. Older sons are screened. "We especially welcome children, because there's no place for them to go." Battered wives not yet ready to flee are also welcome to visit with residents. A very comprehensive program, multiservices, sixty volunteers.

GREENFIELD: (413) 772-0125. New England Learning Center for Women in Transition, 310 Main St. (zip 01301).

HYANNIA: (617) 771-8564. The Cape Shelter, Inc. 54 Main St. (zip 02601).

JAMAICA PLAIN: (413) 522-3417. Elizabeth Stone House, 108 Brookside Ave. (zip 02130).

LOWELL: (617) 453-1771, days, 9:00 A.M. to 7:00 P.M.; (617) 455-5405, 7:00 P.M. to 9:00 A.M. Greater Lowell YWCA, 96 Rogers St. (zip 01852). This is not a shelter for battered wives and cannot take children. However, "without funding, or salaries, we are taking in battered women in crisis. We're all volunteers." (Salvation Army can arrange temporary motel accommodations when there are children.) "This is the sort of altruistic thing most YWs will do."

N.B. When I began my research, I found neither YWs nor Salvation Army residences were aware of the problem, nor prepared to deal with it. By 1977, however, both these groups, in many communities, are frequently leaders in trying to provide help.

NATICK: (413) 872-6161. YWCA Women Against Violence (zip 01760).

PITTSFIELD: (413) 443-0089. Women's Services Center of Berkshire County, 33 Pearl St. (zip 01201).

SOMMERVILLE: (617) 623-5900. Respond, 1 Summer St. (zip 02143).

WILBRAHAM: (413) 596-8449. Heart House, P.O. Box 704 (zip 01095).

WORCESTER: (617) 791-6562. Daybreak, Inc., 93 Grand St. (zip 01610).

MICHIGAN

KALAMAZOO: (616) 343-9496. Women's Crisis Center, 211 South Rose St. (zip 49006).

MARQUETTE: (616) 227-2219. Project Shelter, Women's Center, North Michigan University (zip 49855).

MUSKEGON: (616) 722-3333. Rape/Spouse Assault Crisis Center, 24 Strong Ave. (zip 49441).

PONTIAC: (313) 332-HELP. YWCA of Pontiac, North Oakland Domestic Crisis Shelter, 269 West Huron St. (zip 48053).

YPSILANTI: (313) 668-8888. Assault Crisis Center, 561 N. Hewett (zip 48197). A phone call will activate many supportive services, including emergency shelter in various facilities. The history of this private, nonprofit corporation is significant in the growing movement against wifebeating. This center is an outgrowth of the pioneer Ann Arbor–Washtenaw County NOW Wife Assault Task Force. Its volunteers began taking women into their own homes in 1975, and publishing what continues to be the excellent—and perhaps the only—training manuals on setting up a similar Task Force and on counselor training (see Recommended Publications). Phone referral for the new shelter, Safe House, is (313) 995-5460.

MINNESOTA

AUSTIN: (507) 437-6680. Victim's Crisis Center,

Freeborn Mowe Mental Health Center, 908 NW 1 Drive (zip 55912).

BRAINERD: (218) 828-1216. Mid-Minnesota Women's Center, Inc., Box 602 (zip 56401).

BURNSVILLE: (616) 894-2424. Community Action Council, Inc., 13760 Nicollet Ave., South (zip 55337).

DULUTH: (218) 722-0222. Northeastern Coalition for Battered Women, Inc., 2 E. Fifth St. (zip 55805).

MARSHALL: (507) 532-2350. Southwest Women's Shelter, 111 East Main St. (zip 56258).

MINNEAPOLIS: (612) 827-2841. Harriet Tubman Women's Shelter, P.O. Box 7026. Powderhorn Station (zip 55407). After the Women's Advocates' House was well established in the sister city of St. Paul, Minneapolis observed there was still great need for more refuge. Ellen Pence and other feminist activists interested the Minneapolis Housing and Redevelopment in offering a vacant duplex for $1.00, plus $92,000 of community development funds for rehabilitation. Over $12,000 worth of rehabilitation labor was donated by dedicated women. The present director is one of the original Advocates. Capacity: sixteen. (The city is strict about enforcing the housing code on overcrowding, so—atypically—there cannot be an open-door policy. There is usually a waiting list.) Age limit on sons is pending. Full supportive services of the exceptionally social-service-minded Twin Cities communities are available.

MINNEAPOLIS: (612) 874-8867. St. Joseph's House, 2101 Portland Ave., Minneapolis (zip 55404). Capacity: six women and two babies. This is not a licensed facility, "so we're not involved in politics." Instead, it is run as a private home taking guests by Sister Rita Steinhagen, a charming, dynamic nun who dresses in lay clothing. Patterned after Dorothy Day's Catholic Worker houses, her home is open to anyone in need, not exclusively battered wives.

ROCHESTER: (507) 285-1010. Women's Shelter, Box 61 (zip 55901).

St. Paul: (612) 227-8284. Women's Advocates' House (WAH), 584 Grand Avenue, St. Paul (zip 55102). This is the pioneer shelter in America, run on a nonhierarchical basis, by loving, courageous, idealistic women of many backgrounds and ages. WAH is the mother of all the shelters and services, the model —and yet still struggles for enough funding to be guaranteed operating expenses.

MISSISSIPPI

Hattiesburg: (601) 544-4357. Coalition Against Spouse Abuse, Box 9227 Southern Station (zip 39401).

Tupelo: (601) 842-5222. Aid to Battered Women, Inc., Project SAFE, P.O. Box 334, c/o Information Place (zip 38801).

MISSOURI

St. Louis: (314) 531-2033. Women's Self-Help Center, 27 N. Newstead (zip 63108). Safe Home program.

Cape Girardeau: (314) 334-7794. Women's Center and Safe House, 739 Themis (zip 63701).

Joplin: (417) 782-1772. The Family Self-Help Center, Inc., P.O. Box 1185 (zip 64801).

Kansas City: (816) 931-1653. Rose Brooks Center, Inc. Box 27067 (zip 64110).

Kansas City: (816) 444-4750. St. George's Home for Women, 1600 E. 58th St. (zip 64110).

St. Louis: (314) 533-1219. Raphael House of the Holy Order of Mans, 3740 Grandel Square (zip 63108).

MONTANA

Butte: (406) 792-2616. Community Resources, 1937 Florida (zip 59701).

Glendive: (406) 365-2412. Glendive Task Force Against Spouse Abuse, Hagenston Bldg. (zip 59330).

GREAT FALLS: (406) 453-6511. Great Falls Mercy Home, P.O. Box 6183 (zip 59406).

MISSOULA: (406) 543-8277. This is the Crisis Center, which screens for a new shelter in a donated three-bedroom house, funded by private contributions. Length of stay is "only a few days, because it's being used so heavily." All counseling available.

NEBRASKA

Some shelters are now taking in battered wives and their children, along with their usual population of homeless men and women. They lack the effective supportive services and are unfamiliar with the real dynamics of the problem, but they do provide escape—for which I say thank you.

GORDON: (308) 282-2492. Family Rescue Shelter, 309 North Main (zip 69343).

LINCOLN: (402) 467-2596. Family Shelter, 84th and Adams Sts. Capacity: seven families plus dorm for singles, on forty acres, with pasture for horses. Fifty-four percent of residents are local; 46 percent transient. Religious emphasis: regular chapel, Bible study—"but not pushed at," according to Jim Dunn, whose father, Pastor Jerry Dunn, is the head. "I believe God has established free will." Interdenominational. Supported by United Way. "Of 372 cases last year, 127 were abused wives. We try to find them jobs and reestablish them in their own community, own apartment. We try to keep the family unit together." Even if he beats his wife? "Well, we try to get the wifebeater into counseling."

OMAHA: (402) 496-3300. The Shelter (A Center for Victims of Family Violence), P.O. Box 14510 (zip 68124).

OMAHA: (402) 341-2642. Siena House, 804 N. 19th St. Capacity: thirty people, men, women and children in two connected houses. A Catholic Worker house. No geographical restrictions. Also takes evictions, former mental patients and prisoners—"We don't check backgrounds. . . . We still have to turn people away."

OMAHA: (402) 553-3947. Shiloh House, 1045 N. 34th. Capacity: thirty people. "We're just for people who need food, shelter, gospel talk about the Lord; men, women, children. The Shiloh movement is all around the U.S."

NOTE: For upcoming shelters specifically for battered women, contact Sheri Pond at Commission on the Status of Women, 619 Terminal Bldg. Lincoln, Nebraska 68508.

NEW JERSEY

BURLINGTON: (609) 382-3151. Providence House, Box 424 (zip 08016). Another shelter also in Willingboro.

ELIZABETH: (201) 355-1500. Battered Women's Project, YWCA of Elizabeth, 1131 East Jersey St. (zip 07066). For emergency housing.

GREYSTONE PARK: (201) 267-4763. Jersey Battered Women's Service, Box 7 (zip 07950).

HACKENSACK: (201) 487-8484. Bergen County Community Action Program, 215 Union St. (zip 07601). Not a shelter bldg.; crisis housing is elsewhere.

HACKENSACK: (201) 342-1185. Shelter Our Sisters, 133 Cedar Ave. (zip 07601). This is the private home of Sandy Ramos, who has been single-handedly, without funding, sheltering battered wives and their children. Many diverse ethnic groups have been able to live cooperatively there. Although she has enjoyed the respect of many supportive social agencies, the city government has consistently denied her help. The day I phoned to verify information, she was holding a press conference because the city was trying to close her down for "overcrowding."

JERSEY CITY: (201) 333-5700. Hudson County Battered Women's Project, c/o YWCA, 111 Storms Ave. (zip 97306).

KEYPORT: (201) 264-4111. Women's Resource & Survival Center, 57 W. Front St. (zip 07735). This is the nation's first federally funded relief and emergency assistance center.

MAY'S LANDING: (609) 653-8411. Atlantic County Women's Center, Box 84B, RD 3, West Hickory Street (zip 08330).

NORTHFIELD: (609) 646-6767. Hotline: (609) 822-2178. Atlantic County Women's Center, Abuse Center (zip 08225).

TRENTON: (609) 394-9000. WOMANSPACE, Inc. Box 7182 (zip 08628).

NOTE: To be referred to new local services, call statewide hotline, toll-free, (800) 322-8092, provided by Together, Inc., in Glassboro.

NEW YORK

NOTE: New York State has small shelters opening (and sometimes closing) frequently. Contact the nearest shelter from this list for possible refuge nearer you.

ALBANY: (518) 434-3531. Mercy House, 12 St. Joseph Terrace (zip 12210). Can't take children.

AUBURN: (315) 252-2024. Cayuga County Action Program, 60 Clark St. (zip 13021). Safe Homes.

BINGHAMTON: (607) 772-0340. YWCA of Binghamton, Hawley & Exchange sts. (zip 13901).

BROOKLYN: (212) 449-2151. Park Slope Safe Homes Project, c/o Children & Youth Development Services, 262 9th St. (zip 11215). Excellent program but for Park Slope residents only.

BROOKLYN: (212) 439-7281. Women's Survival Space. Capacity: presently thirty-six beds. The first New York State-funded shelter, privately operated by women, founded by the Center for the Elimination of Violence in the Family. P.O. Box 279, Bay Ridge Station, Brooklyn (zip 11220).

BUFFALO: (716) 884-6000. Haven House, Erie

County Coalition for Victims of Domestic Violence, Box 45, Niagara Square Station (zip 14201).

BUFFALO: (716) 884-5330. Simple Gifts, 80 Richmond Ave. (zip 14222).

CANTON: (315) 386-4130. North Country Women's Center, Box 474 (zip 13617).

CATSKILL: (518) 943-3300. Greene County Dept. of Social Services, 465 Main St. (zip 12414). Emergency refuge.

CORTLAND: (607) 756-6363. YWCA, Aid to Women Victims of Violence, 14 Clayton Avenue (zip 13045). Safe homes.

EAST MEADOW: (516) 542-2594. Coalition for Abused Women, Box 485, Nassau County Medical Center, Nurses Residence (zip 11554).

ELMIRA: (607) 732-0314. The Salvation Army, 414 Lake St., Box 459 (zip 14902).

ENDICOTT: (607) 754-4340. S.O.S. Shelter, Inc. Box 393 (zip 13760).

ISLIP TERRACE: (516) 589-1658. Long Island Women's Coalition, Inc., P.O. Box 183 (zip 11752). Safe homes.

ITHACA: (607) 272-1616. Tompkins County Task Force on Battered Women, 112 The Commons, 1-A (zip 14850). Safe homes.

JAMESTOWN: (716) 484-1820. Women's Resource Center of the Jamestown Girls Club, 532 East 2nd St. (zip 14701).

JAMESTOWN: YWCA, 401 North Main St. (zip 14701).

MANHATTAN: (212) 686-1676. M–F, 10–4. This is the AWAIC number (see chapter 1) which screens for the new DEP—Demonstration Evaluation Program, Protective Shelter and Services program of the Henry Street Settlement House, AWAIC and Human Resources Administration. The phone number at the Urban Family Center is (212) 766-9300.

NEW YORK CITY: (212) 581-4911. Battered Women's Shelter, c/o New York City Human Resources Administration, 250 Church St., 13th Floor (zip 10013). Facility at secret address is so large, almost no one need be turned away, but referral must come from police, Income Maintenance, or Social Service agency.

NYACK: (914) 623-1112. Rockland Family Shelter, Box 517 (zip 10960).

OSWEGO: (315) 342-4474. Farnham Youth Development Center, 145 E. Bridge St. (zip 13126).

PLATTSBURGH: (518) 563-6904. Women Incorporated, Box 44 (zip 12901).

ROCHESTER: (716) 232-7353. Alternatives for Battered Women, Inc., 380 Andrews St. (zip 14604).

SCHENECTADY: (518) 374-3394. YWCA Services to Families in Violence, 44 Washington Ave. (zip 12308).

SUFFOLK COUNTY: (516) 360-3606 VIBS—Victims Information Bureau of Suffolk, 501 Route 111, Hauppauge (zip 11787). The excellent counseling this group does is mentioned earlier in book. No shelter building yet; refuge referrals.

SYRACUSE: (315) 475-1688. Family Service Department of the Salvation Army, 749 S. Warren St. (zip 13032).

SYRACUSE: (315) 422-2271. Vera House, Inc. Box 62 (zip 13207).

NORTH TONAWANDA: (716) 692-5643. YWCA of the Tonawandas, Abused Women Program, 49 Tremont St. (zip 14120).

UTICA: (315) 797-7740. Advocates Against Family Violence, YWCA, 1000 Cornelia St. (zip 13502). Crisis refuge elsewhere.

WATERTOWN: (315) 782-1855. The Jefferson County Women's Center, Inc., YWCA, 50 Public Square (zip 13601).

WAYLAND: (716) 728-5010. Project Reach, Inc., 18 South Lackawanna St. (zip 14572).

WOODSTOCK: (914) 338-2370. Family of Woodstock, Inc., 16 Rock City Road (zip 12498).

YONKERS: (914) 968-4345. The Shelter, Yonkers Women's Task Force, Inc., P.O. Box 395, Main Post Office (zip 10702).

NEW MEXICO

ALBUQUERQUE: (505) 247-4219. Women's Community Association, Inc. Box 6472 (zip 87197).

PORTALES: (505) 356-4779. Battered Families Project, 211 S. Main (zip 88130).

SANTA FE: (505) 988-9731. Battered Women's Project, P.O. Box 5701 (zip 87501).

NORTH CAROLINA

DURHAM: (919) 688-4353. Battered Women's Crisis Line at Hasslehouse, 1022 Urban Ave. (zip 27701).

FAYETTEVILLE: (919) 323-4187. CARE (Citizens Aware & Responding to Emergencies) Center, 108 Highland Ave. (zip 28305).

GREENSBORO: (919) 275-0896. Women's Aid Services for Abused Women, P.O. Box 1137 (zip 27402).

NORTH DAKOTA

NOTE: 1-(800) 472-2911 is the toll-free crisis line, statewide, for after-business hours, of the Abused Women's Resource Closet, 219 North 7th St., BISMARCK (zip 58501). The daytime office phone is (701) 222-8370.

FARGO: (701) 232-2546. Fargo-Moorhead YWCA, 411 Broadway (zip 58102).

FARGO: the statewide after-hours crisis line and the daytime 1-(701) 235-6433. Women Abuse, Children's Village, Family Service, 1721 South University Drive (zip 58102).

MINOT: (701) 857-2000. Women's Action Program, Inc., Services for Battered Women, P.O. Box 881, 400 22nd Ave. NW (zip 58701).

OHIO

NOTE: 1-(800) 282-3040. This is the toll-free number for information on all shelters in Ohio, operated 9 to 5, Monday to Friday, by Women's Information Center (WIC), The State House, Columbus, Ohio 43215. WIC requests all new shelters to send updating for their computer.

AKRON: (216) 923-0174. Furnace St. Mission, Box 444 (zip 44309).

AKRON: (216) 762-6685. M-F, 10-6. Akron Task Force on Battered Women, 146 South High St. (zip 44305).

ATHENS: (614) 593-3402. My Sister's Place, Box 1158 (zip 45701).

CINCINNATI: (513) 961-0680. Alice Paul House, YWCA Battered Women's Shelter, 9th and Walnut sts. (zip 45202).

CLEVELAND: (216) 961-4422. Women Together, Inc., Box 6331 (zip 44104).

COLUMBUS: (614) 294-3381. Phoenix House for Battered Women, Box 8323 (zip 43201).

COLUMBUS: (614) 294-2720. Heidi House, Box 8053 (zip 43201).

FAIRFIELD: (513) 874-3690. Butler County Women's Crisis Shelter, 5021 Fairfield Circle (zip 45014).

MANSFIELD: (419) 526-4450. Richland County Task Force on Domestic Violence, Box 1524 (zip 44901).

NEWARK: (614) 345-HELP. Family Service Assn. 122 W. Church St. (zip 43055).

SPRINGFIELD: (513) 325-3707. Project Woman, 22 E. Grand (zip 45506).

XENIA: (513) 376-2993. Greene County Crisis Center, 53 N. Collier (zip 45385).

OKLAHOMA

NORMAN: (405) 364-9424. Women's Resources Center, Norman Task Force for Battered Women, Box 474 (Peters and Gray) (zip 73070).

OKLAHOMA CITY: (405) 528-5440. YWCA Women's Resource Center, 3626 North Western Ave. (zip 73118).

OREGON

ASHLAND: (503) 779-HELP. Jackson County, Box 369 (zip 97520).

EUGENE: (503) 689-7156. Family Shelter, 367 HWY 99 N (zip 97402).

EUGENE: (503) 485-6513. Womanspace, P.O. Box 3030 (zip 97403).

HILLSBORO: (503) 640-1171. BEWARE, 276 East Main (zip 97123).

NEWPORT: (503) 265-2491. Women's Resource Center of Lincoln for Battered Women, 908 SW Hurbert (zip 97365).

PORTLAND: (503) 232-6562. Address: 200 S.E. 7th Ave.

PORTLAND: (503) 223-4544. Raphael House, Box 10797 (zip 97210).

ROSEBURG: (503) 673-0240. Refuge House, 920 SE Cass (zip 97470).

SALEM: (503) 399-7722. Women's Crisis Center, 617 Cheme Keta, Box 851 (zip 97301).

PENNSYLVANIA

NOTE: A useful reference for up-to-date information on changing conditions is The Pennsylvania Coalition

Against Domestic Violence, 2405 North Front St., Harrisburg, Pa. 17110. Phone: (717) 233-6030.

BEAVER FALLS: (412) 843-6440. Women's Center. 1305 Third Ave. Capacity: twelve. Sons under eight, unless emergency.

BETHLEHEM: (215) 437-3369. Turning Point of Lehigh Valley, Box 5162, (zip 18015). Referrals to limited crisis refuge.

BLOOMSBURG: (717) 784-6631. The Women's Center. 100 South Market Street, Box 221 (zip 17815).

CHAMBERSBURG: (717) 264-4444. Women in Need, Box 25 (zip 17201).

ERIE: (814) 454-1963. Hospitality House, 205 Myrtle Street. Capacity: about six adults, four children. Emergency shelter for all women, mostly battered, but including teens with parental problems, former mental patients. Religious oriented, but nonsectarian. "We are not trained counselors, but give information and referral. We need to read more on this subject."

HARRISBURG: (717) 238-1068. Women in Crisis, YWCA, 4th and Market. Capacity: six families; sons to age fifteen. Serves tricounty area. Re wifebeater counseling—"Most don't ask."

HUMMELSTOWN: (717) 534-1101. Women in Crisis, RD 1, Box 314-A (zip 17036).

LANCASTER: (717) 299-1249. Lancaster Shelter for Abused Women, YWCA, Box 359 (zip 17604). Capacity: twenty. Twenty-four-hour counseling.

MEADVILLE: (814) 333-9766. Women's Services, Greenhouse, Box 637, (zip 16335).

PHILADELPHIA: (215) 843-2905. Box 12233 8–6 counseling and intake. Women Against Abuse. Capacity: twenty-five to thirty. This shelter helped formulate new law, Protection Against Abuse: Anyone beaten in home files petition, must be heard within ten days; abuser, if ruled against, must be out of home up to a year.

PITTSBURGH: (412) 661-6066. Women's Center

and Shelter of Greater Pittsburgh, 661 North High-land Ave. Capacity: ten beds, a few cribs. Sons to eight years old. "No trained counseling, but creative listening." This shelter is secured at theological seminary—a beautiful deed I commend to all seminaries.

ROCHESTER: (412) 775-0131. Women's Center of Beaver County, 175 West Washington St. (zip 15074).

SELLERSVILLE: (215) 257-1088. A Woman's Place. 108 Main St.

ST. MARY'S (814) 834-1227. Elk City Crisis Line, c/o Ruth Arick, Patti Smith, 316 West Theresia Rd. (zip 15857).

STATE COLLEGE: (814) 234-5050. Centre County Women's Resource Center, Rape/Abuse Crisis Line, 108 West Beaver Ave. (zip 16801). Limited refuge in safe homes.

UNIONTOWN: (412) 785-7532. Fayette County Family Abuse Council, 64 S. Beeson Blvd. (zip 15401). Limited refuge in safe homes.

WEST CHESTER: (215) 431-1430. Women's Resource Center of Chester County, YWCA, 123 North Church St. (zip 19380).

WILKES BARRE: (717) 823-7312. Domestic Violence Service Center, Box 1662 (zip 18703).

WILLIAMSPORT: (717) 322-4714. Wise Options for Women, YWCA, 815 West 4th (zip 11754).

RHODE ISLAND

PROVIDENCE: (401) 781-4080. Women's Center, 37 Congress St. (zip 02907). Capacity: fourteen. The first shelter in state. When I called, it had been open six to eight weeks, already had battered wives from Massachusetts and Connecticut. "We are just a group of women who decided battered wives needed a place to go; funded by United Way and donations. No staff for counseling or children, but college students play with the kids."

N.B. Although number is listed, I found this very

difficult to track down. I didn't have the exact name; telephone company had no category for battered women, although supervisor tried alternatives diligently. Then I tried several social agencies and residences who knew but felt they should not reveal possibly secret information. Finally got the number via police. I commend this route to battered wives when trying to find shelter in own community, also try local chapter of NOW. To shelters, I recommend briefing the telephone company thoroughly about women who need your number but may not have your exact name.

PROVIDENCE: (401) 751-1262. Sojourner House, Inc. Box 5667, Weybosset Hill Station (zip 02903).

SOUTH DAKOTA

BROOKINGS: (605) 692-4359. Brookings Women's Center, 802 11th Ave. (zip 57006).

LAKE ANDES: (605) 487-7634. South Central Community Act Program, Box 6 (zip 57356).

TEXAS

AUSTIN: (512) 472-HURT. Center for Battered Women, Box 5631 (zip 78763).

CORPUS CHRISTI: (713) 881-8888. Women's Shelter, Inc., Box 3368 (zip 78404).

DALLAS: (214) 827-5260. Woman's Help, P.O. Box 11449 (zip 75223). This hotline will lead to counseling, information, and what little shelter exists. The Salvation Army, used also for transients, alcoholics, and vagrants, does not take children. They must be sent to children's shelter. Mother must sign waiver that if she can't find permanent housing in a month, child will be placed in a foster home, perhaps put up for adoption. Horrors!

Volunteers from NOW tried crisis intervention, and offered own homes as emergency refuge—but were stopped by dangerously retaliatory husbands. "I almost got shot," said one volunteer. With only small donations, $900 in six months, the present facilities were set up.

DENTON: (817) 387-4357. Women's Services Project, Box 1322 (zip 76201).

EL PASO: (915) 859-4156. Transitional Living Center, Inc., Box 13265 (zip 79912).

FORT WORTH: (214) 336-3355. Women's Haven, Inc., Box 12180 (zip 76116).

GALVESTON: (713) 763-5605. YWCA Women's Resource and Crisis Center, 621 Moody (zip 77550).

HOUSTON: (713) 527-0718. Houston Area Women's Center, Inc., Box 20186, Room E401 (zip 77025).

PALESTINE: (214) 729-6483. Anderson County Shelter. 1504 West Reagan (zip 75801).

SAN ANTONIO: (512) 532-7648. Women's Shelter of Bexar County, Inc., Box 10-393 (zip 78210).

UTAH

OGDEN: (801) 392-7273. Women's Crisis Center, YWCA, 505 27th St. (zip 84403).

SALT LAKE CITY: (801) 352-2804, YW number. YWCA, 322 East 3rd, South (zip 84111).

VERMONT

BRATTLEBORO: (802) 254-6954. Women's Crisis Center, 14 Green St. (zip 05301).

BURLINGTON: (802) 864-5096. Women's House of Transition, Inc., Box 92 (zip 05401).

ST. JOHNSBURY: (802) 748-8645. Umbrella of St. Johnsbury, Inc., 79 Railroad St. (zip 05819).

VIRGINIA

ALEXANDRIA: (703) 360-6910. CEASE (Community Effort for Abused Spouses), 8119 Holland Road (zip 22306).

CHRISTIANSBURG: (703) 382-6553. Women's Resource Center, 203 Phlegar St. (zip 24073).

FAIRFAX COUNTY, Groveton and Mt. Vernon sections: (703) 360-6910. 8 A.M. to midnight, seven days, LEAA-funded to provide temporary shelter in commercial facilities, many supportive services, including wifebeater counseling.

VIENNA: (703) 527-4077. Fairfax County Women's Shelter, Box 1174 (zip 22180).

WASHINGTON, D.C.

(202) 797-7460. House of Imogene, 214 P St., NW, (zip 20001).

(202) 347-0190. House of Ruth, 459 Massachusetts Ave., N.W. (zip 20001). This is a pioneer effort, the first shelter for "shopping-bag ladies" (aging women who carry their life's possessions around with them in shopping bags and sleep in doorways and parks, without money or home). Many of them had fled from a wifebeater years before and never were able to get welfare or any housing or charity. HoR expanded to offer refuge to contemporary battered wives. Now expanding to annex.

(202) 347-9689. New House of Ruth annex, for battered wives and children only. 1215 New Jersey Avenue.

(202) 529-5991. My Sister's Place, Box 3035, (zip 20010).

WASHINGTON STATE

BELLINGHAM: (206) 734-7271. Whatcom County Crisis Services Domestic Violence Program, 124 East Holly (zip 98225).

BREMERTON: (206) 479-1980. ALIVE (Alternatives to Living in Violence), 611 Highland (zip 98310).

EVERETT: (206) 25A-BUSE. Survival Center of Snohomish County, 5205 South 2nd (zip 98203).

OLYMPIA: (206) 352-2211. YWCA Women's Shelter Program, 220 East Union (zip 98501).

PORT ANGELES: (206) 452-8958. Claham County Safe House Program, c/o Vici Roth, Dept. of Social & Health Services, Box 2148 (zip 98362).

RICHLAND: (509) 946-0329. A Woman's Place, 1440 Kimball, (zip 99352).

SEATTLE: (206) 622-8194. New Beginnings, 217 9th Ave. North (zip 98109).

SEATTLE: (206) 322-7959. Catherine Booth House, Salvation Army, 925 North Pike St. (zip 98122).

SEATTLE: (206) 447-4882. Women's Resource Center, Seattle-King County YWCA, 1118 Fifth Ave. (zip 98101). Can't take children.

TACOMA: (206) 383-2593. YWCA Women's Support Shelter, 405 Broadway (zip 98402).

VANCOUVER: (206) 695-0501. YWCA Emergency House, 1012 West 12th (zip 98660).

YAKIMA: (509) 248-7796. Dawson House, 15 N. Naches Ave. (zip 98902).

(206) 454-WASH. WASH is an acronym for Women's Association of Self-Help, and, of course, abbreviation for the state. This Seattle number is the drop-in support center, Coalition Task Force on Women and Religion, 4759 15th Ave., N.E. (zip 98105). It is also the referral for all the growing number of shelters in the state—at this writing, in Tacoma, Olympia, Snohomish, Yakima, Vancouver, Spokane, Bellingham, Everett, and two in Seattle. Comprehensive public education material is being developed to provide fund raising: information on who the abusers are, samples of shelter house rules, procedures, evaluation, and follow-up. One of the real heroines in this work is in Seattle: Barbara Pavey, who has devoted her time since the late 1960s—long before public awareness of the problem—to counseling battered wives from her home and developing public interest in the need for shelters.

WEST VIRGINIA

MORGANTOWN: (304) 292-2121. Rape Information Service, Inc., 221 Willey St. (zip 26505).

MARTINSBURG: (304) 263-8292. Shenandoah Women's Center, Box 1083, 410 West Race St. (zip 25401). Limited refuge elsewhere.

WISCONSIN

EAU CLAIRE: (715) 834-9578. Refuge House, P.O. Box 482 (zip 54701).

ELLSWORTH: (715) 273-4438. Turningpoint for Victims of Domestic Abuse (zip 54011). Safe homes.

GREEN BAY: (414) 432-4244. Women's Service Center Domestic Violence Project, 102 North Monroe (zip 54301).

KENOSHA: (414) 652-1846. Women's Horizon's, 1630 56th St. (zip 53140).

MADISON: (608) 251-4445. Dane County Advocates for Battered Women, P.O. Box 1145 (zip 53701).

MILWAUKEE: (414) 933-2722. Sojourner Truth House. Box 008110 (zip 53208).

RACINE: (414) 633-3233. Women's Resource Center of the YWCA, 740 College Ave. (zip 53403).

SHEBOYGAN: (414) 457-7924. Sheboygan County Advocates for Battered Women, 427 Bell Ave. (zip 53081). Temporary crisis refuge elsewhere.

STEVENS POINT: (715) 344-5759. Task Force on Abused Women, Mental Health Association in Portage County, 945-A Main St. (zip 54481).

WAUKESNA: (414) 547-3388. Waukesna County Battered Women's Task Force 1303 Fleetfoot Dr. (zip 53186).

WAUSAU: (715) 842-7636. National Organization for Women, North Central Wisconsin Chapter, Box 793 (zip 54401).

The three below are clear and helpful, the only handbooks of their kind, written from experience. Available only from the NOW Domestic Violence Project, 1917 Washtenaw Avenue, Ann Arbor, Michigan, 48104.

How to Develop a Wife Assault Task Force and Project, by Kathleen M. Fojtik, 1975. Mimeographed. Clear, step-by-step approach on how to be most effective, directly helping local battered women. Organizational tips, sample questionnaire for victims. $2.00.

Counselor Training Manual #1, by Mindy Resnick, MSW, 1976. Mimeographed. The volunteer peer counselor's role, step by step after the conjugal crime. Glossary of terms, suggested questionnaire and release of information and liabilities form. $2.00.

Counselor Training Manual #2, by Barbara Cooper, MSW, 1976. Mimeographed. Focuses specifically on crisis intervention with families and victims of conjugal crime. Includes crisis theory, ability to respond to stress, perceptions of alternatives, role of volunteer peer counselor/case manager. Flow charts, victim intake questionnaires. $2.50.

Shelters' own histories and ongoing life. For understanding the day-to-day operations of an effective shelter, including the problems of founding, hiring and training, forms and documents needed, mistakes and successes: Women's Advocates House (WAH), 584 Grand Ave., St. Paul, Minnesota 55102. $3.00.

WAH also puts out a newsletter, approximately monthly, on daily life in a crisis center, with current budgets and with announcements of upcoming conferences across the country, pending bills, etc. Very useful. $5.00 a year.

Women's Transitional Living Center, Inc., P.O. Box 6103, Orange, California 92667. $5.00.

(In preparation, probably $3.00.) Coalition Task Force on Women & Religion, 4759-15th Ave., N.W., Seattle, Washington 98105.

NCN (National Communication Network for the elimination of violence against women). A newsletter has started as a vehicle by which groups and individuals across the country, working on wife abuse, can communicate with each other—shared experiences, problems, solutions. Ultimately its hope is to foster a national network of shelters and groups and grow into a political force on behalf of abused women. Published every two months on a rotating basis. For a year's subscription send $6.00 to Joan Valenti, 565 Portland, St. Paul 55102.

The original list of groups and individuals involved in various areas of help for battered women, periodically updated. *Working on Wife Abuse*, c/o Betsy Warrior, 46 Pleasant St., Cambridge, Massachusetts 02139. $3.00 plus $.50 postage.

RESPONSE (to intrafamily violence and sexual assault) is dedicated to increasing public awareness and effecting national policy change. Updating on current and pending programs and funding. Bimonthly. Funded by LEAA. Free from Center for Women Policy Studies, 2000 P St., N.W., Suite 508, Washington, D.C. 20036.

National NOW Times. This is the national newsletter of the National Organization for Women, an organization which can be joined locally for an average of $30. Newsletter reports on progress of legislation, lobbying, etc. Published at National NOW Action Center, Suite 101 425-13th St., N.W., Washington, D.C. 20004. Write for address of nearest local chapter.

A Handbook for Beaten Women, by Marjory D. Fields, attorney. Applies to New York State law, but useful in general. A self-help guide of twenty-nine clear pages, specially designed small and flat, "so it can be hidden in lining of pocketbook, for use when needed." Contents: how to seek the right attorney, how to deal

282

with typical attitudes of police and courts, what questions you will be asked and how to stand up for yourself. Free for picking up at her office or any New York Legal Services offices or NOW chapter. Or send $.25 in stamps to South Brooklyn Legal Services, 152 Court Street, 3rd floor, Brooklyn, New York 11201.

The Battered Women Conference Report. From the AFSC Conference. (See chapter 10.) One of the most comprehensive and insightful collections of understanding I've seen, for readers new to the problem or working on it. Forty-five pages. $1.50. Available from Community Relations Program, American Friends Service Committee, 15 Rutherford Place, New York, New York 10003.

The Bucks Start Here: How to Fund Your Public Service Project, by Kathleen M. Fojtik, a pioneer in this work. For the layperson who wants to start from scratch and develop a program from only a good idea. $5.00, plus $.50 for postage and handling. NOW Domestic Violence Project, 1917 Washtenaw Avenue, Ann Arbor, Michigan 48104.

BOOKS

Battered Women: A Psychosociological Study of Domestic Violence, edited by Maria Roy. A professional reference book with new, unpublished studies. I wrote the opening chapter. Van Nostrand Reinhold, $14.95.

Now the pioneering study, mentioned in this book, is available to the public. "The Assaulted Wife: 'Catch-22' Revisited," by Susan Eisenberg and Patricia Micklow, from *Women's Rights Law Reporter,* spring/summer 1977, Rutgers University, 180 University Avenue, Newark, New Jersey 07102. $7.00.

Battered Wives by Del Martin. The basic feminist overview and analysis of the problem by the co-chairwoman of NOW's Task Force on Battered Women.

1976. Glide Publications, 330 Ellis Street, San Francisco, California 94102. Paperback, $6.95.

Scream Quietly or the Neighbours Will Hear by Erin Pizzey. The experiences of the British founder of the shelter movement. Now published in America. Ridley Enslow, 60 Crescent Place, Box 301, Short Hills, New Jersey 07078. $7.95.

USEFUL ADDRESSES

For clergy interested in understanding and changing the wifebeating pattern, there is nothing in print as yet. But there will be papers coming from a clergywoman (see chapter 10) who is convener of the Task Force in the American Baptist Churches of metropolitan New York, a practicing psychotherapist and facilitator of a seminar in volunteer counseling of battered women. Rev. Sarah L. Darter, Union Theological Seminary, 3041 Broadway, New York, New York 10027.

To follow the New York Class Action Lawsuit on behalf of battered wives against police and Family Court (see chapter 10), as it goes to trial, contact attorney Laurie Woods, MFY Legal Services, Inc., 759 Tenth Ave., New York, New York 10019.

To follow the progress through committees and hearings of the Domestic Violence bills before Congress: Congressman Newton I. Steers, Jr., puts out an occasional newsletter on HR 7927, Domestic Violence Prevention & Treatment Act of 1977, with some updating on shelters, pending state laws and related activities. Phone: (202) 225-5431. Address: Room 510, Cannon House Office Building, Washington, D.C. 20515.

For additional information about programs for battered women from the federally funded Law Enforcement Assistance Administration (U.S. Department of Justice), write LEAA, Special Programs Division, 633 Indiana Ave., N.W., Washington, D.C. 20531.

Means of obtaining help from police and courts differ slightly in details and red tape from one community to another. Even the terms may differ: "Order of Protection" may be called "Restraining Order," "Peace Bond," "Peace Warrant," etc.; "Family Court" may be called "Children's Court" or "Domestic Relations Court." It offers help and civil warnings instead of criminal penalties.

The following is a condensation of a minutely detailed explanation of procedure that attorney Marjory Fields of South Brooklyn Legal Services, New York City, gives for that area. The information in brackets is my own. To find out your own community's procedural variations, call the police precinct, Legal Aid or Legal Services office, or the local chapter of NOW.

[CALLING THE POLICE: Battered women all over the country report that police delay or refuse to come when a woman calls, saying that her husband is assaulting her. In many enlightened states and communities, new laws are being proposed or passed to remedy this situation. Until then, this is a stopgap measure: 1. Alert a neighbor within hearing distance that wifebeating is your husband's habit and ask that he or she phone for you as soon as it is evident. This is because the law or local policy often requires the police actually to witness the violence before they are allowed to take action. 2. Some groups advise saying "a man" is assaulting, rather than "my husband," because police don't like to interfere in "Domestics," but must if the perpetrator is a stranger or unrelated. However, many police are now aware of this ploy, and it may backfire. 3. Ask the local chapter of NOW what works best in your community. 4. Go to the precinct in person, well dressed, on a calm day between assaults, and ask what the policy is. (You could say it's for a friend.) Take the badge number and name of the officer you speak to, so you'll have something to refer to if police don't help you when you need them.]

ARREST: If police refuse to arrest the wifebeater [and most do refuse if they have not actually witnessed the crime in progress, and often even if injuries are apparent], you have a right to make the arrest yourself. The police must assist you in going to the station and in filling out the civilian arrest forms.

COURTS: Courts are empowered to order custody or support for your children, to order that the wifebeater stop his conduct, move out of the home, or stay away from you and the children. [The specifics are in the Order of Protection. Many courts, however, make the procedures very time consuming, delaying, and complex. Some judges, both men and women, clearly are biased toward the theory that the "home is a man's castle, not the woman's."] If you have need of any of these court services, you must go immediately, because the court's clerk will ask you why you didn't come sooner.

[The following material on Order of Protection procedure is for New York State. I am including it, however, to give the reader the full scope of the red tape involved in trying to get legal relief from conjugal crime.]

ORDER OF PROTECTION: To get one, go to Family Court. You will be given an appointment, sometimes two or three weeks in the future, to see an Intake-Probation officer. You have a right to insist on immediate help [although it may not be respected].

You can't get to the judge—who gives the order—yet. First, Probation will ask you to file a petition for it [or discourage you from filing at all] and will want to be supplied with the following: 1. Bruises shown [or photographed]. 2. Witnesses. 3. Proof of medical care. 4. Report of your reporting to the police.

You should demand to see a judge that day and get a temporary order of protection. Whether or not you ask for and get it, you will be given an appointment for a court hearing before a judge several weeks hence. The temporary order lasts until the court hearing.

The clerk will help with filing details. Husband will be served with a summons informing him he must appear on the court-hearing date.

COURT-HEARING DAY: If husband does not appear, case will be adjourned and another date set. If he does appear, the case may be adjourned anyway to permit him to get an attorney. He has a right to a court-appointed attorney; the wife does not.

At each scheduled hearing, you should bring witnesses, medical reports, and show your bruises [or photographs if bruises are faded after all the delay]. The judge will decide whether [or not] to sign an order of protection for you.

REINFORCING THE ORDER OF PROTECTION: If you get it, and husband disobeys it: 1. Police are legally required to arrest him [this time]. Show the order. If police officer refuses, take his or her badge number. The arrested husband will be taken to the police station —and then released [he is free to return home, probably enraged]. He is told he must show up at Family Court the next morning or Monday. Or, because this is a new incident, you may ask that the case be referred to Criminal Court.

2. Or you can go to family court, file a new petition called violation of order of protection. Husband will be served with a summons to return to court for a later hearing.

In either case, there will be a hearing. . . . with right of attorney for husband only. If the judge believes you, he or she may impose stricter orders, such as ordering husband out of home. [Note that at least two occasions of assault and much delay were necessary to achieve this. Some judges simply tell the wifebeater to promise to behave and then send him right back home.]

If you decide on Criminal Court, realize that some district attorneys are not interested in family violence cases, or they may say your case cannot be won.

Ultimately, it is up to the woman to show that she herself continues to be interested, through all the delays and forthcoming court appearances, and to show evidence. The final decision about whether to prosecute, however, is up to the district attorney.

The woman who is not legally married to her assailant may go directly to Criminal Court and make a sworn complaint. She will be given a summons, to be served by the police, and a court date. The judge will listen to both the beater and the beaten and decide if either should be charged with a crime or if the case should be dismissed.

Attorney Fields points out realistically that "it is important that you present your case well. Do not shout, but speak loudly, slowly, and clearly. Practice with a friend. Tell what the man did to you. Tell of your injuries and fear. Show pictures of your injuries. Tell how the beating upset your children. Make it a *short* story. Answer the judge's questions briefly. Do *not* show anger with what the judge asks or says. If you get upset, you can cry.

"Talk only to the judge. The man who hurt you will tell his side of what happened. Do not get angry with him. Do not fight with him or interrupt him, no matter what he says. When he is done, the judge will let you talk again."

Step-by-step details of the New York State procedures are available: See Recommended Reading and Useful Addresses.

[Note that there is no guarantee the woman will achieve any safety via the justice system. It is clear why so many battered wives, already at their wit's end with the nightmare of having to live with the wife-beater, find themselves even more traumatized by the complex, impersonal court procedures. And give up. Some communities provide Victims Advocates, Victims Information Bureau, Victims Assistance Project, or volunteers from law schools or shelters, to guide the frightened woman. These are real lifesavers and many more are needed.]

NOTE: These are outstanding programs with some documented success on record. In time, there will be others. Possible sources of information for future programs are shelters, police departments, YW-YMCAs, and some Family Service Associations.

MVR, Men in Violent Relationships, P.O. Box 14299, University Station, Minneapolis, MN. 55414. PHONE: 874-1985. Free telephone hot line for men who batter, staffed by trained and supervised male volunteers. Callers and counselors are anonymous.

Batterers' Project, c/o Metrocenter YWCA, Family & Child Services of Seattle, 909 Fourth Ave., Seattle, WA. 98104. Group therapy for men who batter, PHONE 774-3646. Funded by United Way. Also couple counseling. Extensive public awareness outreach. Program got 55 calls in its first two weeks. Widely considered an excellent model which new groups elsewhere often adopt or adapt.

Domestic Assault Program, Psychology Service, American Lake Veterans Hospital, Tacoma, WA. 98493. By referral only. Designed by Drs. Anne Ganley and Lance Harris. One of the most innovative in that participants, all volunteers, were required to reside at hospital for "time-out" of four weeks to learn new behavior and attitudes with which to handle anger. Focus is on how the batterer perceives an event, not on the psychodynamics of his marriage. The pilot residential portion was discontinued because the number of beds required by hospital regulations were not filled (typical of the red tape and bureaucracy problems which hamper so many good projects!) Treatment continues on an outpatient basis, though progress is slower. I commend this worthy project to all Veterans Hospitals.

Alternatives to Aggression: An Anger Control Program for Men, c/o Family Service Assn., 214 N. Hamilton St., Madison, WI. 53703. Assessment and orientation interview necessary to join program; for referrals, Dan Saunders, 251-7611. Full range of innovative and non-threatening methods to enhance emotional and physical control.

VIBS, Victims Information Bureau of Suffolk, 501 Route 111, Hauppauge, N.Y. 11787. (516) 360-3606. Couple Counseling. For details, see Chapter 10.

Notes

CHAPTER 1: *Conjugal Crime: It Happens in the Best of Families*

1. Kathleen M. Fojtik, *How to Develop a Wife Assault Task Force and Project.* Ann Arbor-Washtenaw County NOW Wife Assault Task Force, 1917 Washtenaw Avenue, Ann Arbor, Michigan 48104.

2. Linda Bird Franke, "Battered Woman," *Newsweek,* February 2, 1976.

3. Alice Bonner, "Wife Beating on the Rise," *Washington Post,* November 19, 1975.

4. Suzanne K. Steinmetz and Murray K. Straus, eds., *Violence in the Family* (Toronto: Dodd, Mead, 1974).

5. Leslie Maitland, "Courts Easy on Rising Family Violence," *The New York Times,* June 14, 1976.

6. Franke, "Battered Woman."

7. From a George Levinger study, 1966, as mentioned in Steinmetz and Straus, *Violence.*

8. Terry Zintl, "Wife Abuse: Our Almost-Hidden Social Problem," *Detroit Free Press,* January 25, 1976.

9. Sidney Katz, "Battered Wives Seek Refuge," *Toronto Daily Star,* August 23, 1975.

10. Jane Myers, "The Beaten Wife," *Ann Arbor News,* September 18, 1975.

11. Ibid.

12. Kenneth Briggs, "Gallup Poll Finds New Evidence of Pervasive Religious Character of U.S., with Only India More Committed," *The New York Times,* September 12, 1976.

13. Uniform Crime Reports for the United States, 1975. Issued by the Federal Bureau of Investigation, Washington, D.C. 20535.

14. Adolph W. Hart, "Thomas Promised That He Would," Op-Ed page, *The New York Times,* June 10, 1975.

15. Personal communication from Mel Gray, M.A.N. (Man's Awareness Network), St. Paul, Minnesota.

16. Arnold A. Hutschnecker, M.D., *The Drive for Power* (New York: Bantam Books, 1976).

17. "A Report by the Task Force to Study a Haven for Physically Abused Wives," Prepared for the County Council, Montgomery County, Maryland, November 1, 1975.

18. Maria Roy, Ed., *Battered Women: A Psychosociological Study of Domestic Violence* (New York: Van Nostrand Reinhold, 1977).

19. Kathy Fojtik, "Ann Arbor Overview," *Do It NOW*, vol. IV, no. 5 (June 1976) "Stop Household Violence" issue.

CHAPTER 2: *What Kind of Man Would Beat His Wife?*

1. Sheila Rowbotham, *Women, Resistance and Revolution: A History of Women and Revolution in the Modern World* (New York: Random House, 1973).

2. Betsy Warrior, *Battered Lives* (pamphlet). KNOW, Inc. P.O. Box 86031, Pittsburgh, Pennsylvania.

3. From the CBS-TV report on "The Battered Wife," Morning News program, running daily first week in December 1975.

4. Richard J. Gelles, *The Violent Home: A Study of Physical Aggression Between Husbands and Wives* (Beverly Hills, California: Sage Publications, 1974).

5. Private conversation with a battered wife. This illustration—and all other illustrations not drawn from published studies—are disguised in order to preserve privacy and prevent identification.

6. Margaret Ball, ACSW, "Issues of Violence in Family Casework." Paper presented at Metropolitan Detroit Chapter of National Association of Social Workers, December 3, 1975.

7. John E. O'Brien, "Violence in Divorce Prone Families," *Journal of Marriage and the Family,* November 1971, vol. 33, no. 4.

8. P. D. Scott, "Battered Wives," from a report compiled by a committee of the Royal College of Psychiatrists, reprinted in *British Journal of Psychiatry,* 125 (November 1974): 433–441.

9. Unbylined precis, "Black and Blue Marriages," in *Human Behavior* magazine, June 1976.

10. Sue E. Eisenberg and Patricia A. Micklow, *The*

Assaulted Wife: "Catch-22" Revisited (An Exploratory Legal Study of Wifebeating in Michigan) © 1974. Unpublished, University of Michigan Law School, Ann Arbor, Michigan. (Now published. *See* Recommended Books.)

11. Ibid.

12. Gelles, *The Violent Home.*

13. This material is taken from a talk given by Bernard Chodorkoff, M.D., at a Seminar on Violence in the Family, sponsored by Family Service Association of Detroit and Wayne County, October 2–3, 1975.

14. Del Martin, "Beating Her, Slamming Her, Making Her Cry," Op-Ed page, *The New York Times,* October 6, 1975.

15. Scott, "Battered Wives."

16. Bill Peterson, "Battered Wife Syndrome: Shame, Fear Keep Most Women Silent," *Washington Post,* September 13, 1975.

17. Personal communication from Margaret Ball, ASCW, Family Service Association of Detroit and Wayne County, Emergency Counseling Division.

CHAPTER 3: *What Kind of Woman Becomes a Battered Wife?*

1. The survey was taken by Joann Gerardi, Ph.D., and Carol Victor, founders of Growth & Life Center, Inc., New York City, for an early television documentary of wifebeating and then not used "because wifebeating is not A-topic news." I am deeply grateful for being given the material exclusively for this book.

2. Mary Pat Brygger, personal communication.

3. Private conversation with Mel Grey and also notes from the minutes of the Battered Women's Study Committee Meeting, May 6, 1976, in preparation of the detailed copyrighted report, *Battered Women: The Hidden Problem.* Community Planning Organization, Inc., 333 Sibley St., St. Paul, Minnesota 55101.

4. Based on material from Mindy Resnick, *Wife Beating Counselor Training Manual #1.* Ann Arbor NOW Wife Assault, 1917 Washtenaw Avenue, Ann Arbor, Michigan 48104.

5. Hans Toch, *Violent Men: An Inquiry into the Psychology of Violence* (Chicago: Aldine, 1969).

6. Gelles, *The Violent Home.*

7. *The 1974–1975 Committee Report, The Select Committee on Violence in Marriage*, Appendix 5 to the Minutes of Evidence, pp. 490–491, House of Commons, London, England. Available from John Rose, Clerk of the Select Committee on Violence in Marriage, House of Commons, London, SWIA OAA.

8. Eisenberg and Micklow, *The Assaulted Wife*.

9. From an unbylined Associated Press report, "Wife Beating," appearing in the *St. Louis Post-Dispatch*, Sunday, August 3, 1975.

10. Scott, "Battered Wives," pp. 433–41.

11. From Associated Press report, "Wife Beating," *St. Louis Post-Dispatch*, August 3, 1975.

12. Mirra Komarovsky, *Blue-Collar Marriage* (New York: Random House, 1962).

CHAPTER 4: *How Society Keeps Her There*

1. Eleanor Kremen, "The 'Discovery' of Battered Wives: Considerations for the Development of a Social Service Network," a paper read at the American Sociological Association, New York, August-September 1976.

2. Martin Symonds, "The Accidental Victim of Crime," a chapter in *Violence and Victims*, ed. Stefan Pasternak, M.D. (New York: John Wiley, 1975).

3. Cheryl Shaw, "Family Crisis Teams Reduce Wife Battery Problems," Part III, *Lubbock Avalanche-Journal*, May 9, 1976.

4. Helene A. Pepe, Georgetown Law Center, "Wife Abuse: Does the American Legal System Offer Adequate Protection to Abused Wives?" a paper presented at the Conference of the American Sociological Association, New York, August-September 1976.

5. J. C. Barden, "Physically Abused Women Are Subject of Conference," *The New York Times*, February 1, 1975.

6. Eisenberg and Micklow, *The Assaulted Wife*.

7. As quoted in Murray A. Straus, "Sexual Inequality, Cultural Norms and Wifebeating," a talk given at International Institute on Victimology, Bellegio, Italy, July 1–12, 1975.

8. Leslie Maitland, "Courts Easy on Rising Family Violence," *The New York Times*, June 14, 1972.

9. Ibid.

10. Beverly B. Nichols, "The Abused Wife Problem." *Social Casework*, January 1976, vol. 57, no. 1.

11. Eisenberg and Micklow, *The Assaulted Wife.*

12. Jeannette Milgrom, from a paper prepared for Women's Network, St. Paul, Minnesota, August 1975.

13. Morton Bard and Joseph Zacke, "The Prevention of Family Violence: Dilemmas of Community Intervention," *Journal of Marriage and the Family,* vol. 33, no. 4 (November 1971): 677–82.

14. Elizabeth Truninger, "Marital Violence: The Legal Solutions," *The Hastings Law Journal,* vol. 23 (November 1971).

15. Helene A. Pepe, Georgetown Law Center, "Wife Abuse: Does the American Legal System Offer Adequate Protection to Abused Wives?" A paper presented at the Conference of the American Sociological Association, New York, August-September, 1976.

16. *"Rape and Battery Between Husband and Wife," 6, Stanford Law Review 719,* July 1954.

17. Pepe, "Wife Abuse."

18. Ibid.

19. Del Martin, "The Economics of Wife-beating," a paper presented at the Conference of the American Sociological Association, New York, August-September 1976. The material was excerpted from her book *Battered Wives* (San Francisco: Glide Publications, 1976).

20. Truninger, "Marital Violence."

21. Michele Kamisher, "Behind Closed Doors: Battered Women," *The Real Paper,* Boston, February 11, 1976.

22. Lawrence Van Gelder, "Giving Battered Wives a Little Legal Clout." *The New York Times,* November 13, 1976.

CHAPTER 5: *How Does He Get Away With It?*
Historical Precedents for the Toleration
of Wifebeating

1. Robert Graves, *The Greek Myths: 1* (Baltimore: Penguin Books, 1955).

2. Ibid.

3. Eva Figes, *Patriarchal Attitudes* (New York: Stein & Day, 1970).

4. Vern L. Bullough, *The Subordinate Sex* (Urbana: University of Illinois Press, 1973).

5. Steinmetz and Straus, eds. *Violence in the Family.*

6. Paul Tillich, *A History of Christian Thought,* Carl E. Braater, ed. (New York: Simon and Schuster, 1972).

7. Mary Van Stolk, "Battered Children," in *Children Today,* March-April 1976.

8. *Corpus Iuris Canonici,* ed. A. Friedberg, 2 vols. (Leipzig, Germany, 1879–81), vol. I, pt. II, c. 33, q. 5, c. 12, 13, 17, 18. In Julia O'Faolain and Laura Martines, eds. *Not in God's Image* (New York: Harper & Row, 1973).

9. Cherubino da Siena, *Regole della vita matrimoniale* (Bologna, Italy, 1888), pp. 12–14. In O'Faolain and Martines, *Not in God's Image.*

10. The Martin Luther reference is quoted in *Sex and the Church,* eds. Oscar E. Feucht and other members of the Family Life Committee of the Lutheran Church (St. Louis: Concordia Publishing House, 1961), p. 84. In Bullough, *Subordinate Sex.*

11. Joseph Campbell, *The Masks of God: Primitive Mythology* (New York: Viking Press, 1959).

12. Bullough, *Subordinate Sex.*

13. Karen Horney, "The Dream of Woman," *International Journal of Psychoanalysis,* 13 (1932): 348–60.

14. Sir William Blackstone, 1, *Commentaries on the Laws of England,* 444, 1765.

15. *Bradley* v. *State,* Walker, 156, Mississippi.

16. Vincent Cronin, *Napoleon Bonaparte, An Intimate Biography* (New York: Morrow, 1972).

17. Christopher Herold, *The Age of Napoleon* (New York: American Heritage, 1963).

18. Ibid.

19. Ibid.

20. Emil Ludwig, *Napoleon* (New York: Boni & Liveright, 1926).

21. Ibid.

22. Ibid.

23. Ibid.

24. John Stuart Mill, *The Subjection of Women* (1869). Introduction by Wendell Robert Carr (Cambridge, Mass.: M.I.T. Press, 1970).

25. Ibid.

26. Ibid.

27. Ibid.

28. Ibid.

29. Ibid.

30. Michael St. John Packe, *The Life of John Stuart Mill* (New York: Macmillan, 1954).

31. Frances Power Cobbe, "Wife Torture in England," *The Contemporary Review,* 1878, London. (I am indebted

to two British correspondents, Paul Barker, editor of *New Society,* and social historian Pat Thane, for this reference, unavailable in America.)

32. Ibid.

33. Ibid.

34. Ibid.

35. Ibid.

36. Ibid.

37. Ibid.

38. Eisenberg and Micklow, "The Assaulted Wife."

39. Roy, *Battered Women.*

40. Philip Judge, "Rowdy, Rakish Oliver Reed," *Girl Talk,* vol. VII, no. 1, January 1976.

41. Michele Kamisher, "Behind Closed Doors: Battered Women," *The Real Paper,* Boston, February 11, 1976.

42. Susan Braudy, "Bang! A Little Gift from Hollywood," *Ms,* January 1975. P. 36.

CHAPTER 6: *How It Affects the Children*

1. These fragments come from the children themselves, from the children's playmates, from therapists, and family.

2. Ibid.

3. Richard J. Gelles, "Violence and Pregnancy: A Note on the Extent of the Problem and Needed Services," *The Family Coordinator,* January, 1975.

4. Noor van Crevel, "But What About the Kids?" A paper presented to the roundtable session on marital violence at the Conference of the American Sociological Association, August-September, 1976.

5. Ibid.

6. Ibid.

7. Ibid.

8. Ibid.

9. Ibid.

10. Scott, "Battered Wives."

11. Gelles, "Violence and Pregnancy."

12. Terri Schultz, "Though Legal, Abortions Are Not Always Available," *The New York Times,* The Week in Review, January 2, 1977.

13. "Congress Acts on Abortions," *The New York Times,* September 19, 1976.

CHAPTER 8: *A Personal Investigation: One Week in the Life of a Shelter for Battered Wives*

1. Adapted from Susan Ozzanna, "The Battered Woman's 'Only Solution,'" *Majority Report*, January 24, 1976.

CHAPTER 9: *What to Do, What to Avoid: Guidelines to Help for Battered Wives, Wifebeaters, Children, Friends and Family, Counselors and Clergy*

1. Erin Pizzey, *Scream Quietly or the Neighbours Will Hear* (Harmondsworth, England: Penguin Books, 1974). (*See* Recommended Books for name and address of new United States publisher.)

CHAPTER 10: *The Future: The Fastest-growing Social Movement in America*

1. From Lindsy Van Gelder, "Wife-Beater Hit With 3-Year Term," *New York Post*, January 7, 1977, and personal communication with women who were there.
2. Harry Danyluk and Robert Herbert, "Killer of Husband Spared Jail by Weeping Judge," *Daily News*, December 17, 1976.
3. *New York Law Journal*, front page, July 15, 1976.
4. J. C. Barden, "Wives Who Allege Beatings Suing Police and Court," *The New York Times*, December 8, 1976. The facts are taken from the clipping. The editorializing is mine. The states that sent queries about starting a similar lawsuit are: California, Colorado, Florida, Illinois, Oregon, Massachusetts, Rhode Island, Vermont.
5. *RESPONSE*, vol. 1, issue 2, December 1976.
6. Erin Pizzey, from a fund-raising pamphlet.
7. Pizzey, *Scream Quietly or the Neighbours Will Hear*.
8. Terry Davidson, Chapter I. "Wifebeating. A Recurring Phenomenon Throughout History," in *Battered Women*, ed. Maria Roy (New York: Van Nostrand Reinhold, 1977).
9. From Dennis Broe, "Women Charge Rape Program Is 'Hoax,'" *The Gramercy Herald*, Aug. 26, 1977; Judith Kurens, "No Relief! Battered Women Program Is a Farce," *East Side Express*, August 25, 1977; plus conversations with members of the coalition.

10. Betsy Warrior, *Working on Wife Abuse*, pamphlet available from 46 Pleasant Street, Cambridge, Massachusetts 02139. $3.00 plus $.50 postage.

11. This is reported in *UC Clip Sheet*, University of California at Berkeley, March 1, 1977. The researchers are sociologists Sarah and Richard Berk, UC, and Catherine Berheide, Indiana University Southeast.

12. Murray A. Straus, *Sexual Inequality, Cultural Norms, and Wifebeating*. A paper read at the international Institute on Victimology, Bellagio, Italy, July 1–12, 1975.

Index

307